ALL THAT

Jazz

THIS IS A CARLTON BOOK

Copyright © Carlton Books Limited 1996

10 9 8 7 6 5 4 3 2 1

First published in 1996 by Carlton Books Limited

A CIP catalogue record for this book is available from the British Library.

ISBN 0-76519-953-X

Executive Editor: Lorraine Dickey
Art Direction: Zoe Maggs
Design: Sue Michniewicz
Picture Research: Charlotte Bush
Editor: Duncan Noble, Joanna Copestick
Production: Sarah Schuman

Printed in Dubai

The Publishers would like to thank Martin Gayford.

SMITHMARK

ALL THAT

Jazz

The Illustrated
Story of Jazz Music

GENERAL EDITOR: RONALD ATKINS

Contents

A Century's MUSIC

Fifty years ago in South Africa, a boy was growing up in a remote part of the Transkei, where white people were few, and where his father taught in a mission school. The mixture of Protestant hymns and music by the local tribes might have influenced his later career, when he studied the European classics at college by day and played a different type of music around the clubs at night.

The story of Chris McGregor - whose group the Blue Notes, established in the teeth of apartheid, was later exiled in Europe - ties in with what had happened earlier in another vast country, across the Atlantic and several thousand miles to the northwest. A new music emerged from a clash of cultures, in which white hymns and sounds from the black community formed a crucial part of the mix. This took place in what became the U. S., and the outcome was jazz, a name not always popular with those involved but now too established to jettison.

What is jazz? Everyone should at least agree that, musically, jazz is the mother of all hybrids. The U.S. was home to immigrants from all over Europe and beyond, who wished to build a new life, or just needed to escape from the old. They brought their native musical cultures with them, from classical symphonies to polkas to jigs.

One group found life harder. Africans, shipped across to labour on the cotton and tobacco plantations, were second-class citizens, owned by their white masters. They brought their own musical traditions. Many areas of their African homeland were dominated by drums and other percussion instruments. Music tended to have a social or communal purpose, more so than among whites. Jazz and its predecessors were never planned. One cannot say exactly how and when everything happened because techniques of documenting music at the time were primitive compared to today. What we do know is the reason why. Jazz arose from the interweaving of two contrasting cultures, inspired very

largely by the descendants of the slaves. The blending may have spread over a period, but that doesn't make the outcome any less remarkable. Precisely because the fundamental clash was of such seismic proportions, what it produced has the strength of solid gold.

Developed as functional music, from work songs in the cotton fields to galvanizing jitterbugs in the ballrooms, it has gravitated to the concert platform. An orchestral infra-

With the pioneering Fletcher Henderson band, Coleman Hawkins evolved the smooth, breathy, ultimately rhapsodic style other tenor saxophone players copied.

structure, the jazz big band, became the first ensemble since the symphony orchestra to utilize a full range of instruments. Brass and reeds, especially the previously-neglected saxophone, are used in ways far exceeding in scope anything

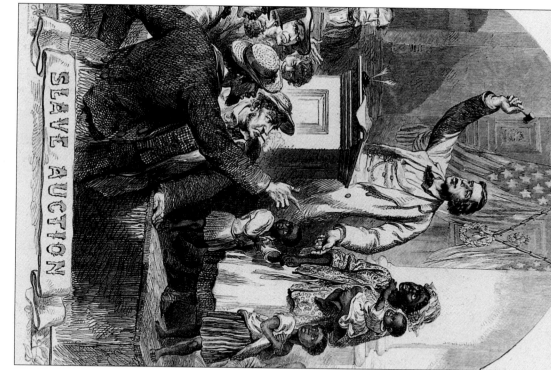

SLAVE AUCTION

Auctioning slaves. In Africa at one time, a good horse was worth several men.

heard before. Just as unique is the jazz rhythm section.

The music demands the highest virtuosity. Yet there are no absolute standards of excellence. Art Tatum's fulsome piano technique has drawn praise from classical pianists. Then you have Jimmy Yancey, who played only a few tunes in a few keys but distilled the last drop of feeling from the blues. Jazz can be worth performing at any level: film director/comedian Woody Allen is just the most famous example of someone

who, after a day's work, enjoys a session with friends.

There are also no absolute rules about how one should sound. Thelonious Monk was once described as treating the piano as an unexplored instrument. Coleman Hawkins and Stan Getz are undisputed masters of the tenor saxophone. Play a representative solo by each, one after the other, and you can hardly believe that the same instrument can produce such utterly different tones.

As jazz changed, diatribes against each change, and diatribes against those who oppose change, have led it to rival the Christian Church in the number of its schisms. Battle lines are currently drawn between those

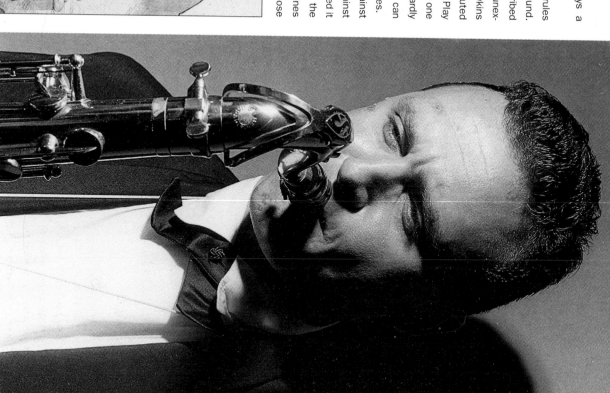

Stan Getz came to the fore by giving his own twist to the prevailing tenor style, Lester Young's, notably through his command of the high register.

exploring the music from within and those reaching outward. As ever, there is a commercial subplot, with one side marketed as being in the 'tradition', the other as pushing back the boundaries through being part of 'world music'.

We probably need both. Art thrives on new ideas. But whenever jazz gets too airy fairy, somebody straightens it out. Musicians understandably decry pigeon-holes, and all would support Duke Ellington's dictum that there are only two kinds of music, good and bad. Yet in a career that evolved over fifty years, Ellington's music remained an identifiable entity. The same

applies to an even more protean figure, Miles Davis, who (in complete contrast to his successor Wynton Marsalis) always looked beyond jazz. Everything he played, not least his more 'European' ventures, was done on his own terms.

History's biggest lesson is one people hate to admit: a century down the line, jazz exists.

The Musical
HERITAGE

"The slave trade was one of those historical phenomena - not unlike the Holocaust - which is extremely difficult to describe in its full enormity."

James Walvin, Slaves And Slavery.

Nobody can dispute the barbarity of the slave trade. Of the twelve million people shipped from Africa to the New World, about 1.5 million lost their lives before they even got there. Some of the slaves were regarded as machines, being worked until they dropped only to be replaced by new ones.

Looking at how the trade affected what became the U.S., one is struck by a set of circumstances and a sequence of events that could almost have been scripted to come together and create something truly extraordinary. These relate to the volume of slaves, the way they were treated and the white culture to which they were exposed.

Jazz fans are used to thinking of the U.S. as the focal point of the transatlantic slave trade. But only about 6% of those who survived the crossing ended up there. Once on the plantations their conditions, however poor, compared favourably with those in the gold mines of Brazil or on the sugar fields of the Caribbean. Within the master-slave relationship, many were treated as human beings and were able to lead something resembling a family life. As a result, the number of people of African descent in the U.S. more than trebled at a

time when the number in Brazil (which had shipped over six times as many) actually declined.

The Americanization of the North American slaves was therefore accelerated because, unlike Brazil, plantation owners had no need to import more from Africa. Without further arrivals from their homeland, they were more isolated culturally and, though a majority in a few states such as South Carolina, were outnumbered four-to-one by whites at the same time, the balance between black and white throughout the New World was about equal, and blacks in Brazil outnumbered whites by nearly three-to-one.

There were revolts, notably those led by Nat Turner in Virginia in 1831 and an earlier one in Louisiana, but few compared to what occurred in the Caribbean, where slaves were more numerous and conditions were worse. Even so, their owners forbade them to use the drum, which was regarded as an instrument of potential subversion. Outside New Orleans and parts of the South close to the Caribbean, there are few legacies of African drumming in the U.S., unlike the Caribbean itself or Brazil.

The polyphony of a percussion choir expresses something deeply

ingrained in the culture of large parts of Africa; instead of merely offering support, the choirs provide the totality of music through overlapping rhythms that are more complex than those you get in jazz from just one drummer. Simply by suppressing the drums, the slave-owners could not wipe out the culture, and the transplanted Africans incorporated this rhythmic complexity into their music. Their work songs, for example, were based on an African tradition of antiphonal chanting. While working in the fields, a lead singer would shout out a verse, probably improvized, and the others would respond by a structured mix of chanting, foot-stamping and flailing axes (or by doing whatever was necessary to add a rhythmic kick to the menial task in hand). Later American versions of what is called the 'field holler', an extended falsetto shout that can elide through several semitones, have been placed on record.

Another legacy of African practice is the religious dance known as the ringshout. This involves two groups dancing in a circle while being encouraged vigorously by those on the outside who beat out a variety of rhythms via hand and foot. Observers have described ringshouts occurring

as part of the Christian services held on plantations during the nineteenth century.

The African tradition of narrative songs and of songs relating to everyday experience led directly to the musical form known as the blues. In the course of time, as these traditions were taken up by American-born slaves and their descendents, these songs would acquire some of the trappings of European music. So far as we know, Africans were used to harmonizing their songs instinctively and would not have been unfamiliar with the basic Western scale - the notion of an African five-note scale clashing with the familiar do-re-me is possibly too simplistic. They were, however, willing to ad-lib at all times and were not inhibited by the letter of the well-tempered scale. Their readiness to bend notes and the ease with which they unearthed microtones that tended to be out of bounds in European music had a profound effect on what followed.

As well as banning drums, and for the same reason, plantation owners discouraged Africans from speaking their native languages. Reacting to this, the slaves seem to have cannily devised a system of using African words that could pass for English. Many of the idiomatic terms linked to jazz and now part of American slang can be traced back: jam, jive, hip, dig and even jazz itself.

Slavery was officially over by 1890, around the time this picture was taken, but many blacks were still employed picking cotton on the plantations throughout the Southern States of the U.S.

The Formal BACKGROUND

Jazz did not emerge overnight. Two completely different cultures had to find each other and, given the master-slave relationship, racial segregation and primitive communications (no trains, cars, radios), there was little chance of a totally fresh musical system suddenly blossoming. If the gestation period was slow, this gave time for the ingredients to come together on the launching pad so that, when the touch-paper was finally lit, jazz took off like a rocket.

the rituals, to which they gave several personal tweaks. Black preachers were popular long before the American Revolution, though their subversive potential tended to keep them off the plantations during the heyday of serfdom.

With hindsight, the choice of Protestant church music as the conduit whereby African musical traditions led to jazz could not be bettered. People from a different background soon pick it up. It is easy to harmonize. In the case of Africans brought up on metres both complex and indeterminate, it drilled into them the most basic and assimilable of European musical structures. After a generation or so, four-in-a-bar and a steady beat would seem to them perfectly natural, if occasionally constricting.

They would, however, draw a line at keeping silent during the lengthy pauses between lines and verses. African rituals of this sort would be highly participative, with any gaps left by the main speakers or singers punctured by cries, comments, asides and exhortations. The degree of preacher and congregation interaction in black churches and of call-and-response routines erupting on all sides during the singing is something we are now familiar with. We don't have recordings of the gospel music of 200 years ago (the spectacular verbal riffs found in modern times are postjazz), but the seeds must have been sown by then. There is also evidence of Negro spirituals existing in 1800.

Gospel Music

Introducing conquered subjects to their own brand of Christianity has been part of the British imperialist tradition: the concept of the meek inheriting the earth perhaps seen as a convenient safety valve, giving people at the bottom of the ladder something to feel good about. The conversion of those working on the plantations of the U.S. was carried out with enthusiasm, especially when the ethical position of slave owners being Christians was resolved to the owners' satisfaction.

It was also a success. The African slaves got the message about salvation and soon identified the Christian God as being on their side. They were also able to identify with

The Blues

The blues might represent an unbroken musical chain linking Africa to the U.S. In his *Savannah Syncopators*, published in 1970, Paul Oliver countered the image of Africa as a drum-happy continent by pointing out that stringed instruments prevailed in areas such as those now

WILLIAMS' COLORED SINGERS

THE WORLD'S GREATEST

HARMONIZING OCTETTE

Chas. P. Williams, Mgr.
6618 Vernon Avenue
Chicago, U. S. A.

Williams & Johnson
Proprietors

Gospel groups such as Williams' Coloured Singers basked in the success of the Fisk Jubilee Singers, whose drawing-room renditions of spirituals greatly impressed the British Queen Victoria.

A country blues singer in relaxed pose. Some used a bottleneck on the left hand for sliding down the strings.

known as Senegal, Gambia and Northern Nigeria. He noted examples of Africans singing and accompanying themselves on various instruments (including the 5-string halam, which Oliver suggests led to the banjo), that bore a close resemblance to field recordings of American blues and other performers.

This applies particularly to matters of pitch and intonation, and use of expressive vocal devices such as falsetto cries. As a way of externalizing emotions of all shades of intensity, the blues song is undoubtedly African in origin, and researchers have since found further musical parallels between Africa and America's Deep South. The structures of the blues form evolved over a period into more regular verse patterns. Someone improvizing a song would hit upon the idea of repeating the opening line, so as to make time for working out the next. If that became the punch line, you would end up with verses of three lines, of which the first two were identical, or at least closely related.

From here, the step to the modern 12-bar blues is short. Earlier three-line narrative songs would, by comparison, have been quite irregular - there are examples of singers accompanying themselves who often vary the length of the line. As backing groups became more indispensable, the need for some kind of metrical discipline inspired a more stable form. The strict AAB blues (the first two lines being nearly the same, musically and verbally, while the third, represented by 'B', supplies the contrast) was very well established at the time of the blues recording boom of the 1920s. By then, the possibilities of a more sophisticated form had already been realized, so that some blues pieces, far from sticking to simple AAB, have a melodic ABC structure that, without being quite so complex, resembles a Charlie Parker blues. But we are jumping ahead of our story.

Instruments &
BANDS

A definition of jazz commanding universal respect has yet to be found. Hardly surprising. Imagine trying to capture in a single paragraph the music played by European symphony orchestras - let alone a bigger slice of Western concert music - and the size of the problem should be clear, even disregarding the question as to whether music in general and jazz in particular can be encapsulated in prose.

be met, and other factors, such as improvization, receive a positive reading, you may well have jazz.

Jazz has unquestionably made massive contributions to the way instruments are used in Western music. On an individual level, the diversity of noise produced by brass and wind instruments contrasts with that found in older-established idioms, where a musician is more likely to mould a sound from some ideal template. Jazz players follow no book of rules. The brass growl, bend notes at will and distort sound via a selection of mutes. These fall into two categories that can even be used simultaneously: the kind you stick into the bell and those manipulated in front of it. Musicians often employ *ad hoc* models, such as a felt hat dangling over the bell.

On a collective level, the styles adopted by big bands, Dixieland ensembles and assorted groups evolved from within (although there are stylistic and instrumental links between Dixieland and the brass and marching bands that preceded it).

Finally, the concept of rhythmic uplift exemplified by the jazz rhythm section that, in its sophisticated forms, does immeasurably more than beat time in the background, has no parallel elsewhere. In earlier jazz groups, a typical rhythm section consists of drums, bass (a brass bass, such as a tuba, replaced eventually by the stringed double-bass), banjo or guitar and piano. Guitar and bass generally pump out a steady, ungarnished beat, though, as essentially melodic instruments, they do so by playing notes that fit the tune being performed.

The drummer employs a mixture of stick on cymbal and foot on pedal-operated high-hat: four even taps to express four beats to the bar, while the high-hat cymbals click together on beats 2 and 4 - the rest of the kit imparts cross-rhythms and embellishments. Over the years, especially following the example of Count Basie, the piano tends to provide accents, behaving more like a brass or reed section and leaving the beat to the others. As the roles of bassist and drummer grow in complexity, the

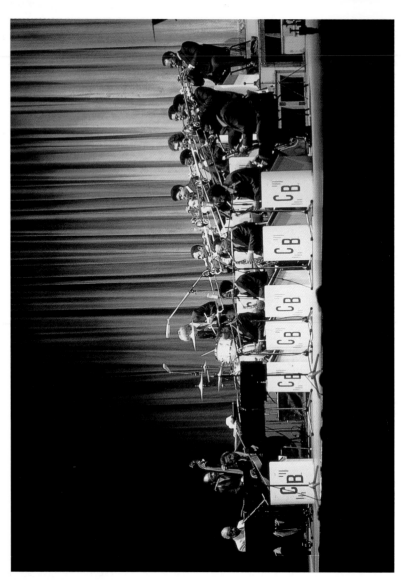

Paradoxically, widening boundaries might be making the task easier, as groups appear that seem, on subjective evidence, to interact much as jazz musicians do. Recent examples could include Whatever, led by British bassist Danny Thompson, and the international trio of Miroslav Vitous, Jan Garbarek and Peter Erskine. Attempting a definition years ago, the French critic Andre Hodeir in his book *Jazz: Its Evolution and Essence* came up with such conditions as 'vital drive', 'relaxation' and 'getting the notes and accents in the right place'. Where these seem to

Count Basie and his orchestra on stage, aligned so each of the four sections - trumpets, trombones, reeds and rhythm - are together.

rhythm guitarist becomes obsolete except as a substitute pianist.

New Orleans seems to have been awash with marching bands, and the archetypal jazz front line of trumpet, clarinet and trombone is the brass band in microcosm: the trumpet punches out the tune, the clarinet weaves ornate counterpoint over and around while the trombone adds guttural, incisive obligatos. The big bands that came after demanded a more structured approach. As the instruments multiplied, you had sections of trumpets, trombones and reeds, the latter consisting mostly of saxophonists who could switch to the clarinet when necessary. Instead of the hierarchical Dixieland approach, there was more variety. One or another section, or a combination of them, could take the lead in presenting the tune, while the rest filled in the background, often by playing what are called riffs: repetitive figures.

Violins have always been present, but there are as yet few equivalents of the European string ensembles. Instead, the saxophone has become the popular image of jazz. Invented by the Belgian Adolphe Sax around 1840, it struggled to break into the well-established classical field. In this new music with no hallowed conventions, the saxophone found the perfect medium. At least four types are regularly identified with jazz: soprano, alto, tenor and baritone, with the last three generally constituting the saxophone section. Differences between each are even more striking than those between trumpet, cornet and flugelhorn. Among leading exponents in each category, in addition to Coleman Hawkins and Stan Getz, you could contrast Sidney Bechet with Wayne Shorter, Johnny Hodges with Lee Konitz and Harry Carney with Gerry Mulligan - and then take account of the technical breakthroughs of people like Evan Parker.

King Oliver's Creole Jazz Band, Chicago 1923. From left to right: Johnny Dodds, Baby Dodds, Honoré Dutrey, Louis Armstrong, King Oliver, Lil Hardin and Bill Johnson. Note the conical mutes on the floor.

Evolution of Jazz

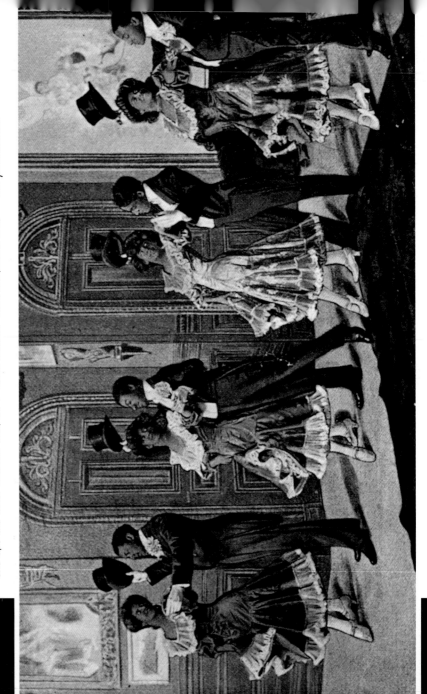

The RAGTIME Era

During the nineteenth century, the pace of progress stepped up all over the Western world. Among the cultural developments in the U.S. were the brass bands of John Philip Sousa, a new type of ensemble, even though the music stayed close to European notions of contrasting themes and formal repetition. By disseminating these forms more widely, the brass bands probably influenced ragtime.

Of the identifiable musical forms that led to jazz, ragtime is the black innovation closest to white practice. Before being identified with the piano, syncopated music had spread through minstrel shows, in which black entertainers would dance a high-stepping jig to a distinctive banjo-led accompaniment. This dance, known as the cake-walk, came out of the old plantation where square dances, jigs and reels were also among the most popular recreations. Slaves would don their best clothes and ape the white masters who, all unsuspecting, donated a cake to the most proficient couple. Translate the cake-walk rhythms to the piano and compose a march around them, and you have ragtime.

It emerged from the wide-open cities of the American mid-West towards the end of the century. Saloons, honky tonks and houses of entertainment gave musicians the freedom of the piano. In this way, ragtime's founder Scott Joplin learned his craft. He began as just one of the hundreds of, mainly, black pianists who ripped through the syncopated treble runs that gamblers and pleasure seekers demanded. But he was able to turn the tunes he and others played into formal compositions.

Classic ragtime piano became an art form that Joplin intended to be played strictly as notated. After the success of 'Maple Leaf Rag', he was composing full-time, and his disciples - including James Scott, the white Joseph Lamb and the half-Indian Louis Chauvin - were composers first, not functional performers compelled to please the barflies. Their main rivals and successors, based in New York's Harlem and enjoying such exotic titles as Abba Labba and Kid Sneeze, were more competitive and more inclined to give themselves licence to improvize. They played in saloons, in halls where people came ostensibly for dancing lessons - permission to run dances was rarely granted to black entrepreneurs - and at innumerable rent parties. The most creative of them, James P. Johnson, describes how a 'tickler', as pianists were dubbed, folded his overcoat on the piano, with the special lining on top, rested his gold-headed cane on the music rack and adjusted his diamond ring for it to flash on the lady of his choice.

The century also saw the spread and codification of the spirituals,

A highly staged version of the cake-walk, a dance that began on the plantations.

songs that had emerged spontaneously - the words of 'Swing Low Sweet Chariot', for instance, had been sung to more than one tune. Eventually, these tunes would be written down and formalized, with such choirs as the Fisk Jubilee Singers and such composers as Stephen Foster playing a role similar to that of W.C. Handy's in relation to the blues. By the turn of the century, ragtime, spirituals and blues could combine to give both emotional and structural depth to what became jazz. The blue tonality, associated most of all with the use of the minor-third interval to impart a sense of sadness, stands out in Handy's multi-themed compositions, some of which are not that far removed from rags.

As a pop version of ragtime took over, thanks to songs like 'Ragtime Cowboy Joe' and 'Alexander's Ragtime Band', black bands and entertainers were at least getting a share of the action. One of the most intriguing was James Reese Europe, whose black Hellfighters captivated French audiences during the First World War. Recordings by Europe's black bands are rhythmically stiff compared to even the earliest jazz, but the use of breaks and flexible tonality show what was just about to happen. Reese was a dynamic leader, whom many think could have become a

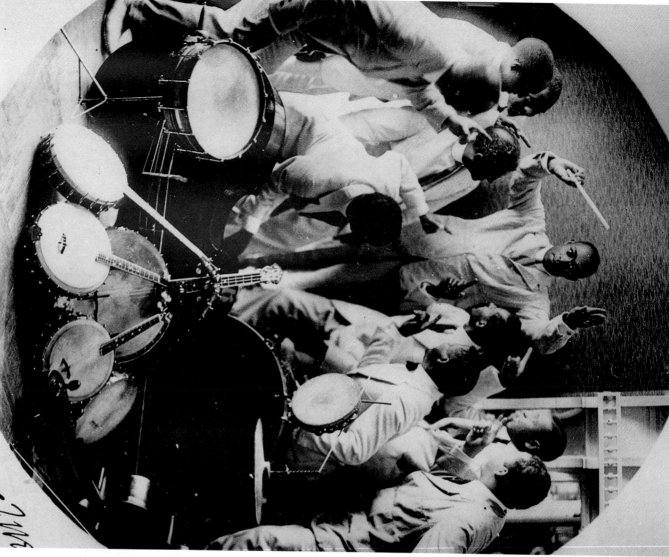

black Paul Whiteman if he hadn't been murdered in 1919. Europe was possibly the first to identify the expressive characteristics of what is now called black music, saying that black musicians should forget about trying to copy whites.

On the often thorny question of race, if one accepts jazz as an inspired and comprehensive fusion, which is the view put forward in this book, surely it follows that who plays it is irrelevant? Things are not that simple. All the impetus for the fusion came from those of African descent, and the continuing rhythmic tradition, expressed most obviously in the rituals of black churches, has no obvious white parallel. The fact of innumerable white musicians throughout the world playing what is recognizably jazz is now accepted and, in many cases, their wider influence acknowledged. But must their style of jazz, for reasons of tradition and upbringing, be different?

As a person's music comes out of his or her experience, differences can be expected and, even, quantified. However, one need only reverse the sometime argument that white people should not try to play black jazz, by applying it to European classical music (some prominent black musicians, especially in the early days, might have been 'lost' to jazz, had discrimination not ruined their chances of making it in the classical field), to realize the futility of setting rigid barriers, whichever direction they face.

The remarkable bandleader James Reese Europe, who later became a Lieutenant leading a black orchestra during the First World War. His vocalist, Noble Sissle (on Europe's left) himself became a well-known bandleader, employing Sidney Bechet and writing musicals with Eubie Blake.

Just as in Louis Armstrong's day, the best-known jazz trumpeter alive comes from New Orleans, Louisiana. The link with tradition symbolized by Wynton Marsalis could not be better timed, given that musicians acknowledge as never before the legacy left them by generations of pioneers.

Did jazz really, as is claimed, begin there? With qualifications, the answer must be yes. You could find syncopated ragtime, improvized breaks and growling through mutes elsewhere. Something was missing, though, an ingredient added by the Armstrongs and Mortons as they travelled and spread the message.

Why New Orleans? Firstly, its cultural heritage was exceptionally diverse even for the immigrant-laden New World. A French colony, it was for a time ceded to Spain, then sold to the U.S. in 1803. Thanks to its position at the mouth of the Mississippi/ Ohio River, it became a booming port.

Compared to the stern Protestant ethic elsewhere in the South, the attitudes prevailing in this Roman Catholic city encouraged dances and music, both functional (parades, weddings, funerals) and for entertainment. Its reputation was such that around 1850 a touring minstrel show called itself the New Orleans Serenaders even though members came from elsewhere, a ploy many bands in far-flung countries have since emulated.

Uniquely in the Southern States, African roots were not suppressed. For several years, New Orleans allowed its black inhabitants to take their drums, of which the plantation owners were so terrified, to Congo Square. In the open, they played and acted out rituals which, despite official church opposition, combined Catholicism and their old religions (given a catch-all name of voodoo).

A mixed-race group known as Creoles lived downtown and developed their own cultural identity. As the surnames made clear, their backgrounds were often French, perhaps the free descendents of wealthy landowners and their black mistresses (long before Abraham Lincoln, New Orleans encouraged the liberation of slaves). They looked to France and Latin Europe in general, and aspired to European standards of excellence.

So far as we know, black, white and Creole bands played similar music, though each did it differently. The repertory would include rags, marches and a spread of popular ditties. Whatever their ethnic origins, these people were working class. A few might be professional musicians, but most players held down ordinary jobs - making cigars seems a vocation favoured among the Creoles, while the leader of one of the early white bands, drummer Jack Laine, was a blacksmith. The black bands were the most expressive, more inclined to diverge from a score, if any existed.

Under these conditions, something had to happen. The catalyst, act of fission, or whatever, which speeded the process was the code discrim-

A marching band in New Orleans, around 1910.

A Storyville landmark. The Arlington Annex of Tom Anderson featured everything from string trios to the Luis Russell band.

The role of the lead trumpeter, the King of New Orleans jazz, as he punches out the melody in spare and direct phrases, is usually traced back to Buddy Bolden. His main rival on cornet around 1900 was probably Manuel Perez, and his successor as King is usually given as Freddie Keppard. Both were Creoles (though, unlike Perez, Keppard didn't read music), so the musical mix was nearly complete.

New Orleans also boasted the first legal red-light district in the Western world. As work-centres for musicians, the brothels of Storyville have been subject to debate: some blame the mass emigration of talent on the district's closure in 1917, others point out that mainly pianists were used for entertaining customers. One can easily imagine, however, musicians in the nearby cabarets and honky-tonks gaining from the snowballing economic effect, only to be the first to suffer, at a later date, when the snow suddenly melted.

Direct African influence is clearly present through the use of the drum. Evolving over a period to fit the 2/4 and 4/4 tempo of the marches and rags and, on the surface, far removed from the complexities of African drumming, it revolutionized popular music as the emphasis changed from military stiffness towards the springy beat we now call swing.

inating against anyone of African descent and aimed deliberately at the Creoles. How ironic that, by forcibly integrating two groups previously wary of each other, a racist law inspired by the White League led directly to this century's most potent, and above all black-inspired, cultural innovation. Competing with the blacks from uptown, the Creoles had to coexist musically. They were conspicuously better trained, notably the woodwind players. But they couldn't improvize.

That soon changed. Alphonse Picou became sufficiently involved to jazz up for clarinet the piccolo part from the march 'High Society', now a jazz standard. Technical skill and, in particular, the counter-melodic role of the clarinet were the Creoles' important contributions.

On the riverboats. Fate Marable (piano), Louis Armstrong (trumpet).

1920S

The Spread of Jazz

In 1916, the Original Dixieland Jass Band (ODJB) came from New Orleans to New York via Chicago and, in the following year, made their first record. Thus did the ball start rolling for the new music, which people throughout the world soon learnt to spell J-A-Z-Z, (some New Orleans musicians of all races continue to use the word 'Dixieland').

The racial politicking around jazz has caused the white ODJB to be undervalued. They didn't invent the music, and many black contemporaries played it better. On the evidence, however, their repertory mix of ragtime and blues, down to the imitation farmyard noises, can be taken as representative of early New Orleans jazz and its offshoots. The front-line of trumpet, clarinet and trombone was the accepted minimum for the Dixieland brass-band effect.

As to how good they were, the respected British writer Iain Lang was genuinely impressed by clarinettist Larry Shields when the ODJB came to London in 1919, while spotting at once that Sidney Bechet, heard in person the following year, was far more gifted.

Records and, very soon, radio broadcasts helped to spread the word and show would-be imitators how far they had to go. But the best lessons were taught by example. Riverboats out of New Orleans and bandleaders such as pianist Fate Marable, hiring top musicians to entertain customers on trips up the Mississippi, are part of the legend. In 1920, Louis Armstrong and his compatriots were treated like messiahs in St. Louis when they

Paul Whiteman, the 1920s 'King of Jazz'. His attempt to merge jazz with Western symphonic traditions would today have made him a cross-cultural hero.

stepped off the boat and played at a dance. What they did, and the locals didn't, was improvize.

Given its ragtime roots, St. Louis had plenty of music. Charles Creath, perhaps the first in a line of St. Louis trumpeters that includes Harold Baker, Clark Terry and Miles Davis, recorded 'Grandpa's Spells' by Jelly Roll Morton in 1925, a year before the marvellous version by Morton's Red Hot Peppers. Clipped and more formal, closer to ragtime, it is worthy enough to invite comparison, not least over the trumpet lead where Creath's playing differs markedly from that of George Mitchell.

For many, the Jazz Age came alive in Chicago. King Oliver drew large crowds to the Lincoln Gardens and, later, it was in Chicago that Jelly Roll Morton made his classic recordings, using mostly musicians from home. The craze for 'hot' dance music throughout the Mid West ensured that bands both black and white had fanatical support, while some of those flocking to hear Oliver, espec-

ially after Louis Armstrong joined him, were there just to study jazz.

Musicians from Bix Beiderbecke, already a favourite for his exemplary lead work at the head of the Wolverines, to Benny Goodman had links with Chicago, so that the city's name has come to stand for the white musicians of the Twenties. The best of them developed their own styles, though the so-called 'white sound' (with connotations of being less expressive) really stems from the pure-toned Beiderbecke and his influence on trumpeters. One could hardly accuse Pee Wee Russell, or even the early Goodman, of putting smoothness above all.

Towards the end of the decade, the spotlight moved away from Chicago. Armstrong and Morton had gone, while touring bands led by Jean Goldkette and Ben Pollack, not to mention the 'King of Jazz' Paul Whiteman, snapped up the top white talent, including Beiderbecke. The concept of jazz as the rhythmic apotheosis of the brass band was also changing. In New York, around the time that Armstrong was tearing things up at the Lincoln Gardens, Fletcher Henderson had tentatively launched the next craze. Played for the dancers thronging the Roseland Ballroom, his music had few

improvized clarinet counterlines. Instead, two saxophones were given arranged ensemble roles alongside two trumpets and a single trombone. Dancers loved it. They turned Henderson into a celebrity, so that Armstrong, when asked to leave Oliver and join the band, felt that he was stepping up. During the year he played in Henderson's trumpet section, he taught the band to swing. Arranger Don Redman freely acknowledged Armstrong's impact upon musicians and upon his own writing, as is clear when you hear the records in date order.

New York increasingly became the place to be. The recording industry was there, and good money could be earned in clubs, not least, as Duke Ellington proved, by drawing white folk to Harlem. Arrangers grew more ambitious, so groups expanded in size to fill out their harmonies. Perhaps more important, the tuba and its brass relations were replaced gradually as rhythm instruments by the string bass. The last impediment to swing had gone.

Kid Ory's Creole Jazz Band, California, early 1920s.

The Vendome Theater in Chicago put on shows aimed at black audiences.

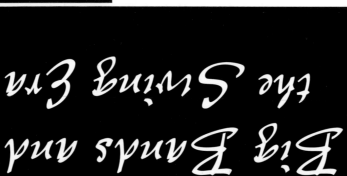

The John Kirby Sextet, New York 1939. From left to right, Kirby (with bass), O'Neil Spencer (drums), Russell Procope (alto saxophone), Buster Bailey (clarinet), Charlie Shavers (trumpet) and Billy Kyle (piano).

T hroughout the Thirties, Duke Ellington remained the jazz composer supreme, working regularly and rarely having to change personnel. His music was inimitable. Paul Whiteman, who had swapped the occasional score with Fletcher Henderson, listened intently to Ellington at the Cotton Club and admitted that he could steal nothing from him.

The outstanding recordings of the Jazz Age, Armstrong's Hot Fives and Sevens, helped define the instrumental solo and hasten the decline, for the moment, of the New Orleans/Dixieland ensemble. They did not otherwise contribute to the *lingua franca* of swing which emerged through trial and error, built around the rhythmic refinement of the call-and-response patterns, in which brass and reed sections counter each other's phrases, the use of repetitive phrases (riffs), to propel the soloist, and the change from a slightly stop-go

2/4 beat to an even 4/4, facilitated by the replacement of the tuba's oompahs by the smoothly-plucked rhythms of the string bass.

Oddly enough, some of the most naturally swinging jazz of the Twenties was recorded in New Orleans, notably the collective improvizations of bands led by trumpeters Louis Dumaine and, especially, Sam Morgan. New Orleans possibly pioneered the string bass: Morgan used one, and such noted bassists as John Lindsay (with Morton's Red Hot Peppers), Pops Foster (in Luis Russell's great band of 1929-30) and Wellman Braud (who joined Duke Ellington in 1927) all came from New Orleans.

By 1930, Armstrong had a band and the swing style around New York, as practised by Henderson, Don Redman and Cab Calloway, was well past the experimental stage. Leaders were not always what they seemed: the Mills Blue Rhythm Band, for instance, fronted by Lucky Millinder, was named after the agent

Irving Mills, who used them as relief for Ellington and other bands in his employ.

While the jazz remained buoyant, the Depression years took their toll. Outside New York musicians hustled, often for little pay. White bands that did well tended to play so-called sweet music, the Casa Loma being almost the only exception, while Benny Goodman and others took refuge in radio bands, an area barred to blacks. Where the pianist/ impresario Jean Goldkette (who had hired Bix Beiderbecke and defeated Fletcher Henderson in a 'battle' at the

Alphonso Trent (centre, with accordion) at the Adolphus Hotel, Dallas in 1925. T. Holder (trumpet) is second from left; Snub Mosley (trombone) is fourth from left.

In the Thirties, swinging jazz became the music to inspire dancers, shown here at the Savoy Ballroom in Harlem.

Roseland) once ran several orchestras, he was by now just an agent.

New York's main rival as a centre for swinging sounds became Kansas City, bossed politically by Tom Prendergast. Thoroughly corrupt, Prendergast nevertheless pitched his appeal to those at the bottom end of the social ladder (using people rather than machines on building work, for instance, all put through his own firm). Because all forms of night life flourished under Prendergast, so did musicians.

If Kansas City was the magnet, good black dance bands proliferated all over the South West. Walter Page's Blue Devils in Oklahoma, Troy Floyd, Don Albert and Alphonso Trent in Texas, Jesse Stone in Missouri and Nat Towles in Omaha were among those most revered. Unfortunately, little of what they did survives. Trent, for instance, broadcast regularly on radio in Dallas but before the days of home taping. The few recordings by Page and Stone give more than a hint of their quality while, from a band that recorded only eight titles, Trent's Clementine is nothing short of magnificent.

The bandleaders who made it nationally were Kansas City's Benny Moten, a canny operator who raided Basie's, which tied a relaxed beat to Page himself, and Andy Kirk with his Clouds of Joy, originally from Oklahoma but discovered by recording executives in Kansas City. Moten's band eventually became Count Basie's, including

arrangements of minimal complexity, embellished by arguably the most gifted bunch of soloists ever meshed in a single unit.

By then, Benny Goodman had been crowned King of Swing, while drummer Chick Webb ruled the Savoy Ballroom and Jimmie Lunceford combined showmanship with impeccable jazz. Artie Shaw and Tommy Dorsey got the highest profiles and the first crack at the Hollywood musicals, but those black bands that had battled through also benefited.

The stature of jazz as an evolving American phenomenon finally sunk in. Benny Goodman's concert at New York's Carnegie Hall paid tributes to everything from the ODJB to Basie and Ellington. The two 'Spirituals to Swing' concerts included a gospel quartet, Sidney Bechet's 'Weary Blues' and the trio of Albert Ammons, Meade Lux Lewis and Pete Johnson playing boogie-woogie, which was nothing more than a marketing term for blues piano. Racially-mixed groups, live and on records, were accepted, at least outside the South. Jazz seemed to be booming. What could go wrong?

T he start of the Second World War did not, on the surface, affect jazz other than by stifling the inevitable spread of the music abroad. Coleman Hawkins and Benny Carter had been among those working and recording in Europe alongside the locals. Quite apart from the amazing Django Reinhardt, such talented musicians as British trombonist George Chisholm and French saxophonist Alix Combelle did not seem out of place.

At least until America entered the war, jazz was cruising into the Forties, outwardly secure, with more records available and more movies to show.

Dizzy Gillespie, foreground with trumpet, and his orchestra of the Forties. The pianist is John Lewis.

The birth of what became known as Bebop (sometimes Rebop, most often Bop) should be seen in that context. Charlie Parker, Dizzy Gillespie and their main disciples all came out of swing bands, and saw their own work as a natural development.

Bop was essentially the handiwork of two men. Parker established the phraseology and created the style, while Gillespie codified it and spelled out the implications. Its essence was a further subdivision of the beat. The 2/4 of Dixieland had been followed by the more even 4/4 of swing. Parker and Gillespie introduced eight even beats to the bar. The fact both could play accurately at great speed and invent melodies drawn from a wider than usual selection of notes (though the likes of Art Tatum and Coleman Hawkins had already shown compa-

rable harmonic sophistication) mattered much less than the way they exploited the rhythmic implications.

In a sense, they followed exactly the principle whereby black gospel groups shake up the rigid, slow-moving hymn form by filling the gaps. These eight beats, which Kenny Clarke, Max Roach and the new breed of drummers tapped out by stick on cymbal, doubled the space available to bop's greatest figures. The irregular length of phrases played at speed - stopping and starting on, off and between beats - gave Parker's solos their remarkable rhythmic momentum. More beats to the bar also allowed more space for the drummers to plug, by abrupt accents or brief drum rolls.

The trumpeter Theodore 'Fats' Navarro, trombonist J.J. Johnson and saxophonist Sonny Stitt were almost

Woody Herman with his Second Herd at the Commodore Hotel, New York, in 1948. Serge Chaloff is at the microphone, Stan Getz (left) and Zoot Sims are shown in the saxophone section.

the only other horns to sound really comfortable playing the new music, while Bud Powell was the giant among a handful of pianists. A short-lived group replacing the extravagances of bop with more subtle textures, the so-called Birth Of The Cool band, hinted at great things to come from Miles Davis, most notable of those who gained prominence in the Forties but matured during the next decade.

The economic bubble sustaining big band jazz burst after the war, a combination of returning servicemen looking for work, increased popularity of canned music and disc jockeys and because former band singers like Frank Sinatra could make it big on their own. Sidemen, especially in black bands, had never been well paid, and soon many swing survivors folded. Gillespie, though, formed a band which triumphed above all in translating bop's anarchic spirit, expressed through wild introductions and zigzag interludes, thereby popularizing its conventions.

The Bunk Johnson band in New York City, 1945. Left to right, Jim Robinson (trombone), Alcide 'Slow Drag' Pavageau (bass), Bunk Johnson (trumpet), Baby Dodds (drums), George Lewis (clarinet).

Woody Herman, launching his series of Herds, Boyd Raeburn and Stan Kenton all reflected bop to some extent, while the sonorous textures Gil Evans conjured up for Claude Thornhill's band inspired, some years later, an approach to orchestration more radical than the Gillespie band's essentially swing-adapted formula.

The most famous teeth in jazz belonged, or rather didn't, to trumpeter Bunk Johnson, figurehead of what became known as the New Orleans Revival. Twelve years older than Louis Armstrong, he was discovered doing odd jobs in Louisiana and given a set of dentures which enabled him to make his record debut at the age of 52. Other veterans were recorded, all leading to a grassroots movement that enshrined the three-piece front line and turned its back on swing.

Because the Revival produced no earth-shattering instrumentalist, it now tends to be ignored. But it made an enormous impact throughout the jazz world. Driven by pundits and fans rather than musicians, it extolled New Orleans-style collective improvisation and non-commercial music at the expense of arranged jazz, which could only be a poor imitation of European classical music - a philosophy in its own way not so different from that which sustained Punk Rock. On the plus side, it gave amateurs a lead-in, though the fanaticism and lack of tolerance shown towards other forms contributed far more than the rise of bop to the internal feuds which, by the end of the Forties, left jazz reeling as though in the aftermath of a three-handed prize fight.

1950s

Cool Jazz, Hard Bop and Consolidation

The Modern Jazz Quartet. Left to right: John Lewis, Percy Heath, Connie Kay, Milt Jackson.

The notion of jazz communicating as self-expression and placing the solo above everything else, rather than as music for dancers, had gradually become entrenched in the Forties. Bands lost their hold on the ball-rooms, and small groups playing in small clubs became the norm. Around the turn of the decade, Dizzy Gillespie reverted to a quintet, Herman and Basie also cut down and only Duke Ellington, Lionel Hampton and a few others were running full-time orchestras.

Just as Sidney Bechet had pressed suits during the Depression, so did J.J. Johnson find a job inspecting blueprints. In another parallel with the Thirties, white musicians took refuge in the studios, but this time in Hollywood working for films and television (the local union was segregated at the time and there were pressures to keep blacks out of studio work). They had access to record companies, from which emerged the so-called West Coast school. Although they tended to play on each other's records - all of which were categorized as part of cool jazz, then something of a fad - one can with hindsight see that Shorty Rogers, Jimmy Giuffre, Art Pepper and the rest were not necessarily trying the same things.

The most popular groups of the early Fifties were from the West Coast though, again, hardly representative of any movement. Gerry Mulligan formed a piano-less quartet featuring Chet Baker, an unknown young trumpeter. Many people likened their often jovial counterpoint to jazz from the Chicago of old, and compared Baker with Bix Beiderbecke. Another quartet, pitting the ultra-relaxed noodling of Paul Desmond on alto saxophone against the two-fisted, classically-inspired improvizations of leader-pianist Dave Brubeck, discovered a new audience around the college circuit.

Back East, two survivors of the early Dizzy Gillespie band formed a group which eventually became the Modern Jazz Quartet, starring Milt Jackson on vibraphone and John Lewis on piano. The classical borrowings found occasionally in Lewis's arrangements, no less than an insistence upon formal dress, upset a few, but they set a standard for ensemble interplay rarely approached, before or since.

Things were getting better. As befits music ten years old, bop became assimilated. The new generation could not only play it but concentrate on different elements, perhaps even look back beyond bop. Some, notably the young trumpeter Clifford Brown, were comparable, as virtuosos, to Parker and Gillespie. Others, including saxophonist Jackie McLean and pianist Horace Silver, took what they could use from, respectively, Parker and Bud Powell, and came up with something simpler, yet personal - in Silver's case, a unique blend of bop and the Kansas City blues. There were those such as trumpeter Kenny Dorham who, while he had made his reputation alongside Charlie Parker, was now far more assured.

Almost coincidental with Parker's death in 1955, they evolved a *lingua franca* for small-group jazz, in the process smoothing bop's more jagged edges. Someone coined the name Hard Bop, perhaps acknowledging the declamatory accompaniment of drummer Art Blakey (though "easier bop" might have done just as well).

This remained the dominant style of the Fifties, soon linked to the modal themes used by Miles Davis, whose tenor saxophonist John Coltrane became a huge influence. With his lightning-fast fingering and asymmetrical phrasing, Coltrane even suggested yet another rhythmic division (from eight beats in the bar to sixteen); in the short term, however, disciples found his tone and his highly sophisticated harmonic sense rather easier to emulate. Add the rediscovery of Thelonious Monk, previously regarded as an obscure bebop pioneer, to the continuing impact made by Sonny Rollins and mid-Fifties modern jazz seemed healthy enough.

As a new generation of fans and critics/reviewers increasingly rejected the old sectarianism, so did a semblance of unity come to pass. Survivors from the swing era were regularly recorded. Just as in the late Thirties, a momentum gathered to celebrate the historical sweep of jazz - in this case, expressed through the growth of the jazz festivals. These events were designed to counter divisiveness by incorporating the lot, from Clara Ward's Gospel Singers to Cecil Taylor. Musicians of all ages and styles were seen to talk to each other and even perform together.

Thelonious Monk, later to appear on the cover of *Time* magazine, took part in the *Sound Of Jazz* TV spectacular, as did Lester Young, Billie Holiday, Pee Wee Russell, Red Allen and many others. The big bands of Count Basie and Woody Herman were back. In Europe and beyond, the influx of American groups ensured that interest in jazz continued to grow. What could go wrong?

Chamber jazz: the Chico Hamilton Quintet, with Jim Hall (guitar) Hamilton (drums).

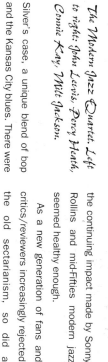

The tenor saxophones of the Jazz Couriers, Ronnie Scott (left) and Tubby Hayes.

1960S

Free Jazz and the African Connection

An exile from South Africa, whose passionate solos lit up the British scene: Dudu Pukwana on the alto saxophone.

Most jazz slanging matches seem odd in retrospect, and none more so than those of the early 1960s. How did the surface unity collapse so quickly? Why couldn't people accept Ornette Coleman's music, whether or not they actually liked it, and get on with whatever they were doing?

One culprit was the theory of progress, a strong undercurrent of the Fifties, under which jazz had to move forward. John Coltrane, Charles Mingus, Miles Davis and a few others had been identified as the vanguard but their influence, strong enough, did not start any violent arguments. Nobody called their albums *The Shape Of Jazz To Come*, whereas from the beginning Coleman was marketed as an iconoclast.

The furore also gained momentum because his music could be made to fit the mood of black nationalism. This had been simmering in the U.S., and it now became an issue as part of the debates over Civil Rights and the pace and reality of racial integration. Simply put, some black intellectuals were seeking an African solution in which the European elements in their culture would be played down, even eradicated. Coleman seemed to turn his back on bar lines, harmonic improvizing and the tempered scale - all of them conspicuously Western inventions.

From nowhere, it seemed, a whole movement emerged. Their credo was summed up in the saying attributed to Albert Ayler, one of the most significant of the so-called New Wave. "It's not about notes, it's about feelings." This tended to encourage the viewpoint that being able to play your instrument properly was a secondary consideration. There is, of course, no evidence that Coleman, Ayler and the others were interested in anything other than making music. They were not responsible for the political subtext, which expanded as pundits, black and white, tried to fit music to fashionable doctrines.

What became known as free jazz spread quickly outside the U.S. and, somewhat perversely, gave impetus to a kind of European nationalism. Put simply, again, European critics had recognised a lack of rhythmic drive in their own jazz compared to the best American product. Now, swing no longer mattered so much and collective improvization was taking precedence over the long solo. German writer Joachim Berendt made a case for the innately collectivist traditions of Europe (unlike the rugged individualism of the New World) coming into their own.

Most countries in Western Europe, and many beyond, developed their own schools of free improvization, often taking the concept of Coleman, Ayler, Cecil Taylor or Archie Shepp as a launching pad before moving on. The British for a time favoured total abstraction. In Germany, Peter Brotzmann seized upon the aggression of what some called 'energy music' and produced the most stentorian

New sounds from Britain. The quintet of Joe Harriott (alto sax), with Coleridge Goode (bass).

saxophone brays in the instrument's history. Equally into aggression, the Dutch then realized that making funny noises on instruments could be made, well, funny; since then, many of their top musicians have well-honed comic personae.

Meanwhile, established stars had continued to thrive. In fact, Mingus, Davis and Coltrane all recorded arguably their finest albums in the early Sixties, without rebuffing older fans, while the front-line of Wayne Shorter and Lee Morgan/Freddie Hubbard turned Art Blakey's Jazz Messengers into his best yet. A style promulgated as Soul Jazz, adapting the secularization of gospel music pioneered by Ray Charles, proved listenable and popular.

Then Davis enticed Shorter away from Blakey and espoused a more abstract group style, often summarised as 'time, no changes', because it largely scrapped harmonic improvizing while maintaining a steady pulse. Coltrane's music became freer, with a touch of mysticism, and Mingus actually dropped out for a while. Jazz as we had known it was leaderless.

Davis, characteristically, inspired the next phase. He was not the first jazz musician to pick up on the technological breakthrough of the

time - the synthesizer and/or the electric keyboard - or to hire the new breed of guitarist. Gary Burton's bubbling quartet of the mid-Sixties had Larry Coryell on guitar and used country-style rhythms. Paul Bley briefly dabbled with a synthesizer, while Sun Ra had played various keyboards before getting organs and synthesizers to enhance the outer-space effects of his music.

What Davis did was ram electronics down the throats of his, initially, reluctant sidemen, who happened to possess musically some of the best brains around. The subsequent achievements and affiliations of Herbie Hancock, Tony Williams, Wayne Shorter, Chick Corea and others who took part in the remarkable series of recordings Davis made in the late-Sixties dominated the music in the following years.

A giant of the New Wave, with an unmistakable 'cry' on tenor saxophone: Albert Ayler.

By the end of the Sixties, the steam had gone out of the free movement. Experience of bebop should have pointed to the danger of using innovation as a selling point - how long can new remain new?. The most distinguished supporter of free jazz, John Coltrane, was dead. The steam had also gone out of jazz as African. We were not too far from the position, expressed with ever-increasing fervour by Art Blakey during the last years of his life, that jazz was the great American music.

This is not to deny the staying power of free improvization. Cecil Taylor, Anthony Braxton, and several Europeans do it at least some of the time, while the style of free jazz - saxophone plus rhythm - introduced by Ornette Coleman is still around. But the impetus lay elsewhere, symbolized by a remark of Chick Corea's when he left Circle, a quartet with deep roots in the progressive soil. In setting up the friendly, electric Return To Forever, he said he no longer wished to play music that, in effect, nobody understood.

A typical group of the Seventies used keyboards and guitars and had drummers often surrounded by tom-toms, each of which they were duty-bound to thwack at least once per set. Weather Report, with Wayne Shorter and Joe Zawinul, were the aristocrats, and demanded most concentration, at least on record. Herbie Hancock, now on keyboards, formed a sextet which contained the seeds of much that is taken for granted today. Then, people found it arid, so he switched to an appealing, if ultimately formulaic, band, patterned on Sly Stone's concept of funk, with which he had several hits.

The most ecstatic audiences were probably those belonging to John McLaughlin's Mahavishnu Orchestra, whose drummer, Billy Cobham, later formed a similar group of his own. Strangely, the man responsible for all this was somewhat in eclipse. Miles Davis toured and recorded, but did not ignite crowds as others did. He retired in 1975, it was thought, then, for ever.

For those unmoved by jazz fusion or jazz-rock, and here we identify the traditional (in the widest sense) jazz fan, one alternative was to keep an eye on Europe. Keith Jarrett, whose European recitals of solo piano were among the phenomena of the time, eventually formed a quartet featuring Norwegian saxophonist Jan Garbarek, a singular talent destined to become one of the big names and whose glacial, haunting sound could fairly be described as evoking Scandinavia. Britain's virtuoso saxophonist, John Surman, used electronics not to make a bigger noise but to enhance the development of his folk forms.

Of the fusion groups, Weather Report were the most consistently inventive. Co-leaders Joe Zawinul (left) on keyboards and Wayne Shorter on tenor saxophone. Jaco Pastorius (right) on bass guitar.

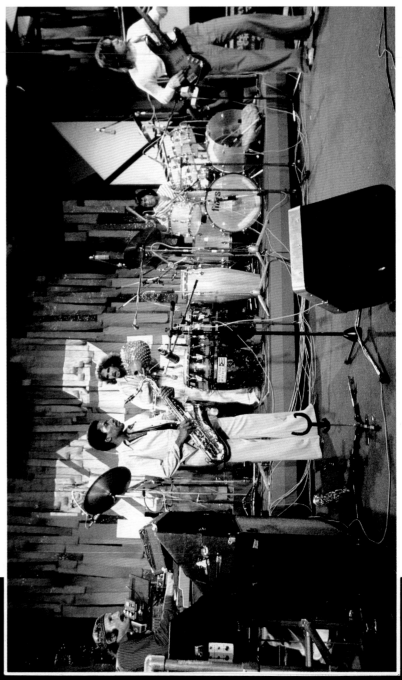

The dream of a world of ethnic impr-ovizers was being realized.

What of straight jazz? It actually survived quite well, mainly because of global demand. The staying power of the big bands was underlined by the Thad Jones-Mel Lewis band, a once-a-week outfit in New York, making international tours. When Duke Ellington died, his son Mercer took over as leader. Touring packages of long-departed groups. In 1967, Paul Desmond had left Dave Brubeck, after sixteen years; by 1972, he was back for a special tour. The Modern Jazz Quartet disbanded in 1974, but the lure of regular gigs brought them back in 1982. It was hard, though, to predict a future for any youngster who just wanted to find a rhythm section and play the blues.

"It was really funny to see us at a concert with the whole groupie bit. The band had nothing to do with it. If you did anything worse than drink a beer you would lose control of the music because there was a lot going by really fast. But the kids - the place would be reeking with all kinds of stuff." Billy Cobham reminiscing about the Mahavishnu Orchestra.

Musicians from the heyday of New Orleans led abstemious lives. Few drank or smoked and, as a result, they often enjoyed ripe old ages. That has not been the case elsewhere. The image of jazz used to revolve around its nightlife connotations - sex, drink and drugs, in changeable order. Dance halls and clubs, often under gangster control, overflowed with booze while the background and lifestyle of some musicians led them to hard drugs at an early age. On a lighter note, a select coterie through-out the world could boast of the time Louis Armstrong let them share his joint of cannabis.

Anyone who spent several years watching jazz would have seen musicians performing when the worse for drink or in various stages of drug withdrawal. Opponents of bebop even tried to correlate it with the drug habits of Charlie Parker and others, claiming that you not only had to be high to play it, but also to wish to do so in the first place.

From about the Seventies, this changed. Perhaps the switch from clubs to festivals, concert halls and general globe-trotting helped, as did the publicized success of John Coltrane and others in kicking their habits. One still hears rumours, but it can be stated with confidence that the seriously addicted jazz performer is virtually extinct.

The Mahavishnu Orchestra, with leader John McLaughlin on guitar in the foreground. Drummer Billy Cobham later formed his own group.

U p to this point, jazz had swung symmetrically with the decades, as even numbers (1920s, etc.) produced the new ideas which the odd ones then consolidated. At first sight, the 1980s broke this sequence, because never before had the tradition of jazz, in something like its fullest panoply, been thrust into public gaze and exposed to such diligent examination.

Why? Could jazz - after Ornette Coleman, Cecil Taylor, jazz-rock and every kind of crossover - have run out of ways to change? That's not correct, though one could put a case for saying it had run out of ways to make itself harder to understand (cf. European music, where atonality and serialism now seem miles away).

More significantly, a generation had arrived, musically literate, looking for role models and sufficiently distant from the past to take an intense, critical look. As pianist Julian Joseph put it, "Miles Davis could see Louis Armstrong and Duke Ellington first hand. Our generation has to understand what they were doing by learning it. When we evolve something of our own as a result, it has a strong foundation."

Joseph may be British, but Americans born after 1960 are equally keen to absorb jazz, not through osmosis, but by study. Their attitude precisely reverses that of the Sixties, when a new generation glanced at jazz, found that there were too many rules and chose freedom. In the Eighties, the notion that 'it's not about notes, it's about feelings' meant little to those well-schooled musicians hooked on jazz and wanting something to get their teeth into. Inevitably, they discovered bebop, arguably the toughest form of improvized music yet devised and one

A new voice making a big impact curing the Eighties: Cassandra Wilson.

Alto saxophonist Steve Coleman inspired new sounds to go with rap vocals.

which had spent 20 years in the wilderness.

The event which launched the decade took place in the summer of 1980, when Wynton Marsalis joined Art Blakey's Jazz Messengers, then hardly at their career peak. A charismatic trumpeter aged nineteen, Marsalis drew media attention to the Messengers and helped give Blakey a platform. As a proselytizer always ready to sell the virtues of jazz, Blakey could convince because he had ignored every craze for fusions and world music. Now, the crowds were willing to listen, while his hiring of gifted young soloists (when Marsalis joined, the musical director was Bobby Watson), which he regularly replaced, fitted exactly the widespread need for a jazz musicians' finishing school.

The sudden surge in popularity of the Jazz Messengers must be due to reasons. Their records and others linked to the old Blue Note record label took off. While his back-catalogue sold in vast quantities, Blakey cut nearly as many albums between 1980 and 1983 as in the entire Seventies.

His records also took off in clubs where new styles of jazz dance emerged. The idiom was mainly hip hop, often fortified by recorded samples taken from Blue Note and its contemporaries and sometimes called Acid Jazz. With the spread of hip hop as a streetwise expression of black American music, saxophonist Steve Coleman and others found a way to improvize around its twitchy rhythms and odd metres. In constructing an instrumental style to underpin the rap vocal, Coleman was smart enough to invent the acronym M-Base (Macro-Basic Array of Structured Extemporization) for reference.

For the first time in 30 years, jazz had a slice of the action in the clubs that succeeded the dance halls of old. Apart from rap and hip hop, the Latin dance music marketed as Salsa

Art Blakey's Jazz Messengers c. 1985. L-r Mulgrew Miller, Lonnie Plaxico, Jean Toussaint, Terence Blanchard, Blakey, Donald Harrison.

as musicians, probably for the same reasons. Their records and others linked to the old Blue Note record label took off. While his back-catalogue sold in vast quantities,

- the latest expression of a link forged long ago between jazz and so-called Afro-Cuban music - spread well beyond its ethnic confines. In commercial terms, the net benefit was to boost the visibility of jazz techniques, of trumpets and saxophones at the expense of twangy guitars.

Coincidentally, among older hands there was a move back towards acoustic sounds. Sonny Rollins played more show tunes and fewer rock ballads. Herbie Hancock and Chick Corea increased the time spent at the piano compared to the electric keyboard. While both contributed positively to jazz fusion, neither had moved an original concept to the next stage. By contrast Joe Zawinul, who always seemed to use electronics with the most resource, has largely stuck with keyboards to this day.

So, the younger generation overturned the ideas of the old. Also, a new slant on improvized music came along to fit a new kind of song and dance. In its capacity to shock, the decade acted true to form after all!.

THE TRADITION
America's Classical Music

As the past continued to expand, repertory bands and live interpretations of jazz classics proliferated: when he directed the Smithsonian Institute's Jazz Repertory Ensemble, Bob Wilber regularly gave concerts that started with Bessie Smith and ended with Coltrane. These still tended to be seen by many as history lessons, and optional at that, rather than as living cultural experiences.

In the Nineties, something strange happened. Musicians did not just acknowledge their (distant) heritage as an influence - there is no significant difference between Ruby

Braff, bypassing bebop and finding a home among swing-era musicians, and youngsters queuing up to join the latter-day Jazz Messengers - they went further, and enthusiastically re-created it.

A new generation has examined the detail of what happened during the previous jazz decades and, in the process, brought the past to life. When a tyro tenor saxophonist takes the advice of Wynton Marsalis to study the work of Eddie 'Lockjaw' Davis (and explains that training exclusively on Coltrane's solos means you rarely get to tackle the

lower registers) one appreciates how much has changed from a time when the practice, notably among black musicians, was to follow fashionable models and learn on the job.

An evangelical figure, Marsalis leads by example. Having played European classics at the highest level, he has the perspective of someone for whom interpretation comes naturally. When asked, he stresses the different skills interpreting jazz demands from a performer, compared to those needed when tackling classical scores. An outsider, though, is more struck by the similarities.

You can't treat jazz as classical music, people would insist, pointing out that Ellington wrote for specific

Trumpeters Lew Soloff (left) and Guy Barker revive Miles Davis-Gil Evans, London 1996.

34

musicians at a specific time. However, the Lincoln Center Orchestra and such projects as the Mingus Big Band and trumpeter Guy Barker's recitals prove it can be done. Having heard Marsalis put his own slant on the trumpet parts of 'Boy Meets Horn' (Rex Stewart) and 'Cornet Chop Suey' (Armstrong), one reckons that these pieces will be on concert platforms a hundred years from now.

Also defying pundits are the big bands themselves. Formed to back floor shows or to cater for dancers in ballrooms long since disappeared, musicians keep them alive as forums for the discipline and the joy of collective music-making - invaluable, now the great leaders have gone. Even card-carrying progressives join in, underpinning the claim by the Lincoln Center's Rob Gibson that the jazz big band is "the American vernacular equivalent of the European symphony orchestra". One would add only that the survival applies equally to Europe.

The big band of British composer/pianist Mike Westbrook.

GOSPEL MUSIC

"Musicians can be successful if they are young, black, erudite, wear a suit really well and claim to stand on the shoulders of the giants." Every style of jazz exists everywhere, but among recent arrivals outside the U.S. there have been few takers for the music implied in the preceding quote (from a very prominent black musician).

Before the Sixties, America ruled. Musicians from Europe and elsewhere were rated on how they might cope in front of a New York rhythm section. Apply this yardstick to someone like Jan Garbarek and you realize how irrelevant it has become.

The stylistic range is ever-widening. Add British guitarist Billy Jenkins and his blues-rock burlesques, the French Workshop de Lyon and the freejazz Globe Unity Orchestra run by German pianist Alexander von Schlippenbach to names mentioned

elsewhere in the book and you barely scratch the surface.

Folk and ethnic music of every kind affect improvizing ensembles - including the Anglo-Celtic Lammas, the Bulgarian Ivo Papasov's Wedding Band, Moldavian pianist Misha Alperin's Moscow Art Trio and many African groups. The spread of a hybrid popular culture in Europe among people of Asian descent promises much. If not as common on jazz gigs as tenor saxophones, such instruments

Wynton Marsalis leads the Lincoln Center Jazz Orchestra.

as uillean pipes, koras and didgeridoos no longer shock.

What strikes home is how much jazz bursts through. Rhythms might change, but the bass-and-drums team still prevails. Themes of 12 or 32 bars no longer dominate, but the approach to improvization resembles what has gone before.

Perhaps that explains why one area where the two sides (if one can so differentiate hard-swinging American jazz from the rest) readily mix is the big band. Similarities between current American and European bands far outweigh differences - compare the Vienna Art Orchestra's performances of Charles Mingus pieces with those by the Mingus Big Band. Frequent collaborations across countries between composers and bands suggest that, here, a common language exists and will continue to evolve.

Audiences are lucky. Instead of spending several hours at a jazz festival listening to assorted hard-bop quintets playing similar tunes, there is infinite variety. Conversely, after several hours of impeccably modulated ethnocentric music, nothing sounds better than a group swinging the 12-bar blues.

Jazz Giants

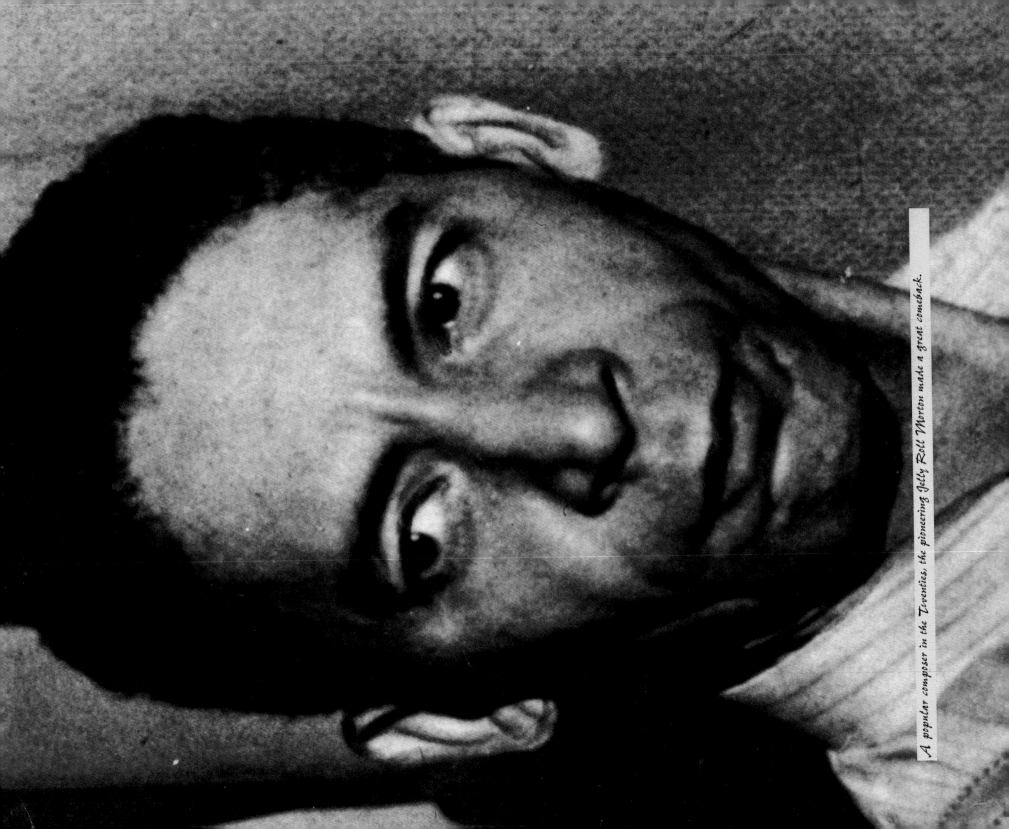

A popular composer in the Twenties, the pioneering Jelly Roll Morton made a great comeback.

Sidney Bechet

A cosmopolitan musician from youth, Sidney Bechet gave rise to the first serious instance of jazz criticism. In 1919, he was the clarinet soloist of the Southern Syncopated Orchestra led by composer Will Marion Cook, who refused to use the word "jazz" but made a point of featuring Bechet. Swiss conductor Ernest Ansermet heard the orchestra several times in London and wrote about Bechet, "[He] can say nothing of his art, save that he follows his own way... perhaps the highway the whole world will swing along tomorrow".

A musical prodigy, Bechet was born in New Orleans, to a Creole family, in 1897. He joined the exodus to Chicago in 1917, and worked there with two celebrated exiles, trumpeter Freddie Keppard and pianist Tony Jackson. With Cook, he travelled to London, where he discovered the soprano saxophone, a more dominating instrument than the clarinet, and one which readily produced his trademark throbbing vibrato.

Deported from Britain, for fighting in a hotel, Bechet moved to New York, where pianist Clarence Williams made a point of recording him, most notably alongside Louis Armstrong: an early meeting of jazz giants. However, he was soon in trouble once again, and he returned to Europe, spending four years with the Black Revue, starring Josephine Baker. While Armstrong was making his classic recordings, his main rival as a jazz soloist was touring Europe and Russia.

More trouble, this time prison, for a shooting in Paris, led eventually to a return to the US. Bechet worked steadily throughout the 1930s, less in the limelight than his talent deserved. Towards the end of the decade, stirrings of the so-called New Orleans revival led to an interest in pre-swing styles and Bechet enjoyed a much higher profile. Among his colleagues on record were Tommy Ladnier, Mezz Mezzrow, Muggsy Spanier and, later, Bunk Johnson and Wild Bill Davison.

After a triumphant return in 1949 for the Paris Jazz Festival, he decided to live in France. There, Bechet became a Gallic superstar (wife in the country; mistress in Paris), lording it over his accompanists and drawing vast crowds. His tune 'Petite Fleur' became a hit worldwide, though he was probably most proud of ballet scores such as 'La Nuit Est Une Sorcière', tuneful if a touch over-sweet in the manner of Charlie Chaplin's film music. Since his death in 1959, a statue of him has stood in a park in Antibes.

Domineering is a word often used of Bechet's music. His various scrapes are testimony enough to a short fuse. This comes over in solos that are often soaring and passionate, direct rather than ornate, and quite unmistakeable. Early recordings show him as Armstrong's equal, and, as he commands the ensemble with his burnished sound, his timing seems more in keeping with a trumpet lead than with the contrapuntal line usually adopted by saxophones and clarinets.

It would be wrong, however, to regard Bechet's work as merely a display of musical autocracy. This is particularly true before his move to France, and especially so of his work on clarinet. With Muggsy Spanier, a sensitive but far from powerful trumpeter, he is a model of restraint. Even the veteran Bunk Johnson, pretty frail by 1945, is free to play a commanding lead in settings close to the New Orleans ideal of relaxed counterpoint.

His greatest recordings would include the remarkable trio 'Blues In Thirds' with Earl Hines and Baby Dodds, 'Blue Horizon', 'Out Of The Gallion' with Mezz Mezzrow and any version of 'Summertime' or 'Weary Blues', a tune that could have been written with him in mind.

CLASSIC *Recordings*

The Legendary Sidney Bechet, RCA Bluebird. Includes the early Feetwarmers and 'Blues In Thirds'.

Sidney Bechet In New York, JSP. Includes reunion with Louis Armstrong.

The King Jazz Story Vol. 4, Storyville. Best of the Bechet-Mezzrows.

Jazz Classics Vol. 1, Blue Note. Includes Bunk Johnson, Albert Nicholas.

1917	Comes to Chicago.
1919	With Will Marion Cook, travels to Europe.
1923	Works with Duke Ellington and records with Louis Armstrong.
1926	Travels with Sam Wooding band to Moscow.
1929	Jailed in Paris.
1932	New Orleans Feetwarmers tracks with Tommy Ladnier.
1938	Records again with Ladnier as interest in pre-swing jazz revives.
1950	Tours Europe, and makes home in France.
1952	First recording of 'Petite Fleur'.
1953	Ballet suite 'La Nuit Est Une Sorcière' premiered in Paris.

Duke Ellington fed on the personalities of his musicians, as expressed through the music they played.

Duke Ellington

For about 50 years, Duke Ellington led an orchestra that toured the world and for which he composed most of the material. A favourite choice among pundits for the title of the greatest of all jazz musicians, he was a supreme manipulator of orchestral sounds.

Edward Kennedy Ellington was born in 1899 into a middle-class family in Washington. At first, he inclined towards art as a career, but he drifted into music, and by the mid-Twenties found himself leading a group then called the Washingtonians. The music he was asked to provide, notably at the famous Cotton Club, was intended to transport white Americans to the Deep South and into the depths of the African jungle. He backed the cabaret turns, and when you hear pieces called 'Jungle Jamboree' or 'Song Of The Cotton Field' it's easy to visualize the floor show.

Ellington's genius lay in exploiting an empirical approach to instrumental sound, characteristic of a music for which there are no rules, where lesser men in his position might ignore or even suppress the individuality of their musicians. For instance, his early band included trumpeters Bubber Miley, a specialist in violently abrasive solos, and Arthur Whetsol, who embellished a tune with the kind of plangency that would, Ellington claimed, send tears running down

people's faces. Similarly, in the trombone section, he had Tricky Sam Nanton and the suave-toned Lawrence Brown. It seems so natural today for Ellington to have nominated Miley and Nanton for the jungle effects, while saving Whetsol for 'Mood Indigo'.

Pre-war, Ellington was already unique, and some of his impressionistic studies, in particular, were hardly part of the mainstream, yet it was simply a case of him being first among the many flourishing bands of the Swing Era. Around 1940, with bassist Jimmy Blanton adding extra lift to the rhythm section, Ellington brought together the many strands of his music to produce such masterpieces as 'Concerto For Cootie', 'Ko-ko' and 'Harlem Airshaft'. He also hired Billy Strayhorn, composer of the band's theme 'Take The A Train', to collaborate on the orchestrations, and they formed such a close working relationship that their contributions were sometimes difficult to tell apart.

After the war, as others disbanded, he carried on. The style of his performances never changed significantly, except that, as the 3-minute record gave way to the long-player, Ellington became even more inclined to write extended works. 'Tone Parallel To Harlem', of 1950, remains perhaps his most sustained effort, but the suites he poured out during his exceptionally prolific final period are held in increasingly high critical esteem.

Throughout, the baritone saxophone of Harry Carney remained constant, as did the alto of Johnny Hodges, apart from a few years in the early Fifties. Certain sounds never left his palette, even when instrumen-

talists moved on. Cootie Williams took Bubber Miley's place in 1929, remained until 1940 and returned in 1962. During his absence, the heavy growl effects were given mainly to Cat Anderson.

Ellington's piano playing, once ignored, began to register strongly, his ringing chords on 'Ko-ko' adding a fresh tonal palette to the band. An influence on Thelonious Monk, he recorded duets with Strayhorn and as a trio with Charles Mingus and Max Roach.

Ten years before his death in 1974, he was, incredibly, turned down for a Pulitzer Prize. Was it racial discrimination, or couldn't the committee take seriously a composer of something called 'Doing The Chocolate Shake'? Ellington, as ever the ultimate in urbanity, shrugged it off, observing that fate was kind in not wanting him to be too famous too young.

1923	Arrives in New York.
1927	First Engagement at the Cotton Club.
1931	'Creole Rhapsody' is first composition by jazz musician in extended form.
1933	Tours UK and Europe.
1939	Billy Strayhorn and Jimmy Blanton join the band.
1943	Premiere of 'Black, Brown and Beige'.
1959	Film score for *Anatomy of a Murder*.
1963	State Department tour of Asia.
1968	Second Sacred Concert.
1969	Awarded Presidential Medal of Freedom by President Nixon.

CLASSIC *Recordings*

Early Ellington,
RCA Bluebird.
Includes many of the early classics.

Duke Ellington 1935-36,
Classics.
Includes 'Reminiscing In Tempo'.

The Indispensable, Vols. 5-6,
RCA.
Includes the best of the best.

Such Sweet Thunder,
Columbia
One of his best-loved suites.

The Far East Suite,
RCA Bluebird.
One of the most successful later suites.

Playing the trumpet or singing, Louis Armstrong won fans from all over the world.

1 Louis Armstrong

Louis Armstrong, if anyone, invented the jazz solo. With his Hot Fives and Hot Sevens, recorded between November, 1925, and December, 1928, he changed the musical landscape, putting his distinctive jazz trumpet style on a par with the brilliance expected from a European classical virtuoso. Over the next forty years, his influence spread far beyond jazz, and he became one of the world's best-loved entertainers.

Born in 1901, in the Storyville district of New Orleans, he appears to have sailed through his childhood, though it seems quite grisly on paper. Possibly illegitimate, his mother left him for a time in the care of his grandmother, and may have been an occasional prostitute. His formal education was sketchy, but, left to run the streets, he was exposed to the rich musical life of his neighbourhood.

Committed to the Coloured Waifs' Home, he responded well to the discipline and joined the band. Starting on alto horn, his ability developed rapidly, and he was soon promoted to the post of bugler. His story from then on encapsulates that of jazz: work on the riverboats, the summons to join King Oliver in Chicago, the chance to show the Fletcher Henderson band how to swing, followed by stardom and a decade leading a big band.

One can trace the process on the records. His chorus on Oliver's 'Froggie Moore', a rag written by Jelly Roll Morton, set the style that led inexorably to the great titles under his own name. By this time, Armstrong could produce beautifully rounded tones over a considerable range, and you can actually hear the range expand year by year as he switches from cornet to trumpet. There's his rhythmic assurance, the way the notes swing whether on the beat or in between, and his marvellous timing as he turns the traditional two-bar break into a whole chorus backed by only the occasional chord, a routine tested on 'Cornet Chop Suey' and gloriously perfected on 'Potato Head Blues'.

In pianist Earl Hines, Armstrong at last found a musician on his wavelength. Their labyrinthine duet on 'Weather Bird' underlines that the jazz repertory in those days often resembled a multi-thematic rag, rather than the simple pop songs and riffs common in the Thirties. As for technique, his sensational opening cadenza to 'West End Blues' led to Roy Eldridge and Dizzy Gillespie, while the emotional depth and sense of drama of his solo on 'Tight Like This' look ahead to Miles Davis.

By the early Thirties he was fronting a big band and touring Europe. Singing became an increasingly important component of his work, though the best of the trumpet features had acquired an even greater majesty. In the 1940s, he gave up the band for the All Stars, a New Orleans-type group which, in various guises, lasted until his death. Earl Hines came back for a while, and trombonists included Jack Teagarden, whose voice matched Armstrong's in uniqueness, and Trummy Young. On clarinet, Barney Bigard was followed by Edmond Hall. If the group rarely pulled its full musical weight, there were always moments to treasure.

By now a familiar figure on the screen in such films as *High Society*, he toured the world, often under the auspices of the US State Department. Known familiarly as Satchmo, a name he didn't encourage but was able to bear, he rose to the top of the pop charts with 'Hello, Dolly' and 'Wonderful World'. After his death in 1971, more than twenty thousand people came to pay respects as his body lay in state, and his funeral was covered on television.

CLASSIC *Recordings*

Hot Fives & Sevens, Vols. 1-3,
JSP.
The classic sides.

Louis with Fletcher Henderson,
Forte.
The birth of a big band style.

Louis and Luis,
ASV.
The virtuoso soloist.

The California Concerts,
GRP.
The postwar small groups.

Louis Armstrong & Duke Ellington, Roulette.
Ellington tunes, with Duke at the piano.

1919	Works the riverboats with Fate Marable.
1923	Leaves New Orleans to join King Oliver in Chicago.
1924	On tour with Fletcher Henderson.
1925	Start of recording series by Hot Fives and Hot Sevens.
1931	Forms own big band. Makes first film.
1933	Launches two-year European tour in London.
1946	Debut of Louis Armstrong All Stars.
1960	Begins intensive touring under US State Department.
1964	Tops the charts with 'Hello Dolly'.
1968	Last British tour.

During the Twenties, Coleman Hawkins perfected the style that other saxophonists tried to copy.

Coleman Hawkins

Invented by Adolphe Sax around 1840, the saxophone at first struggled to find a niche outside military bands. Jazz, with its free-thinking attitude and, in New Orleans, the link with brass bands, provided an obvious outlet. By the Twenties, there were several performers on all varieties from soprano to bass. Coleman Hawkins specialized in the tenor and, apart from Sidney Bechet, was probably the first saxophonist to build a coherent and, ultimately, influential style.

His family were secure and relatively prosperous. Encouraged by his mother, he studied music and eventually fixed on the tenor saxophone. A life-long listener to classical music of all kinds, Hawkins had a grasp of conventional musical theory beyond that of Bechet or Louis Armstrong. On

Precocious and talented, Hawkins rapidly gained a place in the music business, and by 1924, when Armstrong joined the Fletcher Henderson band, he was already installed as its star. Within a year, Armstrong had turned the band round, Hawkins as much as anyone. The industrious slap-tongued soloist had discovered how to relax and swing.

Henderson's band of the time did not provide ideal conditions to display this, and a totally satisfying example of his new maturity did not emerge on record until 1929, when he made 'Hello Lola' and 'One Hour', the first of many luxuriant ballad solos, under

the other hand, he lacked their intuitive understanding of the jazz and blues traditions.

years were spent playing in and recording all over western Europe, notably with guitarist Django Reinhardt and a fellow American, the alto saxophonist Benny Carter. English fans could hear him, not only with Jack Hylton's band but in clubs where, ostensibly demonstrating Selmer saxophones, he would improvize on one tune for thirty minutes and more.

When he returned to the US in 1939, at the age of 35, he was treated as an old master. In the interim, his style had grown more convoluted and, soon afterwards, he made the first and best-known

the leadership of Red McKenzie. These set the trend of Hawkins's playing thereafter. On fast numbers, he surged forward with a multiplicity of notes that propelled the beat; at a ballad tempo, the lines became sensuous and rhapsodic. His tone on both was splendidly rich and ripe at all times, but its velvety texture on ballads remains his most identifiable trademark.

By the time he left the Henderson band in 1934, he had reached a peak which signified change, in a way later repeated in the careers of both Miles Davis and John Coltrane. The next 5

of his recordings of 'Body and Soul'. It became a hit, and remains the ultimate Hawkins ballad solo, identified with him forever.

While bebop upset some older musicians, Hawkins was sympathetic because he understood it. He hired Thelonious Monk as early as 1943, giving him his first chance to record in a studio, and thought nothing of having Howard McGhee, Dizzy Gillespie, Miles Davis or Fats Navarro as a trumpet partner. Rhythmically, however, he remained a swing man, and for much of the Fifties he worked in tandem with Roy Eldridge, in New York clubs and on tour.

His later work parallels in some way the development of Sonny Rollins, in that his tone lost subtlety and shading but gained in sheer brutality. In his final years, beset by melancholia and drinking even more brandy than before, he no longer had the breath for long, flowing lines. But the magic never left. Shortly before he died in 1969, he came to Ronnie Scott's in London and played 'Body & Soul', now bereft of all embroidery, in a stuttering but defiant undertone that had musicians and fans glued to their seats.

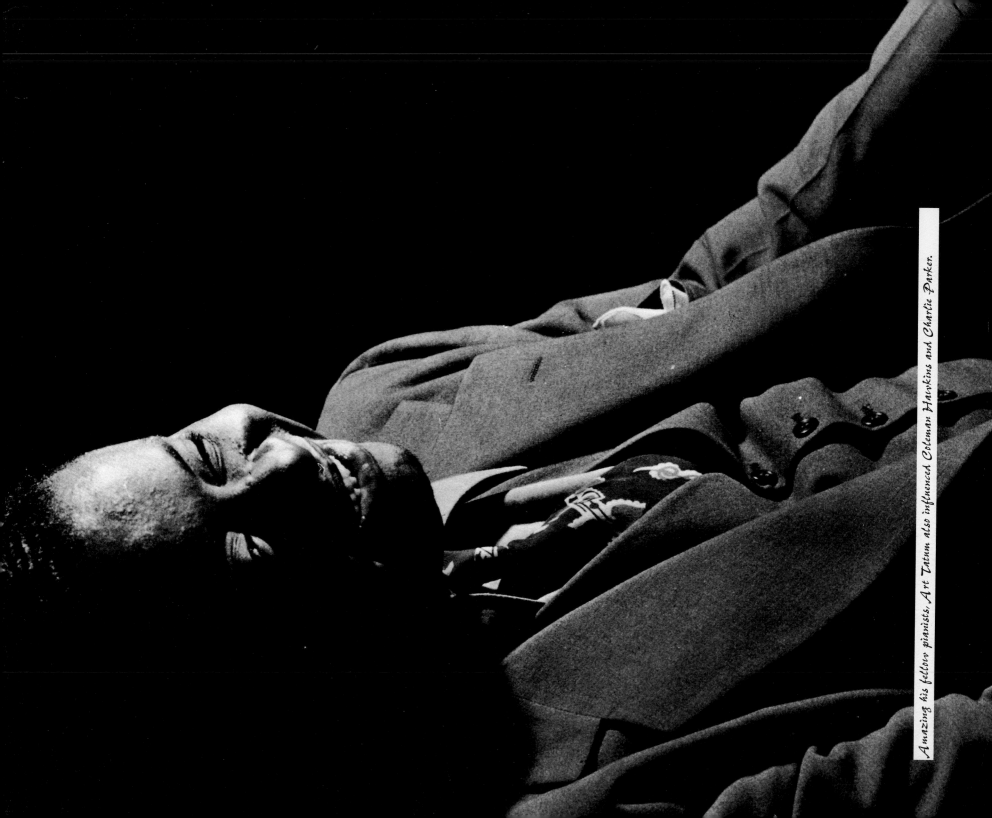

Amazing his fellow pianists, Art Tatum also influenced Coleman Hawkins and Charlie Parker.

Art Tatum

Ask a musician to name the greatest of them all and, if you are talking to a piano player who goes back a few years, the answer could well be Art Tatum. Speed of execution was merely the most obvious facet of his artistry at the keyboard. Yet he remained in the shadows, rarely interviewed or filmed during his lifetime, and taken for granted in the 30 years since his death.

1926	First professional engagements in Toledo.
1932	Arrives in New York as accompanist to singer Adelaide Hall.
1933	Makes first recording of piano solos.
1938	Toured UK and Europe.
1943	Formed most famous of his groups, a trio with Tiny Grimes (guitar) and Slam Stewart (bass).
1947	One of his few filmed appearances, a brief spot in *The Fabulous Dorseys*.
1953	First of a mammoth series of piano solos recorded for Norman Granz.

He was born in Toledo, Ohio in 1909. Cataracts in both eyes left him almost blind, and his parents sent him to a school for the handicapped, where his extraordinary gifts were developed. Starting as a stride pianist influenced by Fats Waller, he had perfect pitch, reharmonized any tune the instant he heard it and could tell the amount of beer left in his glass from the sound of it when tapped. He never forgot a voice, and eye, or a tour of the all-night clubs his mind retained enough sporting statistics to fill an encyclopedia.

His first major job was accompanying singer Adelaide Hall. After that, he usually worked under his own name as a solo performer, or that. Coleman Hawkins, already the first titan of the tenor saxophone, is said to have revamped his approach after hearing Tatum in Toledo around 1929. The teenage Charlie Parker washed dishes in a New York restaurant just because Tatum was playing there.

Though he was said to have ambitions to become a composer, defined in jazz terms. Instead, he chose the after-hours life where he was able to unwind at the piano, croon the blues if he felt the urge and drink his beer in peace.

Though he was said to have ambitions to become a composer, his stock pieces tended to be the popular songs of stage and screen, apart from a few showpieces such as Dvorak's 'Humoresque' and the occasional blues. His work in clubs was broken by the odd concert. In his later years, he was systematically recorded by Norman Granz for his Clef and Verve labels. The

where pianists congregated, Tatum always let the rest play first, as no-one dared follow him.

To the casual listener, a typical solo consisted of very fast runs filling the gaps between the melody. In fact, far from just embellishing it, Tatum often took quite amazing liberties with the tune, completely altering the harmonies or rattling off passages of fearsome complexity in the strictest tempo without ever stating the beat. His technique seemed to owe little to European music in that he kept his fingers flat over the keys, as Monk and others did, perhaps as a means of ensuring that even the beat-up pianos invariably set aside for jazz gigs would produce a sound worth hearing.

A few pianists reproduce some of his runs with conviction, but his influence went much deeper than that. Coleman Hawkins, already the first titan of the tenor saxophone, is said to have revamped his approach after hearing Tatum in Toledo around 1929. The teenage Charlie Parker washed dishes in a New York restaurant just because Tatum was playing there.

For all his ability, by the time of his death in 1956 Tatum had failed to make much impression on the public at large. Perhaps he didn't care. He could be a witty and articulate speaker, but he probably did not fancy the compromises needed to attract a mass audience even as defined in jazz terms. Instead, he chose the after-hours life where he was able to unwind at the piano, croon the blues if he felt the urge and drink his beer in peace.

output included the equivalent of 13 LPs of solo playing, with the rest featuring star musicians mostly of his own generation. Of these, the most successful paired him with Ben Webster, who kept it simple and swinging, produced his most gorgeous sound and wisely made no attempt to match Tatum for speed.

CLASSIC *Recordings*

Classic Early Solos, GRP. Most from 1934.

The Standard Transcriptions, Music and Arts. Taken off the air.

Complete Capitol Recordings, Vol. 1. Capitol. First of two CDs with his later trio.

Complete Pablo Group Masterpieces, Pablo (6 CDs). Includes Ben Webster and Benny Carter.

The Tatum Solo Masterpieces, Vol. 1, Pablo. The first solo session.

An original from top to toe, Lester Young preferred to tilt his saxophone at an angle.

Lester Young

If the lives of some leading musicians seem tragic, Lester Young's was probably the most poignant of all. A peaceful soul who only wanted to make music beautiful, he repeatedly found himself the centre of controversy through no fault of his own. The gradual but horrific decline of his last years suggested that being at odds with the world finally got to him.

His artistry was the most magical and elusive of them all. Where others drove hard and bore down on the beat, his phrases floated on air, symbolized by the way he twisted his saxophone at a horizontal angle high above the floor. With his cloudy tone and oblique phrasing, he seemed to distance himself from his improvizations in a way that was unprecedented among his contemporaries, and even among those hundreds he later influenced.

Born in Woodville, Mississippi, in 1909, he was brought up in New Orleans and his laid-back approach, not least the limpid 'creole' tone he produced on clarinet, has some of that city's musical characteristics. His father ran a family band which toured with carnival minstrel shows, and gave Young his introduction to the music business at the age of ten. As an alto saxophonist, he admitted to being influenced by the Chicagoan

Frank Trumbauer. By 1930, he had switched from alto to tenor but kept the essentials of his style.

The tale of how he was hounded out of Fletcher Henderson's band by, among others, Henderson's wife, who force-fed him Coleman Hawkins records in the hope he would somehow develop a big and breathy sound, set the pattern for a career littered with misunderstandings. However, the immediate future was bright. In Count Basie's saxophone section,

he was admired for his own qualities. Paired with Herschel Evans, a Hawkins man, he demonstrated nightly how and why he differed from everyone else, and his fortunes rose with that of the band which, by 1940, had acquired a national reputation.

Many classic sides, among them 'Every Tub', 'Jive At Five', 'Taxi War Dance' and 'Texas Shuffle' (with Young on clarinet), are enhanced by his solos, perfectly poised and not a note wasted. There were also the collaborations with Billie Holiday, who nicknamed him 'Prez' for President, so that within a four-year period he starred on some of the best big-band and small-group sessions in the whole of jazz.

Both his style and his equally inventive use of slang – "I feel a draught" and "no eyes" have passed into the language – were copied by others. Even if many reviewers savaged him for not sounding like Hawkins, his new status and the resultant acclaim continued into the Forties, until the fateful day he was suddenly conscripted into the Army

and sent to a camp in Georgia. Totally unsuited to military life, especially in the Deep South, he was caught smoking pot, court-martialled and sentenced to a spell in detention barracks.

Things were never quite the same afterwards, though he still had years of good music ahead. Recordings in the late Forties reach a high enough standard, but the world had changed and Young had no place in the squabbles between supporters of the New Orleans revival and bebop. Affected by excessive drinking, his health deteriorated during the Fifties, until he could hardly blow.

His standing had been low when he died in 1959, and did not rise for several years. Suddenly a shoal of tenors have arrived, who think before they play, leave gaps between phrases, craft their solos meticulously and, in his own immortal words, try to tell a story.

CLASSIC *Recordings*

Lester Young Story, Jazz Archives. Early compilation, including Young on clarinet.

Complete Lester Young, Mercury. Small group from Forties, with Buck Clayton.

Lester Young Trio, Verve. All the tracks with Nat King Cole, plus others.

Complete Aladdin Recordings Of Lester Young, Blue Note (2CDs). Many post-war classics.

The President Plays, Verve. With Oscar Peterson Trio.

1934	In Fletcher Henderson's band as replacement for Coleman Hawkins.
1936	Joins Count Basie for the second time. Records with Basie quintet.
1939	First recording of 'Lester Leaps In'.
1944	Makes memorable appearance in the film *Jammin' The Blues*. Conscripted.
1945	In detention barracks in Georgia for possession of marijuana.
1946	Start of regular series of tours with Jazz At The Philharmonic.
1956	Records *Jazz Giants* album, one of his final classics, followed by a quartet album with Teddy Wilson.
1959	Gave memorable last interview while working in Paris.

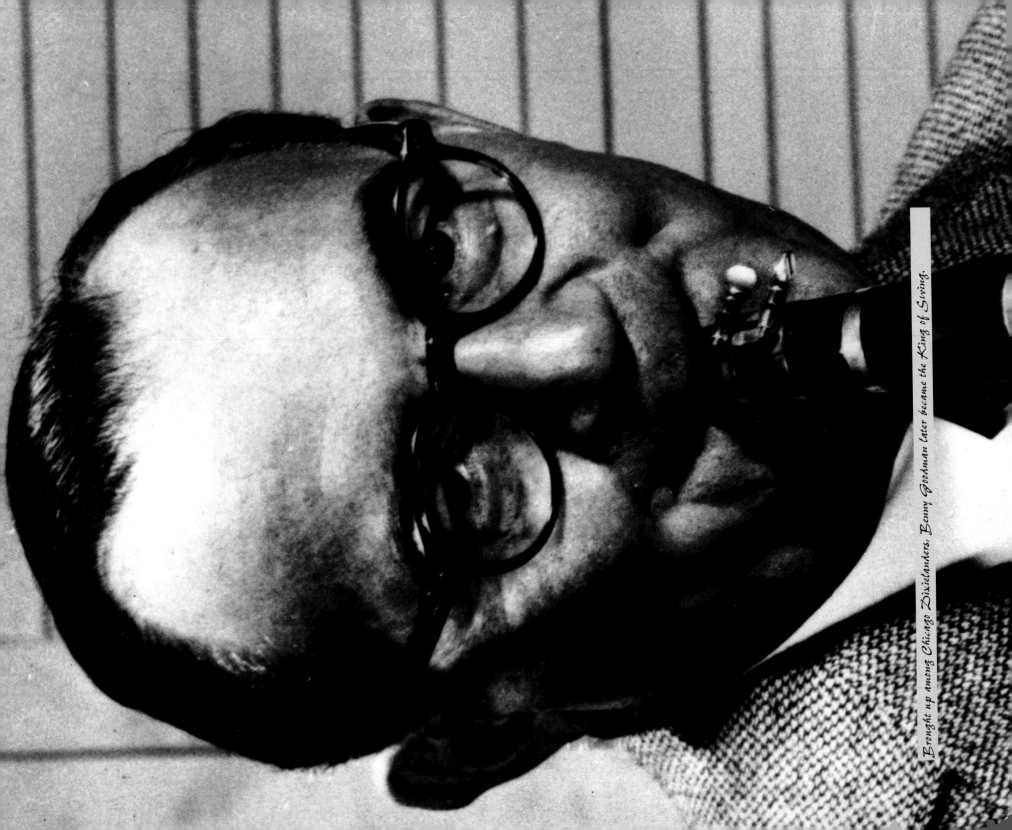

Brought up among Chicago Dixielanders, Benny Goodman later became the King of Swing.

Benny Goodman

If you saw the film, you know jazz history was made one evening in August 1935 when Benny Goodman (played by Steve Allen) and his orchestra came to the Palomar ballroom in Pasadena. Their tour had been a disaster, so in a devil-take-the-hindmost mood, Goodman kicked off with one of his hottest numbers. Instead of dancing, the mainly young crowd gave a mild foretaste of what journalists in subsequent decades would call the rock 'n' roll riot. From that moment, Goodman became King of Swing.

A prodigy, born in 1909, he studied clarinet under Franz Schoepp, the top classical instructor in Chicago, who also taught Buster Bailey and Jimmy Noone. Playing around Chicago in the early Twenties, Goodman performed with the urgency and tonal roughness of other local clarinettists like Frank Teschmacher. But by the mid Thirties, this had been replaced by his immensely influential mature style, much smoother and with a cool sense of swing.

He worked with Ben Pollack and Red Nichols before starting a band that broadcast a weekly hour of swing music. That influential patron of jazz John Hammond, who later became Goodman's brother-in-law, advised him to get Fletcher Henderson as arranger. Henderson's basic but ultra-effective scores – blending brass, reeds and rhythm in a seamless amalgam of solos, riffs and back-grounds - and the influx of such future stars as drummer Gene Krupa and trumpeter Harry James helped Goodman's rise to the top. Breaking the colour bar imposed on jazz from outside, he also hired Teddy Wilson, Lionel Hampton and, later, Charlie Christian and Cootie Williams.

In the 1940s, his band continued to develop for a time, using arrangements by Eddie Sauter and Mel Powell which were more sophisticated than those from the swing era. After a brief flirtation with bebop, which he did not enjoy, he cut down his jazz activities and devoted more time to his parallel career in straight music.

Goodman's hour in the vanguard had passed. However, to the end, he remained a formidable musician. In 1962, the US State Department sent him to Russia with a big band. He was one of the first Americans to perform his music in Europe leading a band made up largely of British musicians. Few bandleaders re-create their past satisfactorily but, ever the perfectionist, he got the old Henderson scores to swing at the correct tempo, and they sounded just as good as the old records.

Given the black-white confrontations that often simmer when jazz is discussed, Goodman's position as King of Swing has not surprisingly raised hackles. Of course, he did not invent the music, any more than he claimed the title. He did, though, introduce big-band jazz of top quality to a majority of Americans. And whereas a tune-by-tune comparison of recordings by Fletcher Henderson's 1934 band and those by Goodman would favour Henderson (that was a truly amazing, if short-lived band), one suspects a gig-by-gig comparison might have different results.

Between the bandleading abilities of the two, there was no contest. Along with Tommy Dorsey, Goodman was known as the ultimate disciplinarian. From various accounts published over the years, many who passed through his band resented this. But he always maintained the highest standards, while in its own way his clarinet playing has never been surpassed. Appropriately enough, swing was its most important component. A natural classicist, one cannot imagine him artfully milking a good tune for all its worth, as his big rival Artie Shaw did. Seldom flashy for all his technique, Goodman's best solos are about grace, taste and timing.

CLASSIC Recordings

BG And Big T in NYC, GRP. Early Goodman and Teagarden.

The Harry James Years, Vol. 1 RCA Bluebird. Recordings by the classic big band.

Live At Carnegie Hall, Columbia (2 CDs). The famous concert.

The Small Bands, Vol. 1, RCA Bluebird. Classic small groups.

Benny Goodman in Hi-Fi, Capitol. Includes Ruby Braff and Charlie Shavers.

1925	Travels to Los Angeles to work in Ben Pollack band.
1930	In Broadway band for Gershwin's *Strike Up The Band*.
1934	Forms own band.
1935	King of Swing. Records trio with Teddy Wilson and Gene Krupa.
1936	Radio show on CBS. First film.
1938	Gives first jazz concert at New York's Carnegie Hall.
1947	New band with bebop arrangements.
1962	Takes big band to Russia for State Department.
1978	Concert at Carnegie Hall, forty years on.

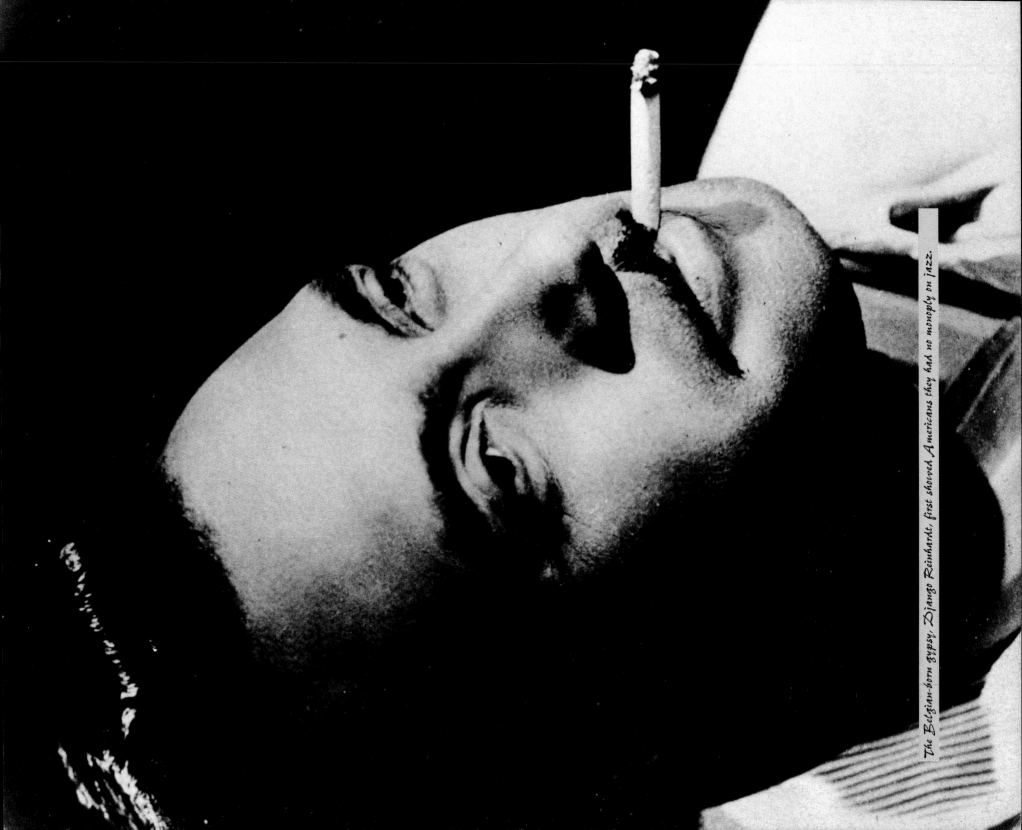

The Belgian-born gypsy, Django Reinhardt, first showed Americans they had no monopoly on jazz.

Django Reinhardt

Jokes about naming famous Belgians fall rather flat in jazz. True, Django Reinhardt was a Gypsy and, by definition, hardly a native of the low countries or of anywhere else. He was, however, born near Charleroi in 1910 and it cannot be wholly coincidental that Belgium has since produced more than its share of top jazz guitarists.

Reinhardt became the first European jazz musician to win an international reputation and to have Americans acknowledge him, either as an influence or as someone of whom they were definitely aware. He achieved all this despite his injury in a caravan fire in 1928, which left him, at the age of 18, without feeling in two of the fingers of his left hand, a tragedy he surmounted by developing a technique that even incorporated these fingers in locked positions.

Before the meeting with Stephane Grappelli, Reinhardt's most prestigious job had been as accompanist to the popular French crooner Jean Sablon. The Quintet of the Hot Club of France, with Grappelli on violin, Louis Vola on bass and Joseph Reinhardt, Django's brother, as one of the two rhythm guitars, gave jazz a fresh, frothy excitement laced with a delightful Gallic charm that was quite unlike anything coming from America. They were popular all over Europe, not least in Britain where they would top the bill in variety shows. Leading American swing stars such as Coleman Hawkins, Benny Carter, Bill Coleman and Dicky Wells all recorded with Reinhardt in Paris. Their personalities off stage were poles apart and this was reflected in the music – elegant violin phrases pitted against exuberant guitar which is why Grappelli and Reinhardt sounded so good together. While the violinist stayed in London during the 1939-45 war, Reinhardt moved between Paris and those parts of Europe where he could avoid the Germans. His most regular colleague became Hubert Rostaing, who played clarinet and alto saxophone and therefore made a very different partner from Grappelli.

After the war, he travelled to the US, having been invited by Duke Ellington for a series of concerts. For some reason, they were not a great success. Perhaps the guitarist's lifestyle was catching up on him. Perhaps, also, he was growing bored with the same routines and, unlike Miles Davis, was unable to do anything about it. An intuitive musician, his natural feel for harmony might have pushed him in the direction of classical music, which he loved, but his complete lack of formal training was a handicap.

Very aware of bebop, he also switched gradually to the amplified guitar. Reinhardt's playing of this instrument has been much criticized, and unfairly so, as the comparison is always with his acoustic playing. While he occasionally tried to copy the followers of Charlie Christian or insert a bebop lick, he usually played in a style that somehow looks forward to the twangy postbop music produced by guitarists who stand up to play. Barrages of chords also remind one of Wes Montgomery, who was almost certainly a Django fan.

Forty years after his death, in 1953, from a stroke, Django Reinhardt appears more in demand than ever, to judge by the number of his disciples all over Europe. His tune 'Nuages' became a hit, and, in contrast to his own childhood, gypsy parents today get their offspring to rattle off those slithery guitar runs he invented before they can walk. Several have gone on to become famous, such as Fapy Lafertin and, especially, Bireli Lagrene, a formidable technician who, on the amplified guitar, seems to start where Reinhardt left off.

CLASSIC Recordings

Django Reinhardt Vol 1,
JSP.
Early recordings of the Hot Club.

Swing From Paris,
ASV.
Mixture of prewar tracks.

Django's Music,
Hep.
Made in France during the war.

Swing De Paris,
Arco.
Post-war assortment.

Peche A La Mouche,
Verve.
Some of his best amplified efforts.

1922 First paid job as a musician.

1928 Caught in a camp fire and loses use of two fingers of left hand.

1933 Records with singer Jean Sablon.

1934 Partners Stephane Grappelli in Quintet of the Hot Club of France.

1937 Records in Paris with Coleman Hawkins and Dicky Wells.

1940 With Grappelli remaining in London, forms new group in Paris, with Hubert Rostaing on reeds.

1946 Tours US with Duke Ellington's Orchestra. Takes up amplified guitar.

1951 Emerges from semi-retirement to work in Left Bank Club.

Billie Holiday could interpret ordinary songs in ways that imparted touches of greatness.

Billie Holiday

Anyone seeking an iconic jazz singer need look no further than Billie Holiday. This has nothing to do with quality of voice as normally understood. Even during the early part of her comparatively short life, her range was limited. But her timing was unerringly right. She knew instinctively when to slur and when to delay; while her knack of completely rearranging the contours of a tune, as written, without seeming to try, gripped audiences to a degree beyond that of other singers with, seemingly, more to offer.

Much has been made of her deprived childhood in forming the background both to her singing style and to the subsequent disasters in her personal life. Born in Baltimore in 1915, her mother was unable to keep her consistently and she was often put in care. A man was convicted after raping her when she was eleven. All the time, intent on escaping poverty and becoming a star, she absorbed records by Louis Armstrong, Bessie Smith and other singers.

She moved to New York in 1929, singing in local bars and restaurants, and made her first records four years later with Benny Goodman. Her big breakthrough came with a series of recordings starting in 1935 when four sides, including 'What A Little Moonlight Can Do' and 'Miss Brown To You', led to a contract for her to record under her own name. These records were not identified as being in the fast lane of the hit parade - record companies reserved those for the top white singers. From the start, though, Holiday could make silk purses out of musical sow's ears. Sung by anyone else, 'Miss Brown To You' would by now be forgotten, instead of being an integral part of any worthwhile record collection.

The groups backing her included many of the best musicians around, from Teddy Wilson, who was often the leader, to Benny Goodman, Ben Webster and Roy Eldridge. The partnership that counted most with listeners, though, involved Lester Young. Whether taking a solo or entwining his phrases with hers, he breathed as she breathed. One of the best of many duets occurs on 'This Year's Kisses', another unremarkable song they transform into a thing of beauty. She named him 'Prez' and he responded with 'Lady Day'.

She worked for a time alongside Young in the Count Basie band, and later sang with Artie Shaw, an early example of a black singer on the road with a white band. The style of her records changed, with more formal arrangements, and fewer solos, though there was no loss of quality and her voice had if anything grown stronger. From this period comes the classic anti-racist 'Strange Fruit'. She had a prominent role in the film New Orleans, playing the statutory maid.

For the rest of her life, she worked mostly as a single. On record she was backed by strings or big bands, but occasionally she revived the jam-session format. Her voice may have grown heavier and her mannerisms more predictable, but she could still pace a lyric. Sessions she made for Verve in the Fifties are among her best, while, however croaky her voice, the last recordings, particularly 'Lady In Satin' from 1958, are tremendously moving.

Her later years were dogged by problems caused by drink and periodic drug addiction. Even her death, in 1959 from lung congestion, occurred while she was under house arrest on a narcotics charge. For those who loved her singing, there is an unmissable legacy of this period: the television show Sound Of Jazz that reunited her with Lester Young, on which they both managed to rouse themselves from their own final [...]

CLASSIC *Recordings*

The Quintessential Billie Holiday Vols. 3&4, Columbia. Two albums including many pre-war classics.

The Complete Original American Decca Recordings, GRP (2CDs). Some of her first records with strings.

Songs For Distingué Lovers, Verve. Excellent small-band acompaniment.

The Great American Songbook, Verve (2CDs). Some well-known jazz standards.

Lady In Autumn, Verve. From her Verve years, a compilation.

Timeline

- **1929** Moves to New York.
- **1937** First recording with Lester Young in backing group. Joins Basie.
- **1938** Joins Artie Shaw band.
- **1939** First recordings for Commodore, including 'Strange Fruit'.
- **1946** Appears in the film New Orleans in which she plays a maid.
- **1947** Committed to hospital after drug arrest.
- **1948** Two sellout concerts at Carnegie Hall.
- **1952** First records for Norman Granz's Clef label.
- **1956** Publication of her autobiography Lady Sings The Blues.

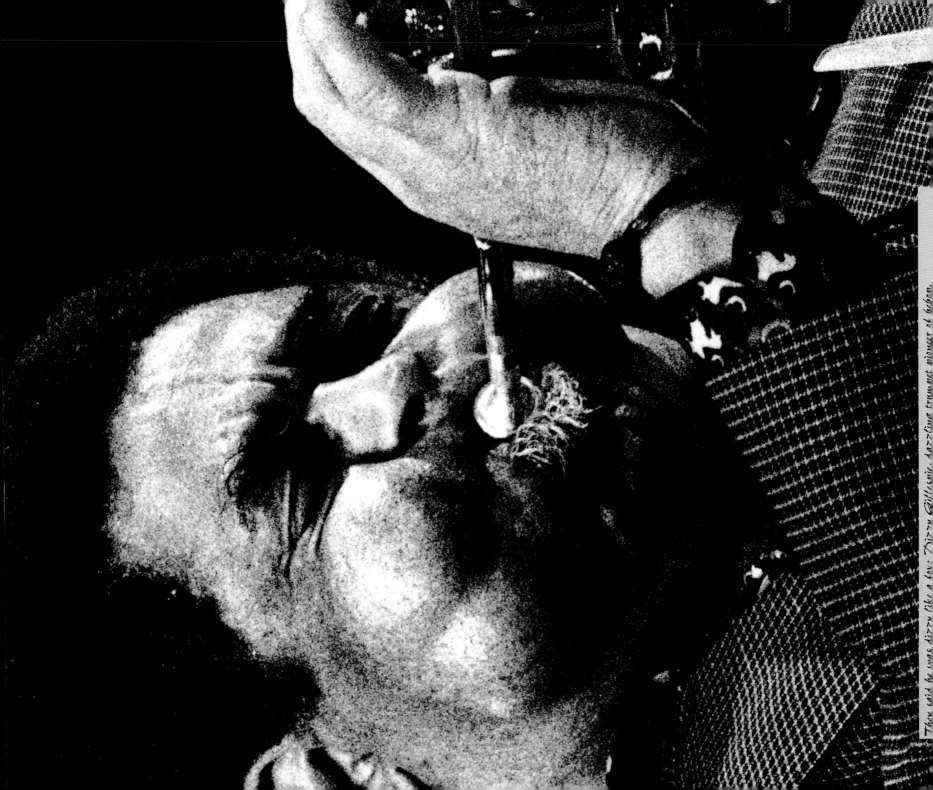

They said he was dizzy like a fox. Dizzy Gillespie, dazzling trumpet pioneer of bebop.

Dizzy Gillespie

John Birks "Dizzy" Gillespie constituted the other half of the bebop equation. He admitted that Charlie Parker put the final gloss on the new music he was working towards. But he was already an original trumpet stylist and a theoretician who knew exactly what he did and was able to explain this to others keen to learn. He got his nickname because, it was said, he was dizzy like a fox, and for all his on-stage clowning, there was no doubting his keen musical brain any more than one could miss his bravura technique.

From Cheraw in South Carolina, born 1917, he started out as a fiery young trumpeter at the height of the swing era, his model being the pace-setter of the time, Roy Eldridge, the fastest and one of the highest around. He even took Eldridge's place in the Teddy Hill band, coming with them to Europe and making his first records. By the time he joined Cab Calloway in 1939, he was bidding for one of the top places, though a well-publicized disagreement with Calloway, and his own leanings, took him to the small New York clubs in which new ideas were being worked out.

Eventually, he got together with Parker, notably in the band led by Billy Eckstine. They recorded together and formed a group that played in New York before moving west for a memorable gig in Los Angeles. While Parker stayed, Gillespie returned to New York and formed his second and more significant big band (the first had lasted for a few months in 1945). With its dazzling ensemble work laced with comic vocals and spiced by the leader's trumpet pyrotechnics, this was the band that put the word bebop on the musical agenda. Gillespie was also the first to underpin big-band bop with Latin rhythms, hiring the Cuban percussionist Chano Pozo and inspiring the fusion that underlies the Latin jazz of today.

In the Fifties, he led a small group for a time, but was then encouraged by the US State Department to put together a new band for the first officially sponsored overseas tour. This lasted for a couple of years, after which he mostly reverted to quartets and quintets, the best of them with James Moody on flute and saxophones. Special projects included a big band featuring musicians from many countries, with which he toured not long before his death in 1993.

Gillespie's most audacious solos date from the 1940s, alongside Parker or with his own group. However, his peak as a trumpeter arguably came in the Fifties and Sixties, by which time his tone, rather strident in earlier days, had rounded out and caught up with his technique. If he never managed the Miles Davis trick of continually surrounding himself with musicians whose eyes were on the future, he was the most extravagant improviser jazz has known, describing his method as, more or less, picking notes out of the air and making them fit whatever rhythmic pattern he dreamed up. He invariably had the musical know-how and, for most of his career, the range and stamina to pull it off.

The tune everyone knows is 'Night In Tunisia', though he was also wholly or partly responsible for other so-called bebop classics including 'Salt Peanuts', 'Groovin' High', 'Blue 'n' Boogie' and 'Woody 'n' You', originally for Woody Herman. Outside of these, the Gillespie composition most frequently played today is the Latin ballad 'Con Alma', which he wrote in the Fifties. For most of his career, Gillespie used a distinctive trumpet with an angled bell, designed in the days before clip-on microphones existed, to help him to hear the notes as they erupted.

1937	Makes first record as part of Teddy Hill trumpet section.
1941	Recorded at Minton's, legendary birthplace of bebop.
1944	Joins Billy Eckstine orchestra, as trumpeter and musical director.
1946	Forms second big band.
1948	Performance with big band in Sweden and France. Cuts down to quintet.
1950	Cuts down to quintet.
1956	Forms new orchestra for State Department tour.
1961	Performs and records Gillespiana suite.
1975	New York tribute concert.
1992	Final recordings at 75th birthday commemoration concerts.

CLASSIC Recordings

Groovin' High, Savoy. Early big band, plus groups with Parker, Stitt etc.

The Complete RCA Victor Recordings, RCA Bluebird (2CDs). Includes his Teddy Hill solos, plus big band and small groups.

Big Band In Concert, GNP Live performance from Pasadena, 1948.

Birks Works, Verve (2CDs). Includes the State Department band.

Gillespiana/Carnegie Hall Concert, Verve. Includes suite by Lalo Schifrin.

Thelonious Monk, who composed 'Round Midnight' and many others, always kept faith in his own tunes.

Thelonious Monk

One way of describing Thelonious Monk is as an eccentric genius whose untold quirks and foibles were definitely skin deep. Behind an inscrutable and rather shambling facade lay one of the sharpest minds to be applied to jazz. When analyzed, his work as pianist and composer revealed a craftlike logic compelling enough to affect an entire generation.

Born in 1917 in North Carolina, Monk was brought up in New York and ideally placed to participate in the music that became bebop. His first appearance on record is with Charlie Christian on a gig at Minton's Playhouse, bebop's birthplace of popular legend. He played piano in Dizzy Gillespie's first big band in 1945, and his best-known tune, 'Round Midnight', rapidly became a jazz standard of the Forties.

However, he was always the individual, too utterly absorbed in his own music to become identified with any school. Though his recordings for Blue Note and Prestige are widely hailed as classics, they were ignored by most critics and fans until, in the mid-Fifties, the world started to catch up with him.

While speed of execution was a characteristic of all the leading beboppers, notably so in the case of Bud Powell, a younger colleague who

set the pace for piano players, Monk had different priorities. Judged by normal standards of accuracy and evenness of touch, his playing could be described as slipshod. Yet he forged out of it a method that deployed rhythmic accents and improvised around thematic material in a way that was totally engrossing and had a profound impact on many

who heard him, among them Sonny Rollins and Steve Lacy. Fans also cherished those moments during someone's solo when Monk's coruscating piano chords crashed through the background.

Everything that made him great was achieved by 1960, after which he enjoyed being discovered by the wider audience. By the end of the decade, his influence was acknowledged worldwide. He appeared occasionally at the head of a larger group that always included at least one transcription of a piano solo in its repertory, but his regular touring outfit was a quartet, usually with Charlie Rouse as the featured saxophonist. All tunes were by Monk, except for a handful of ballads he fancied, 'I'm Getting Sentimental Over You' being one of them. He also carried in his head a mixed bag of forgotten pop songs to play unaccompanied as an encore.

A documentary film compiled after he died in 1982 revealed that he was often mentally ill during his final years. He made progressively fewer

public appearances and there were rumours that he had lost interest in playing. Around this time, he said that he had blazed his own trail and it was now up to the youngsters to surpass him (one felt he regarded such an event as highly improbable).

Monk had no reputation as an orchestrator, and he was not a prolific composer. His repertory, standing at between sixty and seventy compositions, is not a large one. He excelled as a writer of themes that burrowed themselves into the mind and whose jagged edges offered the acute improviser unlimited scope. 'I Mean You', 'Evidence', 'Let's Call This' and the masterful ballads 'Ruby My Dear' and 'Crepuscule With Nellie' are just a few examples that make the point. Before he formed the Modern Jazz Quartet, Milt Jackson was one musician who seemed inspired when working with Monk, and there is also a version on Blue Note of 'Reflections', on which this seemingly guileless ballad is cajoled, by Monk and Rollins, into revealing unsuspected depths.

CLASSIC *Recordings*

Genius Of Modern Music Vol 1, Blue Note. Early classics, including 'Epistrophy' and 'Round Midnight'.

Thelonious Monk/Blue Monk Vol 2, Prestige. Mainly trios, including the original 'Blue Monk'.

Brilliant Corners, Riverside/OJC. Includes Sonny Rollins.

At Town Hall, Riverside. High on atmosphere, notably on the 'Little Rootie Tootie' transcription.

The London Collection Vol 1, Black Lion. Solos and trios, among his last recordings.

1941	Recorded at Minton's Playhouse with Charlie Christian.
1947	First recordings under his own name for Blue Note.
1951	Arrested, wrongly, on drug charge and New York licence withdrawn for six years.
1953	Appears as soloist at Jazz Fair in Paris.
1954	First version of 'Blue Monk' for Prestige label.
1957	Leads quartet at New York's Five Spot, with John Coltrane on saxophone.
1959	Forms quartet with long-serving Charlie Rouse on saxophone.
1964	Records with larger group. Appears on the front cover of *Time* magazine.
1971	Tours as part of Giants of Jazz sextet, including Dizzy Gillespie and Art Blakey.

Charlie Parker

Legends tend to accumulate about the very greatest jazz musicians, especially those seen as leading short and scary lives. Charlie Parker was more than the titan of bebop. He became a symbol of defiance, the black hedonist who cocked a snook at white society and went down with guns blazing. Of all the major figures, though, Parker, perhaps even more than Billie Holiday, seems the one beaten by the system.

Parker was born in Kansas City, Missouri, in 1920. Whatever natural talent he had on the alto saxophone was boosted by a fanatical regime of practice. He worked with several local bands, most significantly with the Jay McShann orchestra where he made his first records and acquired his nickname of 'Yardbird' or 'Bird'. In the early Forties, he joined the bands of Earl Hines and Billy Eckstine, the two large orchestras in which bebop was first noted. His partnership with Dizzy Gillespie in 1945 introduced the new music in pure form to New York's club clientèle.

After a disastrous stay in Los Angeles that ended with him in hospital, he returned eventually to New York and formed the most renowned of his quintets. Miles Davis and Max Roach were the key personnel, Tommy Potter played bass and Duke Jordan, John Lewis or Al Haig took turns on piano. Their records for the Savoy and Dial labels are bebop's answer to Armstrong's Hot Fives and Sevens. Parker departed from the quintet or quartet format only during the brief period when he toured with a small string section, by which time he was recording mostly for Verve.

Anyone seeking a short cut to Parker's genius can ignore the many superb solos in between and go straight to his tunes. The best – boasting a direct rhythmic character, which include 'Moose The Mooch', 'Klactoveesedstene', 'Confirmation', 'Cheryl' and most of the 12-bar blues – pack a concentrated punch quite unlike anything in Western music, let alone the jazz that came before him. The fact he probably wrote many of them a split second before the deadline, in true Fats Waller tradition, makes them seem even more remarkable.

Apart from his studio recordings, complete with rejected versions of the same tunes, Parker's discography bulges with airshots and unauthorized tapings. Only on the very last recordings does he show a significant decline.

In 1951, the New York liquor authorities withdrew his club licence on the recommendation of local drug squads, who had never even managed to arrest him. As a result, he was forced to scuffle for work around the country and rely on local rhythm sections. This happened at a time when he badly needed money for his young daughter's medical bills. The guilt aroused by her death two years later finally broke him. When he died aged 34, the doctor who examined him estimated his age at 60.

Parker introduced a rhythmic language more complex than before, but one that in his hands swung in a manner that actually seemed to increase as he took more frontal liberties with the beat. While his surging melodic lines interlocked in a whirl of rhythmic intensity, their emotional flavour came straight from the Kansas City blues he was brought up to play (and which the McShann band consistently featured).

Early in his career he had become a heroin addict. With a regular intake, addicts can function normally and by all accounts he was no exception. Unfortunately, he operated under a system that drives the user to the black market where supply and quality are unreliable. His erratic behaviour and increasingly disorganized life-style can also be explained by the vast amount of alcohol he consumed as a substitute for narcotics.

Parker's genius can ignore the many

CLASSIC *Recordings*

The Charlie Parker Story, Savoy. The session with 'Koko'. All the versions originally released.

The Dial Masters, Spotlite. Some of his greatest live recordings.

Live Performances, ESP.

News The Time, Verve. The later small groups.

Jazz At Massey Hall, Debut/OJC. The legendary concert.

One of the great bass soloists, Charles Mingus wrote unforgettable tunes that bands play today.

Charles Mingus

Composer and bassist, Charles Mingus was one of the more controversial figures in jazz, though few will deny him a place among the most gifted. Both Mingus and his music were subjects for lively debate, even during periods when his career seemed in eclipse. Legends tell of his volatility, his fights, not always metaphorical, with other musicians, and of his hassles with various authorities.

Born in Arizona in 1922, he was brought up in Los Angeles, where his musical studies led him from cello to the double bass. At various times, he never identified closely with bebop.

Later, his bass playing was well featured with the popular Red Norvo trio. The Fifties, however, began with disillusionment among jazz musicians and Mingus decided to work for the Post Office, from which he was prised, it is said, by none other than Charlie Parker. Mingus, incidentally, became the bassist (and recording engineer) at the famous Parker-Gillespie concert at Massey Hall.

His career and creativity blossomed with the jazz resurgence, and the decade from about 1955 became his Golden Age. Experiments with other adventurous spirits coalesced at this point in his recording of *Pithecanthropus Erectus*. This intro-duced several devices — tempo changes, static harmony, triple time, hard-hitting gospel backbeats and freak instrumental noises - com-monplace within a few years but rarely heard before. They had certainly never been heard as organic parts of a jazz masterpiece designed to give the performers unprecedented freedom within a controlled frame-work.

Mingus developed these charac-teristics further and introduced many of his lyrical, endlessly evolving melodies on such albums as *East Coasting*, *Tijuana Moods*, *Mingus Presents Mingus* and *Mingus Dynasty*, a series that culminated in his *Black Saint And The Sinner Lady*. He was said to discourage musicians from learning his pieces from a score, preferring to bellow instructions during a performance.

The future might have looked rosy, but he hit a period of depression that lasted, on and off, for most the Sixties. He came back in stages, and the quality of his work soon recaptured much of the old flair. Unfortunately, a terrible and debili-tating illness stopped him playing and soon he could only compose for his death.

'Mingus Fingers', an impressively futuristic score. These gigs were outside what was then the modern mainstream, which may explain why

others. By the time of his death in 1979, he was confined to a wheelchair.

Bassists today can play at least as fast, but he stamped his personality on such pieces as 'Haitian Fight Song' to a degree few have even begun to emulate. Though compared to Duke Ellington, with whom he once played and for whom he had the greatest admiration, most of his best-known compositions were performed during his lifetime by smaller groups. After his death, Gunther Schuller put together 'Epitaph', a suite in several movements of which a fragment had been recorded in 1962, and gave a full premiere in 1989 that was both televised and recorded. This led to the Mingus Big Band, a kind of New York rehearsal band that began by playing the few surviving Mingus scores and went on to produce their own excitingly turbulent arrangements of his other tunes. These come over exactly as one imagines they would with Mingus in charge and make this project by far the most creative attempt yet to preserve a jazz com-poser's work as a living entity after his death.

he played in bands led by Louis Armstrong and Kid Ory, and had a two-year stint with Lionel Hampton's band, with whom he performed his composition (and bass feature)

1946	First recorded version of 'Weird Nightmare'.
1947	Plays with Lionel Hampton.
1950	Member of Red Norvo's trio.
1953	Records Massey Hall concert with Parker and Gillespie.
1956	New direction launched with *Pithecanthropus Erectus*.
1963	Records *Black Saint And The Sinner Lady*.
1964	Tours Europe with sextet including Eric Dolphy.
1966	Start of period during which he hardly performed.
1973	Formation of group with George Adams and Don Pullen.
1977	Gives up bass playing because of illness.

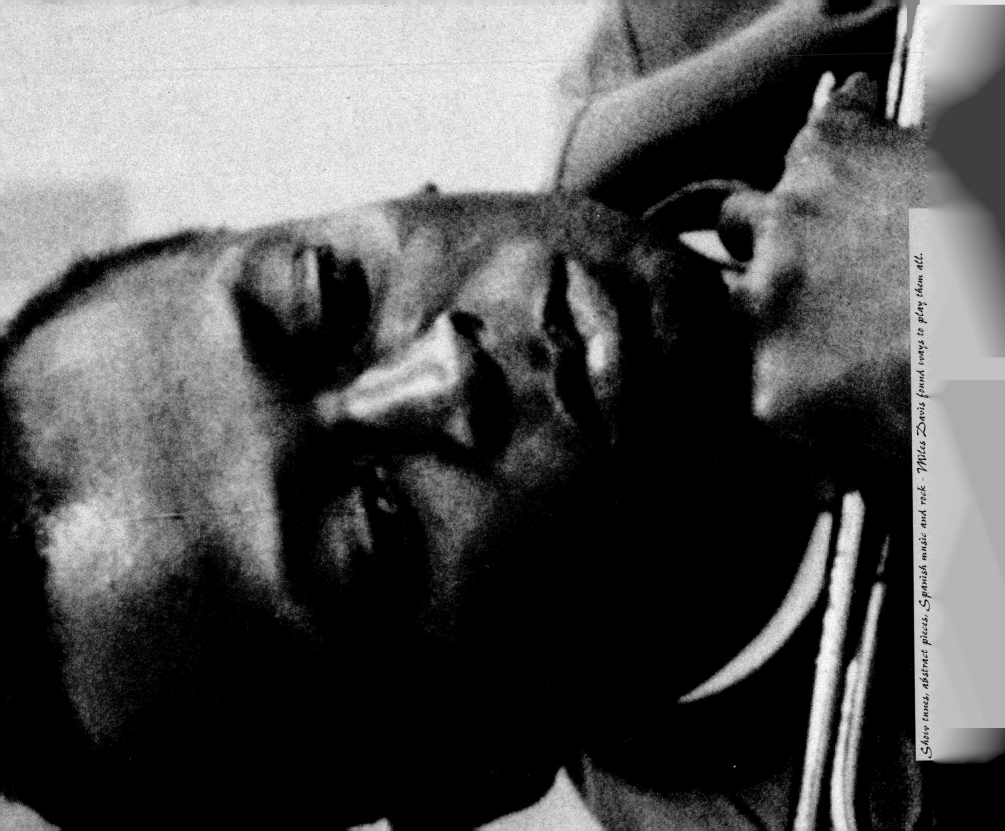

Show tunes, abstract pieces, Spanish music and rock - Miles Davis found ways to play them all.

Miles Davis

Including the years he never played a note in public, Miles Davis maintained the highest profile in jazz. Columnists dwelt obsessively upon his taste in clothes and cars, his wives and lady friends. Apart from his musical stature, he made excellent copy, because, like Frank Sinatra, he seemed to live in the fast lane and to attract controversy. He was beaten savagely in the street by a policeman incensed at seeing an immaculately-dressed black man escorting a white woman. Gangsters shot him in the legs. He survived at least one bad car crash.

Miles Davis (born Illinois, 1926) went to New York, aged 18, ostensibly for formal study. But nightly exposure to Charlie Parker's saxophone solos, when barely out of his teens, provided musical lessons of a kind money cannot buy. The nonet he formed in 1948, after leaving Parker's quintet, driven by the arrangements of Gil Evans and Gerry Mulligan, played a handful of gigs, but its fame lives on through the recordings known as Birth Of The Cool. While they became the talk of jazz, Davis himself went into something of a decline, racked by problems associated with drug addiction.

As he got a grip on his personal life, so his music took off again. Now a more assertive trumpeter, whose belllike clarity in the high register gave a new authority to his playing, he grabbed attention both for his quintet with John Coltrane and for a series of recordings at the head of a large orchestra directed by Gil Evans, renowned for Evans's endless variations on a range of pastel tones. Over the next 15 years, his consistency and range of expression have rarely been equalled. When playing ballads with the mute pressed against the microphone, he evoked a sense of skittish abandon one minute and utter desolation the next.

In the 1960s, Davis formed a new quintet powered by teenage drummer Tony Williams. Following on from the modal base of his earlier group, he adapted to the move towards musical freedom ushered in by Ornette Coleman, but did it in his own way. Then, a liking for James Brown and Jimi Hendrix gradually brought about the change to electric keyboards and guitars.

On records made in 1969-70, Davis applied jazz techniques within a context then associated with electric funk. So many fresh ideas erupted from these sessions that, as they moved on, each participant was able to develop a different strand. By the early 1970s, Davis was filtering his trumpet through a wah-wah pedal and had turned his music around yet again. Ensemble textures evolved continuously, unlike the days when Davis habitually left the stage each time the saxophone took a solo.

In 1975, partly through illness, Davis stopped playing (he describes the next five years largely in terms of sex and drugs). Helped by actress Cicely Tyson, to whom he was married for a time, he got himself into shape to resume his career. His group was still amplified and percussive, but with a difference mirrored exactly in his own behaviour: aloof before the public earlier in his career, he now acknowledged applause and filmed interviews. He published an autobiography, controversial but full of fascinating insights into an exceptional musical mind, and even acted on TV, in an episode of Miami Vice.

The strength of character that once helped him overcome a drug habit, by virtually locking himself in and throwing away the key, drove him to renew his music relentlessly. A list of some of his finest albums - Birth Of The Cool, Walkin', Kind Of Blue, Miles Smiles, Bitches Brew - underlines how he would reach a kind of perfection and then move on.

CLASSIC *Recordings*

Birth Of The Cool, Capitol. Summed up by its title.

Bags' Groove, Prestige. Includes the session with Monk and Milt Jackson.

Kind Of Blue, Columbia. The birth of modal jazz.

The Complete Concert, Columbia. Davis at his peak.

Bitches Brew, Columbia. The jazz-rock classic.

1945	First recordings with Charlie Parker.
1949	Records the first of the Birth Of The Cool tracks.
1955	Impresses fans and critics at Newport Jazz Festival.
1957	Records Miles Ahead, the first collaboration with Gil Evans.
1963	Unveils new rhythm section of
1966	Williams, Carter and Hancock. Miles Smiles album confirms new, more abstract direction.
1969	Next new direction launched with In A Silent Way.
1975	Final concert recordings before retirement.
1980	Resumes career and records The Man With The Horn.

John Coltrane influenced countless saxophonists and did much to further the cause of free jazz.

John Coltrane

Since Charlie Parker, only John Coltrane has made such a direct impact on what jazz musicians play. Taking a broader perspective, one could cite Miles Davis and Ornette Coleman as wielding more influence, but it was Coltrane's solos that others copied, and his ideas, spiritual as well as musical, that they sought to emulate.

Coltrane, nicknamed 'Trane', was a contemporary of Davis, though he took much longer to make an impression. Born in North Carolina but coming of musical age in Philadelphia, he joined Dizzy Gillespie's big band in 1949 and remained when Gillespie reduced it to a quintet. He then worked with Johnny Hodges and Earl Bostic, before being hired by Miles Davis in 1955.

Clearly influenced by the strong-toned Dexter Gordon, his early solos did not strike the casual listener as exceptional. But Davis knew how good he was, and other tenor saxophonists were already looking to him as a model. To some extent he acted as a foil for the leader: Davis's trumpet lines were lyrical and spare, whereas Coltrane, as he developed his skills, became exceptionally voluble, the modern counterpart of Coleman Hawkins (and, as with Hawkins, his ballads were beautiful). The contrast between them comes

over superbly on a Swedish live recording made in 1960, when their partnership was all but finished.

Coltrane readily acknowledged the influence of Thelonious Monk, with whom he worked for several months during an absence from Davis's quintet, though the most obvious element of his first mature style was harmonic exploration, allied to the modal forms favoured by Davis. The

chord pattern of the title tune from the album *Giant Steps* still provides the ultimate challenge for many jazz musicians.

Coltrane left Davis to form the band that became, with Elvin Jones, Jimmy Garrison on bass and the young McCoy Tyner on piano, his classic quartet. With Jones, on drums, implying all sorts of massive poly-rhythms, his tenor became even more aggressive. At the same time, he took up the soprano saxophone and developed a formula of surrounding popular ditties with a repetitive vamp. His version of 'My Favourite Things', arranged in this way, became excep-tionally popular, and led overnight to the biggest boost for the soprano sax since Sidney Bechet's adoption of the instrument forty years previously.

The soprano features co-existed with the headlong 'Chasin' the Trane', a 12-bar blues from which harmony had been all but jetti-soned. Spiritual values, it became increasingly apparent, meant a great deal to Coltrane, and their incorporation into his music was realized most convincingly in the 1964 masterpiece 'A Love Supreme',

with its unison chants and sections the album *Giant Steps* still provides with such curious titles as 'Acknow-ledgement', 'Resolution', 'Pursuance' and 'Psalm'.

The quartet eventually started to pull in different directions, and Coltrane entered a new phase, symbolized by the replacement of Jones and Tyner by, respectively, Rashied Ali and Coltrane's wife, Alice, who were less musically assertive, and therefore allowed Coltrane greater freedom. His support of such newcomers as Albert Ayler, Archie Shepp and Pharoah Sanders helped legitimize free jazz in the minds of sceptics, and increased the reverence felt for him by a new wave of fans and pundits, as well as musicians.

As to his own examples of free jazz, there is still a consensus that he did not live long enough to produce work comparable with his best in other genres. Coltrane died of liver cancer in 1967, and subsequently became, almost certainly, the only jazz musician to have a church founded in his memory. A modest man, one wonders what he would have thought of the honour.

Admired for his skill at presenting a tune, Stan Getz reached new heights in his last years.

Stan Getz

For most of a career that began as a teenage member of Stan Kenton's saxophone section, Stan Getz received his due as an innovative soloist, admired by colleagues but also appealing to a wider audience. The highest level of adulation, however, came at the end. Not because he had become a venerable figure (he was only 64 when he died), but in recognition of the marvellous playing that characterized his final decade.

Born in Philadelphia in 1927 and one of the 'Four Brothers' who recorded that title for Woody Herman, his first real breakthrough came on Herman's 'Early Autumn', recorded in 1948 when he was just 21. It captured his first maturity as a soloist, characterized by a hard, pure, perfectly controlled sound mainly in the high register. John Coltrane was to do something similar in the mid-Fifties (and confirm an admiration for Getz), but for the time it was unique. Quite separate from either the Miles Davis band or from what was about to come out of the West Coast, Getz's solos represented one of the peaks of the cool movement.

Getz soon demonstrated another characteristic. If not considered a pacesetter, he was always alert to changes in fashion, if only as a means of keeping stagnation at bay, and he ceded nothing to Miles Davis as a spotter of talent. Having done well for a couple of years with quartets that nurtured the refinements in his own playing, he hired pianist Horace Silver, then completely unknown but already a probing and restless accompanist, who pushed and swung Getz into a more forceful style.

The benefits were evident on his numerous recordings for the Verve label, where he was paired with most of the big names. Out of action for a while following a celebrated drug case, he spent a brief period in Europe before returning to make two contrasting albums: *Focus* (1961), arguably the finest jazz-plus-strings album, with arrangements by Eddie Sauter, and *Jazz Samba* - followed by *Getz/Gilberto* - which put bossa nova

on the jazz map and took Getz to the top of the pop charts.

In the next few years, he appeared in all manner of contexts, leading an excellent quartet with the young Gary Burton on vibraphone and touring with French organist Eddie Louiss. For a while, his playing lacked consistency and he admitted to trying new things that did not always come off. Eventually, he settled into the memorable form of his final decade. Never at his most convincing at a fast tempo, or when battling through complex harmonies, Getz now concentrated on tunes with a strong melodic content, and exploited his tone, by now one of the most extraordinary sounds ever produced from a tenor saxophone.

One could trace the hard outlines back to his cool period, but his sound now packed far more resonance, billowing outwards and upwards and then hovering in the air so as to induce the most pleasurable frissons in the audience. The outstanding musicians who backed him, including pianist Kenny Barron and drummer Victor Lewis, must have realized they were on to something very special.

Apart from a time in the Fifties when tenor saxophonists, especially in Europe, tried to emulate his tone and phrasing, Getz had few direct disciples. There was, though, his effect on John Coltrane, which led to a whole school of tenors who rarely plunged into the bottom register. Another showing the influence from time to time has been Joe Henderson, and it's surely no coincidence that Henderson has become a leading advocate of the music of Antonio Carlos Jobim, reviving several tunes Getz recorded 30 years ago.

CLASSIC *Recordings*

The Best Of The Roost Years, Roulette. A good mix of ballads with sturdier fare.

Focus, Verve. The ultimate with-strings session. Arrangements by Eddie Sauter.

Sweet Rain, Verve. The quartet with pianist Chick Corea.

The Dolphin, Concord. One of the first of the great last recordings.

Anniversary, Emarcy. His working quartet with Kenny Barron and Victor Lewis.

Those who claimed Ornette Coleman would change the shape of jazz have been proved right.

Ornette Coleman

Perhaps the most genuine visionary of them all, Ornette Coleman's impact on jazz remains as strong today as when he first hit the headlines. His influence has less to do with direct copying (he never had that many saxophone disciples) than with the way his ideas seep into the system, often long after their formulation.

Coleman was born in Fort Worth, Texas, in 1930, and spent his late teens playing with R&B bands, mainly on tenor saxophone. He became interested in bebop through the influence of Red Connors, a tenor player with a big local reputation. In the early Fifties he ended up in Los Angeles, where his emerging ideas about music attracted few followers and he was thrown off more than one bandstand. Eventually, he started

playing regularly with drummers Ed Blackwell and Billy Higgins, trumpeters Don Cherry and Bobby Bradford and bassist Charlie Haden.

In 1958, Coleman, now on alto saxophone, made his first recordings with Cherry, Haden and Higgins, in a quintet led by Paul Bley at the Hillcrest Club in Los Angeles. It was many years before these tapes were released, but, in the same year, Coleman recorded two albums for Contemporary, his first as a leader. He took the Hillcrest group, minus Bley, to New York's Five Spot for arguably the most controversial gig jazz has known. Unlike, say, the Parker - Gillespie stint at Billy Berg's in Los Angeles, this was conducted with maximum media publicity, as famous jazz musicians continually gave their views on Coleman, for and against.

During this period, he recorded the albums for Atlantic which epitomize the first part of his career. All the

trademarks are there. Improvization, over a fairly constant rhythmic drive, was neither based on chords nor built directly on the tune's structure. Some tunes were tear-ups, some were heart-wrenching dirges, and others were melodic pieces with odd twists and accents. Far from being conspicuously cerebral, the music often exuded a low-down warmth, closer to the country blues than to its urban successor.

Similar strains can be heard today, notably in groups led by guitarists with some country and western influence, such as John Scofield and Bill Frisell. Coleman soon added brief but frenzied interludes of trumpet and violin, imparting new tone colours and leading directly to the freakouts that took hold of free jazz in the following years. His own Free Jazz, recorded with a double quartet, inspired works as diverse as Coltrane's 'Ascension' and Peter Brötzmann's 'Machine Gun'.

Apart from some compositions in a classical vein (an area in which he still works), Coleman did not significantly alter his music until the early Seventies, when he formed Prime

Time. The style of this group was derived, in part, from his experience of recording with musicians from Joujouka in Morocco, and was also a practical expression of his theory of harmolodics (a portmanteau of harmony, movement and melody) in which instruments renounce their harmonic or accompanying roles and instead provide melodies and rhythm on equal terms. He typically chose two electric guitars, two electric basses and two drummers (one of them his son Denardo) to interweave with his saxophone, and again found a mixed response among audiences and critics.

However, the impact long-term was marked. From guitarist James Ulmer, who studied with him in the Seventies, to the M-base movement of today, Coleman's seemingly wild notions have crept into the mainstream. 'Prime Time' itself has mellowed. The latest stage show enjoyably combines Coleman's ever-lyrical alto with dancers, rappers, a highly professional video display, and much less strident input from the group's guitars.

Raised in New York in the shadow of bebop, Sonny Rollins had a decisive influence on younger players.

Sonny Rollins

More than anyone playing today, Theodore "Sonny" Rollins embodies the concept of jazz as a legacy handed down. Growing up in New York, where he was born in 1930, he would chase Coleman Hawkins for his autograph. Always identified with post-war sounds, he became nevertheless the first tenor saxophonist to build on the substance, rather than the style, of Lester Young. In a career lasting close on 50 years, he has accommodated elements of free jazz and fusion without changing his approach significantly.

By his early twenties, he had already recorded with Bud Powell, Miles Davis and under his own name, though the stylistic breakthrough came after he appeared on a couple of Thelonious Monk sessions. As he matured and his tone lost its rather querulous edge, he learnt how to adapt Monk's tunes for themselves as much as for their harmonic structures. Although he could rattle off notes at speed, a subtle sense of space and rhythm and a feel for melody permeated the more successful solos, such as 'But Not For Me' with Miles Davis.

In 1954, he took the first of those working sabbaticals that punctuate his career. Soon after he returned, playing better than ever, he joined the Max Roach-Clifford Brown quintet. As part of the group over the subsequent two years, both before and after Brown's death, and under his own name, with Roach on drums, he made his most impressive series of albums. *Saxophone Colossus* includes the much-analyzed 'Blue Seven', on which he and Roach elaborate a mere

better than ever, he joined the Max Roach-Clifford Brown quintet. As part of the group over the subsequent two years, both before and after Brown's death, and under his own name, with Roach on drums, he made his most impressive series of albums. *Saxophone Colossus* includes the much-analyzed 'Blue Seven', on which he and Roach elaborate a mere

conservative than before, though

Coltrane, and this may have contributed to another withdrawal from the scene, lasting two years and enlivened subsequently by accounts of him practising in the middle of New York's Williamsburg bridge.

On return, he confounded speculation by sounding nothing like Coltrane. If anything, his playing was more conservative than before, though

handful of phrases over the entire performance, something totally new for the bebop era.

Anticipating the move to look beyond common time, he recorded the first jazz waltz of the modern age on *Sonny Rollins Plus Four*. But his position as the most admired saxophonist around was usurped by John

He gradually cut down on club bookings in favour of one-off concerts, filling the larger halls with his sound - harsher than before and projected consistently through a microphone attachment that enabled him to traverse the stage while playing. His solos expanded, mostly as variations on the tune but mixed with passages no-one could predict, possibly not even Rollins. A repertory including songs made famous by Al Jolson, on which he used to elaborate at length, he now often encapsulated in spectacular introductions or codas.

For a while, Rollins embraced some of the jazz/rock conventions, though this was more pronounced on record than in his live performances. Frequently overwhelming in their impact, these stand apart from anything else currently on offer, though his example has led younger saxophonists once again to place the development of motifs above technical flourishes.

marked by an even greater mastery of the saxophone. He could not, though, ignore what was happening in the Sixties, replacing his guitarist Jim Hall with trumpeter Don Cherry, who had recently made his name alongside Ornette Coleman, and also hiring Coleman's drummer Billy Higgins. The resulting compromise between free improvizing and the need to keep a tune ticking over had its moments; in the longer term, it also inspired those unaccompanied, stream-of-consciousness passages now part of the Rollins legend.

1951	Makes first record under his own name.
1954	Records with Thelonious Monk before retiring to Chicago.
1956	Joins the Roach-Brown quintet. Records 'Blue Seven'.
1959	Retires again. Practises on one of New York's bridges.
1962	Don Cherry added to group.
1965	Contributed to score for film *Alfie*.
1972	Comeback recording, after two years away from music. Begins to use electric instruments.
1985	Makes album of unaccompanied tenor saxophone solos.

Acclaimed as a trumpeter in jazz and classical fields, Wynton Marsalis is also an important composer.

Wynton Marsalis

Even more than Benny Goodman, Wynton Marsalis enjoys a high reputation in parallel fields. This he underlined in 1984, by winning Grammy awards as the best soloist on both a jazz and a classical record – he did it again in 1985. The controversy surrounding him, among jazz musicians and fans, derives less from this dual role than from what he plays and what he says.

Upon the way people think about jazz, Marsalis has made a greater impact than anyone since Ornette Coleman. Whereas Coleman convinced a generation overwhelmed by technicalities that they could move ahead by simplifying and diversifying, Marsalis arrived on a scene dominated by fusion and cross-cultural endeavours, and said that the future lay in the stuff of jazz itself.

Because of his birthplace (New Orleans, 1961) and because his father Ellis is a widely admired pianist and an experienced music teacher, Marsalis has obvious links with the jazz tradition. However, the dedication necessary to become such a skilled classical trumpeter so young – to judge by his father and brothers, dedication to the job in hand runs in the family – gave him a very unusual perspective on that tradition, one that eventually bore fruit. While studying at Juilliard in

1980, he joined Art Blakey's Jazz Messengers and toured with them, on and off, for two years. His own group, featuring his brother Branford on saxophones, then took the mid-Sixties Miles Davis quintet as its starting point. Kenny Kirkland (piano) Robert Hurst (bass) and Jeff Watts (drums) expanded collectively on the old Hancock-Carter-Williams formula and Marsalis, especially in that context, showed an obvious Davis influence, though the singularity of his technique, no less than the puckish sense of humour that often spills over, gave a substantially different cast to his solos.

Each album seemed an advance on its predecessor as Marsalis's invention became more audacious. At some point, though, he took a decision that has profoundly affected the jazz of the past ten years. He re-formed with a septet that bore little relation to his previous groups. Replacing the super-

charged intensity produced by Watts and Hurst came a relaxed rhythmic team from – inevitably – New Orleans, while the front line was there as much to interpret scores and add colour as to take solos. Between them, Marsalis and his trombonist must have carried a dozen mutes on stage.

The obvious debt to Duke Ellington and parallel attempts by Marsalis, through his role as the Lincoln Center's jazz advisor, to promote recitals of jazz from Jelly Roll Morton and Louis Armstrong onwards caused a storm, as did the notion that great jazz should be studied the way students could almost describe the suites Marsalis wrote, 'Citi Movement' and 'In This House, On This Morning', as his collective answer to Ellington's 'Harlem Suite': they cover a similar terrain, from swinging street scenes to solemnity.

Now writing for the Lincoln Center Jazz Orchestra, Marsalis's 'Blood On The Fields', his musical depiction of slavery, lasts for three hours and includes voices as well as the band. All that, and he is still a world-class trumpet player.

Debussy and Webern. It's possible that Marsalis took these steps because he realized, perhaps subconsciously, that they presented the right route forward for him. Challenged by the spread of material attempted, his playing gained in expressiveness; his tone grew even more incandescent, without losing the pliant quality that adds a subtle dynamic shading, beyond that of most who merely play either softer or louder.

Marsalis set a demanding level of ensemble togetherness for his septet, the vehicle for his new (self-taught) urge to compose. Duke Ellington became increasingly influential, not least for his dramatic imagery. One

---

CLASSIC *Recordings*

Standard Time, Columbia. Showing his class on familiar material.

J Mood, Columbia. The best of the quintet with Branford.

Live At Blues Alley, Columbia. Club session, trumpet fireworks.

Citi Movement, Columbia. Colourful ballet score with septet.

In This House, On This Morning, Columbia. The same group on a programme built around a church service.

A–Z *Jazz Players*

Toshiko Akiyoshi, bebop pianist who now leads her own big band.

MUHAL RICHARD ABRAMS

One of the leading lights in the Association for the Advancement of Creative Musicians set up in Chicago during the Sixties (other AACM notables included Roscoe Mitchell and Joseph Jarman), Muhal Richard Abrams had previously started the Experimental Band, a rehearsal group which included most of the city's avant garde. Born a Chicagoan in 1930, he is credited with launching many careers as teacher and all-round guru. Since moving to New York and joining the touring network, his piano playing and open-ended approach to composition have been heard more widely. (Muhal Richard Abrams: *Blu Blu Blu* Black Saint).

JULIAN 'CANNONBALL' ADDERLEY

'Cannonball' Adderley (short for 'cannibal' – he enjoyed eating) was one of the leading alto saxophonists of the generation after Charlie Parker. A fine technician, his lines were as mobile as Parker's, though less intense: a slightly creamy tone gave his solos an air of avuncular good humour. Born in 1928, he organized high-school bands in his native Florida before coming to New York in 1955, impressing everyone, not least Miles Davis, who persuaded him to join what became the classic sextet which recorded *Kind Of Blue*. The Adderley Brothers quintet, with brother Nat on cornet, drew on the soul and gospel background to jazz and became one of the most popular bands of the Sixties – 'Mercy, Mercy, Mercy!', in particular, rising high in the U.S. charts. Adderley died from a stroke in 1975. (Cannonball Adderley (with Miles Davis): *Somethin' Else* Blue Note).

TOSHIKO AKIYOSHI

Toshiko Akiyoshi has had two distinct careers. Born in Manchuria in 1929, her piano playing made her one of the stars of Japanese jazz, and in the Fifties she was encouraged by Oscar Peterson to try her luck in the U.S.. Very much in the Bud Powell tradition, she made several records and formed a quartet with Charlie Mariano, to whom she was then married. On and off for the past twenty years, she has run a big band, usually in conjunction with her second husband Lew Tabackin. Writing most of the arrangements, she has taken elements from Gil Evans and others to come up with something her own. (Toshiko Akiyoshi: *Carnegie Hall Concert* Columbia).

GERI ALLEN

Geri Allen gained her first jazz experience around Detroit (she was born in Pontiac in 1957), but she does not stem obviously from the Hank Jones-Tommy Flanagan school of long, lyrical lines. Closer to the probing, rhythmically complex approach linked to such New Yorkers as Monk, Herbie Nichols or Elmo Hope, both as pianist and composer, she has worked with Lester Bowie and once fitted in naturally with Steve Coleman's M-Base movement. Her horizons have since broadened to include an excellent trio with Charlie Haden and Paul Motian, and she has successfully recorded several albums of her own. (Geri Allen: *The Maroons* Blue Note).

HENRY 'RED' ALLEN

Born in New Orleans (1908), Henry 'Red' Allen was one of the most original trumpeters to come from New Orleans – or from anywhere else. Obviously influenced by Louis Armstrong, his style was more mercurial, full of trills and slurs that carried enormous rhythmic impact. Some of his greatest solos erupt from the trumpet sections of Luis Russell, Fletcher Henderson and other bands. Much of his later career was spent playing Dixieland at New York's Metropole, but he made some

Julian 'Cannonball' Adderley (left), with brother Nat on cornet.

splendid records, especially after being rediscovered by a new breed of critics. Loved by fans for his warm personality, he toured regularly almost up to his death, from cancer in 1967. (Henry 'Red' Allen: *World On A String* RCA Bluebird).

Mercurial New Orleans trumpeter Henry 'Red' Allen.

Contemporary star Geri Allen at the piano.

MOSE ALLISON

Mose Allison memorably called one of his compositions 'Ever Since I Stole The Blues', which sums up both his appealingly dry humour and the attitude adopted by some (in this case, a Britisher) towards white singers who, as Allison has always done, feature songs associated with black artists. From Mississippi (born 1927), Allison takes material from the blues and country tradition and puts it across with the same lazy drawl he uses on his own songs, rather like a more rustic Hoagy Carmichael. By contrast, he hammers the piano keys to produce intricate solos somewhat in the style of Mal Waldron's. (Mose Allison: *Creek Bank* Prestige).

ALBERT AMMONS

Towards the end of the Thirties, there somehow developed a craze for eight-to-the-bar blues, sometimes transplanted from its pianistic origin to the big swing bands and promoted under the name Boogie Woogie. A Chicagoan, born 1907, Albert Ammons was sucked into the movement and often joined with Meade Lux Lewis and/or Pete Johnson in some powerfully rolling blues – their skill strikes home when one hears others attempt four-handed boogie. His various solo performances suggest Ammons, who died in 1949, was boogie's most majestic stylist. (Albert Ammons: *1936-39 Classics*).

GENE AMMONS

Just as Albert Ammons, a genuine all-rounder, became linked to a certain type of piano playing, so was his son Gene identified as a tenor saxo-phonist with a following in the Rhythm & Blues field. Born in Chicago in 1925 and nicknamed 'Jug', he was in Billy Eckstine's legendary bebop band, and later spent some months with a Herman Herd. His style was a breathier version of Lester Young's and best suited to the simpler ballads and blues, though, in the grand tradition, he once had regular tenor jousts with the fleeter-fingered Sonny Stitt. He remained popular up to his death in 1974. (Gene Ammons: *Jammin' With Gene* Prestige).

RAY ANDERSON

Ray Anderson made his first impact on record alongside Anthony Braxton, but his subsequent career has been more left of centre than way out. As a young trombonist in Chicago (born 1952) he was exposed both to the AACM and to the local blues scene; whatever the context, his measured phrasing and rather gruff tone continue to evoke an early influence, Vic Dickenson. His exceptional technique, including steely-tongued blasts and a battery of growls, is put to its most jocular use in such as the Slickaphonics and more recently his

Alligatory Band, though humour surfaces in all his projects. (Ray Anderson: *Big Band Record* Gramavision).

LOVIE AUSTIN

Apart from singers, the first women to make their mark in jazz were pianists. This reflected society at large, where the boys were supposed to train for a proper job, but learning the piano was suitable for young ladies. Pioneers include Lil Hardin, who married Louis Armstrong, the little-known Mazie Mullens, who accompanied silent films in Harlem and impressed Fats Waller, and Lovie Austin. Born Cora Calhoun in Tennessee, Austin (1887-1972) accompanied blues singers and variety artists, ran her own groups and later conducted a pit band in Chicago. A role-model for the likes of Mary Lou Williams, she was, musically, a formidable talent. (Lovie Austin: *1924-26* Classics).

TEODROSS AVERY

From California's Bay Area, where he gained a reputation in local bands and took a few lessons from Joe Henderson. Teodross Avery (born 1973) is the youngest musician in our list. Having finished studying at Berklee, and with two records, already, as leader for a major label, great things must be expected. On the tenor saxophone, he does seem to have that bit extra: a well-nourished tone, a secure technique throughout the range and, perhaps most significant, the ability to make his own space even at a lively tempo. Both albums show how well he writes and plays in a straight-ahead context, while the second also stretches beyond this. (Teodross Avery: *My Generation* Impulse).

ALBERT AYLER

Although tenor-player Albert Ayler seemed to come from nowhere to burst onto the free jazz scene in 1963, he had previously spent time on the rhythm-and-blues circuit. Working from simple themes to elaborate, torrential improvizations with a hard, powerful tone, his initial impact can hardly be overstressed. Later, forming a band with his brother Donald, his music developed a sometimes ritualistic format of hymn-like lines and wild improvization. Towards the end of his brief career, there were indications that he had lost his way. At his best, however, he was a thrilling and absorbing musician. Born in Cleveland in 1936, he died in rather mysterious circumstances in New York in 1970. (Albert Ayler: *Spiritual Unity*, ESP).

BUSTER BAILEY

The first important jazz clarinettist not from New Orleans, William 'Buster' Bailey shared a teacher with Benny Goodman and ended up with a similarly immaculate technique. Born in Memphis in 1902, he worked with W.C. Handy, and then with King Oliver and Fletcher Henderson as a contemporary of Louis Armstrong. He survived Henderson's various crises and then took a leading role in the first John Kirby Sextet, one of the first small groups to feature tricky arrangements and build a large following. After the war, till his death in 1967, he was often part of New York's Dixieland scene. (John Kirby: *The John Kirby Sextet* Columbia).

DEREK BAILEY

Along with drummer John Stevens, trombonist Paul Rutherford and saxophonists Trevor Watts and Evan Parker, Derek Bailey was among the first free improvizers in Britain. He became both the most dedicated (never using written scores) and the furthest removed from jazz. Avoiding regular groups, he seeks partners from all music where improvizing flourishes and, for many years, featured them during his annual Company Week in London. As a guitarist (born in Yorkshire in 1932) who had worked in theatres and variety halls, he re-taught himself, developing from a rather scratchy sound to a melodious richness comparable, in its way, to flamenco. (Derek Bailey and John Stevens: *Playing* Incus).

CHET BAKER

Originally from Oklahoma, Chet Baker (born 1929) came to Los Angeles, impressed Charlie Parker on a fleeting West Coast visit, and shot to prominence with the Gerry Mulligan Quartet of 1952. His pure open tone on trumpet reminded some of Bix Beiderbecke, though his main influences were Miles Davis and Kenny Dorham and, apart from crooning ballads wistfully, he spent his career

Chet Baker towards the end of his extraordinary career.

KENNY BAKER

One of the finest swing-style trumpeters outside the U.S., Kenny Baker was born in Yorkshire in 1921. After working around London, he joined the Ted Heath orchestra after the war and consolidated his reputation both as an arranger and as a soloist/lead trumpeter. In the 1950s, his excellent Baker's Dozen existed more on radio than in person, because, by then, he was part of the lucrative session scene, in demand for films and, later, television. In recent years he has recorded whole albums of Louis Armstrong solos and, after 30 years, re-formed the Dozen for live gigs, one of which has been recorded. (Kenny Baker: *The Boss Is Home Big Bear*).

IAIN BALLAMY

A London-based musician who came to prominence with Loose Tubes, Iain Ballamy (born in Surrey, 1964) has had a long association with Django Bates. Apart from Loose Tubes and the later Delightful Precipice, they were both members of drummer Bill Bruford's Earthworks, and Bates was in the quartet that recorded the album cited below. In recent years, Ballamy has recorded in New York with John Donaldson, Ray Drummond and Victor Lewis, and been part of Hermeto Pascoal's UK orchestra. His laid-back, somewhat quirky lines on the various saxophones have a melodic cast all

their own. (Iain Ballamy: *All Men Amen* B&W Music).

BILLY BANG

Among the newer breed of violinists, Billy Bang (real name William Vincent) is the most versatile. He has been linked to the freer end of jazz, as befits a former pupil of Chicagoan Leroy Jenkins and an admirer of Ornette Coleman, but also plays the kind of music expected from someone who has recorded a tribute to Stuff Smith. Born in Alabama (1947), he didn't turn professional until the Seventies. For several years he was part of the String Trio of New York, very much a chamber ensemble, and a regular partner has been drummer Dennis Charles, with whom he has recorded as a duo. (Billy Bang: *Live At Carlos 1* Soul Note).

PAUL BARBARIN

New Orleans music is rich in dynasties. Drummer Paul Barbarin, born in 1899, was the son of Isidore,

a brass-band specialist (usually found on tuba-like instruments), while his brother Louis also played the drums. Having built his local reputation, Paul followed the Chicago trail, to work with Freddie Keppard, Jimmy Noone and King Oliver. He later teamed up with fellow-exiles in New York, producing, as part of Luis Russell's rhythm section, some of the most swinging big-band jazz ever recorded. Based again in New Orleans, he regularly led bands in clubs, marched them on parades and occasionally went out on tour. He died in 1969. (Paul Barbarin: *Paul Barbarin And His Band* Storyville).

CHRIS BARBER

Chris Barber represented the extrovert end of British revivalism, as opposed to his former boss, trumpeter Ken Colyer, who stood for the purity of New Orleans. Born in Hertfordshire in 1930, his band of the Fifties, complete with three-piece front line, banjo and blues singer Ottilie Patterson, paved the way for

the brief but momentous Trad boom, during which he, Acker Bilk and others invaded the charts. Since then, his broad musical outlook typifies the MJQ's John Lewis wrote a piece for him), has had continued success by pushing against the boundaries of traditional jazz (Chris Barber: *The Great Reunion Concert* Timeless).

GATO BARBIERI

Born in Argentina in 1934, Leandro 'Gato' Barbieri was living in Rome when he met Don Cherry and became a member of his group, appearing on Cherry's finest Blue Note albums. Regarded as part of the freejazz scene, Barbieri then rediscovered his roots and formed several bands dedicated to a powerful jazz-Latin American mix, over which his full-throated, highly charged tenor saxophone playing rose to thrilling heights – finding different ways to present a tune has always been his strong point. He has also contributed notably to works by Carla Bley and Charlie

Count Basie, with long-time colleague Freddie Green (guitar).

Haden. (Gato Barbieri: *Chapter 3* Impulse).

DANNY BARKER

Banjoist Danny Barker, who took few solos, recorded with Louis Armstrong, Dizzy Gillespie, Bunk Johnson and Wynton Marsalis – even with Herbie Nichols. He was brought up in New Orleans (born 1909), a member, through his mother, of the Barbarin family – in New York, he worked for his uncle, drummer Paul Barbarin, amongst others, and later as guitarist with Cab Calloway's band while Gillespie was there. When swing bands became unviable, Barker switched to Dixieland and also promoted the career of his wife, blues singer Blue Lu Barker. Back in New Orleans, he worked as assistant curator in the Jazz Museum and published his autobiography. He died in 1994. (Cab Calloway: *Best Of The Big Bands* Columbia).

GUY BARKER

Born in London in 1957, Guy Barker played in the National Youth Jazz Orchestra (where his promise was spotted by Clark Terry). He has since been part of bands led by Stan Tracey, has twice played with Ornette Coleman in London and currently runs an excellent quintet in which his front-line partner is Icelandic saxophonist Sigurdur Flosason. As a trumpeter who has assiduously studied the past, he often gives recitals featuring the music of everyone from Louis Armstrong and Bix Beiderbecke to Clifford Brown. His own style is notable for a pure, singing sound and great fluidity of line. (Guy Barker: *Into The Blue* Verve).

ALAN BARNES

Few British jazz musicians have cast their net as wide as Alan Barnes. Born in Cheshire in 1959, he played pastiche dance music with the Pasadena Roof Orchestra, then joined the neo-bop quintet of drummer Tommy Chase, followed by Humphrey Lyttelton's band. With a reputation as a hard-swinging saxophonist, good at motivating audiences, some of his best work is done on clarinet, while he has made a delightful duo record with pianist Dave Newton. His current projects include The Mike Westbrook Orchestra, Kenny Baker's Dozen and the quintet he co-leads with trumpeter Bruce Adams. (Alan Barnes: *Thirsty Work* Fret).

KENNY BARRON

Kenny Barron, whose elder brother Bill (a saxophonist) was quite prominent in the Sixties, was born in Philadelphia in 1943. Having worked with several musicians around New York, he joined Dizzy Gillespie in 1962 and remained in his quintet for

Bix Beiderbecke gave jazz a new trumpet style and composed impressionist piano pieces.

four years. He spent roughly the same time with Freddie Hubbard, Yusef Lateef and Ron Carter, since when he has combined touring with a university teaching post. His considerable all-round piano skills are greatly admired by fellow-musicians; one example was Stan Getz, who regularly played his tune 'Voyage' and in whose groups Barron received some deserved popular adulation. (Kenny Barron: *Wanton Spirit* Verve).

GARY BARTZ

Gary Bartz's career follows closely the jazz experiences of the last 30 years. From freeish improvizing plus politics, to a spell with an early Miles Davis fusion group, then a deeper dig at disco fusion before his current stance as a modern mainstreamer, blowing hard through some of the tunes that have served jazz well throughout the period. Born in Baltimore in 1940, he generally sticks with the alto saxophone, producing a satisfyingly searing sound and rarely overplaying. (Gary Bartz: *West 42nd Street* Candid).

COUNT BASIE

One of the great bandleaders, William 'Count' Basie epitomized the jazz of the South West: ultra-relaxed and ultra-swinging. He was born in New Jersey in 1904, but settled in Kansas City and rose to fame after taking over Bennie Moten's band in 1935. The music seemed to play itself, mainly blues pieces and simple riff tunes which were carried along by a superb rhythm section and elaborated by outstanding soloists. His second great band, from the Fifties onwards, relied more on arrangements (notably by Neil Hefti and Ernie Wilkins) and on ensemble excellence, but carried equal conviction. At the piano, Basie was laconic and intensely rhythmic, using as few notes as possible. He died in 1984. (Count Basie: *The Complete Atomic Mr. Basie* Roulette).

DJANGO BATES

Possibly the brightest talent to emerge in British jazz since the Sixties, Django Bates, born in Kent in 1960, first made waves with Loose Tubes, the co-operative big band that produced a frequently intoxicating mix of traditional scoring and snatches of everything from rock to Latin. Bates played piano and also contributed many scores. He has also run a small group, Human Chain, worked with leading musicians from the U.S. and elsewhere, written pieces for modern-classical pianist Joanna MacGregor and formed his own big band, the Delightful Precipice, writing typically hustling post-Stravinsky scores one minute and engaging parodies the next. (Django Bates: *Winter Truce (and homes blaze)* JMT).

GORDON BECK

Gordon Beck (born 1938) has developed from a stalwart of the London scene into a world-class pianist. Technical skill was obvious from the start, but there was otherwise little to distinguish him from other postbop pianists. He was able, however, to pick up early on the new, more lyrical styles ushered in by Bill Evans, while his international profile rose when he joined Phil Woods's European Rhythm Machine. In recent years, he has spent much time in France, while collaborating with musicians from the US and elsewhere and giving solo recitals. (Gordon Beck: *For Evans' Sake* JMS).

HARRY BECKETT

Born in 1935 and based in the UK since 1954, Harry Beckett comes from Barbados, and his music evokes a feeling of sunshine even if it rarely evokes anything specifically West Indian. A ubiquitous figure in 1960s London, he worked in Graham Collier's various groups and in several big bands, including the Brotherhood of Breath. He has since been involved in projects all over Europe, including the Danish New Jungle Orchestra, while his own groups have included one with four flugelhorns. As to his trumpet solos, with their instantly recognizable twists and turns, they can be described by the name of an earlier group of his – Joy Unlimited. (Harry Beckett: *Passion And Possession* ITM).

BIX BEIDERBECKE

Born in 1903 in Iowa, Bix Beiderbecke discovered jazz when the Mississippi river boats stopped at his home town of Davenport. Also inspired by the ODJB, he developed their music as lead trumpeter of the Wolverines, showing a marvellously assured touch for a 20-year-old. With the bands of Frankie Trumbauer, Jean Goldkette and finally Paul Whiteman, he gave jazz a new trumpet style: a clear, rounded tone and slightly wistful lyricism, while some of his angular phrasing anticipated bebop. He also wrote a few impressionist piano pieces which reflected an increased preoccupation with European music. The original doomed young 'man with the horn', and an alcoholic, he died in

Guitarist George Benson became a popular soul singer.

HAN BENNINK

In the Sixties, Han Bennink, born in Holland in 1942, was often the drummer of choice for visiting Americans, and he played with everyone from Ben Webster to Eric Dolphy. He soon became identified with the Dutch free-improvizing scene, being a founder, along with Willem Breuker and Misha Mengelberg, of the Instant Composers Pool. All have contributed their own brand of deadpan humour; Bennink's routines have included twirling bags of maize around his head, blowing down giant alpen-horns and exploiting the comic potential of bow against saw. He can also be a hard-swinging, straight-ahead drummer, and he excels in both roles as part of the trio Clusone Trio: *I Am An Indian* Gramavision).

GEORGE BENSON

Around his native Pittsburgh in the early Fifties, and still short of his tenth birthday, George Benson (born 1943) used to sing and accompany himself on the ukulele, later replaced by a guitar. He then built a national reputation with organist Jack McDuff as an excellent guitarist in the Charlie Christian mould. Often using the same organ-guitar format, his own groups gradually became more commercial, culminating in the big-selling *Breezin'* album. When his vocal on 'This Masquerade' became a hit single, he developed his career as a major soul singer, though the guitar still cuts through, notably on unison lines with the voice, that change with each performance. (George Benson: *The New Boss Guitar* Prestige).

BOB BERG

Born in New York in 1951, tenor saxophonist Bob Berg has been

LOUIS BELLSON

Louis Bellson is an archetypal big-band drummer, but one who also composes and arranges. Born in Illinois in 1924, he could be found propelling the likes of Tommy Dorsey, Benny Goodman and Harry James. Then he became part of what was known as the "great James robbery", when he and saxophonist Willie Smith left James for Duke Ellington. Bellson's 'The Hawk Talks' and 'Skin Deep' became popular drum features, and he also set the percussion standard for Ellington's 'Harlem Suite'. Since then, he has worked with several big bands, including his own, and supplied the backing for his late wife, singer Pearl Bailey. (Louis Bellson: *Hot Bellson* MusicMasters).

1931. (Bix Beiderbecke: *Singing' The Blues, Vol.1* Columbia).

through all the phases. He was an early convert from free jazz, working with Jack McDuff and later touring with Horace Silver and Cedar Walton, playing in a hard-toned attacking style, somewhere between John Coltrane and Mike Brecker. Since then, he has worked in both acoustic and electric contexts, most famously in the latter case with Miles Davis, when John Scofield was part of the band. (Bob Berg: *Riddles* Stretch).

CHU BERRY

While Coleman Hawkins worked in Europe, his natural successor on the scene as the breathy-toned tenor saxophonist was reckoned to be Leon 'Chu' Berry. Born in West Virginia in 1910, he slotted into the big swing bands of Benny Carter, Fletcher Henderson and Teddy Hill, perhaps making his biggest impact during a spell with Cab Calloway. His sound, somewhat darker than that of Hawkins, and his well-constructed solos also enlivened many small-band recordings, notably those by Lionel Hampton. Bebop might have beckoned, but he died in 1941 after a car crash. (Chu Berry: *The Chu Berry Story* Jazz Archives).

BUNNY BERIGAN

Bunny Berigan produced, in 'I Can't Get Started' (1937), one of the great declamatory trumpet solos of the swing era, combining Armstrong's grand manner with a touch of Beiderbecke lyricism. Born in Wisconsin in 1908, he also became a star of the early Benny Goodman and Tommy Dorsey bands, recording superb solos with both, and when leading a band of his own. Unfortunately, he followed Beiderbecke in being an alcoholic, and the booze finally killed him in 1942. (Bunny Berigan: *Portrait Of Bunny Berigan* ASV Living Era).

TIM BERNE

Alto saxophonist Tim Berne can be described as part of the second wave of free-jazz players, pushing the boundaries but recognizably part of the jazz tradition. Born in New York in 1954, he studied saxophone with Anthony Braxton in 1974 and then became a pupil of Julius Hemphill. His associates, in person and on record, include Paul Motian, Ray Anderson, trumpeter Herb Robertson, drummer Joey Baron, cellist Hank Roberts and, more recently, guitarist Marc Ducret. He has also recorded Ornette Coleman's tunes with John Zorn. (Tim Berne: *Diminutive Mysteries (mostly Hemphill)* JMT).

Bunny Berigan, trumpet star of the swing era, whose dazzling career was cut short.

EMMETT BERRY

Born in Georgia in 1915, Emmett Berry was of the right age to be influenced by Roy Eldridge, whose place he took in Fletcher Henderson's trumpet section. During the war, he worked in radio bands, and then spent five years with Count Basie. In the Fifties, he was one of the beneficiaries of the renewed interest in jazz from the swing era and made several records, though usually under someone else's name. A mainstay of bands large and small and able to hold his own with any trumpeter, he neither sought nor was offered the chance to impose himself as a leader. (Roy Eldridge: *The Swing Trumpets* Mercury).

BARNEY BIGARD

Born into a musical family in New Orleans in 1906, Barney Bigard was, initially, a reluctant musician, but he eventually acceded to family wishes. Joining King Oliver in Chicago in 1925 as a saxophonist, he moved to the Ellington band in 1927 as a clarinet soloist. With Ellington, his classically liquid New Orleans style became invaluable and he assumed immense importance in the development of the 'jungle band' style at the Cotton Club. Leaving Ellington in 1942, he led various bands before forming another lengthy association, this time with the Louis Armstrong All-Stars between 1946 and 1962, after which he retired from touring. Bigard died in 1980. (Duke Ellington: *Jubilee Stomp*, Bluebird).

ED BLACKWELL

Associated with 'free' jazz as Ornette Coleman's drummer, Ed Blackwell (1929 – 1992), who was born in New Orleans, nevertheless retained many traditional aspects of his home town in his drumming: an unusual rhythmic

Ragtime pioneer Eubie Blake was a big star several decades before this picture was taken.

ART BLAKEY

Art Blakey (1919-1990), from Pittsburgh, was the drummer in Billy Eckstine's pioneering bebop big band, but he came into his own in the Fifties, first on records with Miles Davis and then at the head of his Jazz Messengers. His mature style, characterized by a propulsive cymbal beat, massive cross-rhythms behind the soloist and a liking for African effects, was one of the most identifiable and exciting jazz has known. In nearly 40 years of the Messengers, he continually hired young musicians, giving the best of them, successively, the job of musical director. A tremendous publicist for jazz, he was lionized throughout the world during his final decade. (Art Blakey: *Free For All/* Blue Note).

TERENCE BLANCHARD

When Wynton Marsalis left the Jazz Messengers, Art Blakey went back to New Orleans for his replacement. Terence Blanchard, born in 1962, had studied with Ellis Marsalis and then won a music scholarship to Rutgers University. After they left Blakey, he and his compatriot Donald Harrison formed a quintet, and Blanchard, now a much stronger trumpeter, reflecting the best qualities of Woody Shaw and Freddie Hubbard, has since participated in films by Spike Lee and written the score for *Malcolm X*, while continuing to tour with his own group. (Terence Blanchard: *The Billie Holiday Songbook* Columbia).

JIMMY BLANTON

Though his life was tragically short – born in 1918, he died of tuberculosis in 1942 – Jimmy Blanton exerted an

EUBIE BLAKE

Lapping up his role as a delightful anachronism, whose life stretched back to the time jazz began, Eubie Blake died eventually in 1983, just days after his 100th birthday. Born in Baltimore, he became a virtuoso ragtime pianist who worked everywhere from sporting houses to touring medicine shows. In the Twenties, he and partner Noble Sissle wrote the hit Broadway musical *Shuffle Along*, starring Florence Mills, while his best-known song, 'Memories Of You', was written for *Blackbirds Of 1930*. Enticed out of retirement by renewed interest in ragtime, he still had thirty years left, and he lived them up to the hilt, appearing at festivals, writing a book and having his songs performed on Broadway. (Eubie Blake: *Blues & Rags Vol. 1* Biograph).

sonority within the complexities of modern rhythm. He first became known when he joined Coleman's quartet in New York in 1960; later, he worked with Booker Little, Eric Dolphy, and, frequently, with Don Cherry in the band Old And New Dreams. Though his career was inhibited by the kidney disease that led to his early death, he leaves a strong recorded legacy. (Old And New Dreams: *A Tribute To Blackwell/* Black Saint).

Canadian-born pianist Paul Bley was one of the early free improvizers and among the first to experiment with synthesizers. He now often plays solo or in duets.

...nfluence on jazz bass-playing which resonates still as the century ends. A superb technician with an unerring sense of time, his dexterity was complemented by his use of the full range of his instrument, initiating its solo potential, as well as anchoring the music and contributing to its tonal palette. With Duke Ellington from 1939 to 1942, he was, during that period, a significant factor in the development of what may have been the most complete jazz orchestra of all. (Duke Ellington: *The Blanton-Webster Band*, Bluebird)

CARLA BLEY

Born in Oakland in 1938, composer, pianist and bandleader Carla Bley began early in her career to control all aspects of her work, rarely dealing with material outside her own and, after membership of the Jazz Composers Guild from 1968 to 1972, establishing her record label, Watt. Her 1970s group, The Carla Bley Band, gave way to a sextet in the 1980s, to be followed, as she entered her artistic maturity, by The Big Carla Bley Band and, in the 1990s, by the Very Big Carla Bley Band. Influenced by sources as disparate as European cabaret, opera and Ellington, she has found a clarity of expression and depth of texture which mark her out as a true original. (The Big Carla Bley Band: *Fleur Carnivore*, Watt).

PAUL BLEY

Born in Montreal in 1932, Paul Bley created a distinctive piano style, rhythmically and harmonically complex, yet retaining melodic linear constructions which ensured that his work remained easily approachable. Stylistically secure, he was able to work in a wide variety of experimental settings throughout the 1960s, including a brush with synthesizers. His *Open, To Love* recording in 1972 indicated something of a watershed, introducing two decades of majestic, often solo, performances within which original material, standard works, bebop and Ellington songs, as well as the compositions of two of his ex-partners, Carla Bley and Annette Peacock, are exhaustively analysed and reconstituted. (Paul Bley: *Tango Palace*, Soul Note).

ARTHUR BLYTHE

Born in Los Angeles in 1940, Arthur Blythe worked locally with pianist Horace Tapscott before moving to New York in the early Seventies. He shared the alto saxophone duties with David Sanborn in what was probably the best band Gil Evans led, while making some excellent small-group recordings in company with the likes of cellist Abdul Wadud and tuba player Bob Stewart. His unique piercing-yet-pure saxophone sound has more recently been heard to good effect in such all-star groups as The Leaders and Roots. (Arthur Blythe: *In Concert* India Navigation).

BUDDY BOLDEN

Meticulous research by biographer Don Marquis exploded many of the myths about the first trumpet King of New Orleans. What nobody knows is how he played, because a rumoured record remains untraced. Charles Bolden was born in 1877 and worked in guitarist Charlie Galloway's band, taking it over before the turn of the century. He probably mixed rags and blues, with embellishments rather than sustained improvizations, and everyone agrees he played loudly and pleased the crowds. The suggestion is he could not handle the pressures of the music business, spending his final years in a mental home. He died in 1931, no doubt unaware of the fuss to come.

Mainstay of the Art Ensemble of Chicago: Lester Bowie.

LESTER BOWIE

Lester Bowie's early career was spent

Cornetist Ruby Braff modelled his playing on stylists from the big-band era.

in St. Louis, where he had moved from his native Maryland (born 1941). Eventually, he formed the Great Black Music Orchestra, and was therefore almost preordained to join the AACM when he moved to Chicago in the mid-Sixties, after which he co-founded the Art Ensemble of Chicago. His role within the group was often that of the fundamentalist preacher, his trumpet tone big and broad (though with a roughness that somehow looked back to New Orleans parades – no doubt inspiring him, later, to form the 10-piece Brass Fantasy) and his phrases often basic and bluesy. (Lester Bowie: *The Fire This Time In & Out*).

JOANNE BRACKEEN

As pianist Joanne Grogan (born in California in 1938), she accompanied leading West Coast musicians before marrying saxophonist Charles Brackeen. Retiring for a few years to raise her four children, she moved to New York and gradually resumed her career. She worked with the Jazz Messengers and then Joe Henderson and Stan Getz, touring Europe with both of them and drawing attention to her solos – swinging, full of imagination and expressed with abundant technique. She has since worked at the head of a trio. (Joanne Brackeen: *Havin' Fun Concord*).

RUBY BRAFF

The trumpeter and (mostly, now) cornet player Ruby Braff was a pioneer, the first to conspicuously break the rule that jazz historically has to move ever onward. Born in Boston in 1927, he is a contemporary of the cool and hard bop players of the Fifties, yet he modelled his highly mobile and technically adept style on Louis Armstrong. He starred on several of the so-called mainstream recordings of the Fifties, but later cut down on the number of jazz standards in favour of a repertory of show tunes and popular songs, of which he has become one of the most distinguished interpreters. (Ruby Braff: *Bravura Eloquence Concord*).

ANTHONY BRAXTON

Chicago-born in 1945, saxophonist, composer and bandleader Anthony Braxton's work reflects something of the isolation, independence and

experimentalism of his fellow Chicagoan Sun Ra. Buttressed by implacable intellectuality, however, rather than by Ra's B-movie melodramatics, he has produced a massive and diversified body of work, from elaborately scored works for large ensembles to string quartets and solo performances. Through all this runs a consistent thread of work within a jazz quartet line-up of horns and rhythm which both sustains and extends that tradition. It seems likely, also, that the energetic and open-minded Braxton's work is by no means yet complete. (Anthony Braxton: *Seven Compositions (Trio)* 1989 hat ART).

MICHAEL BRECKER

The dominance of the saxophone scene by John Coltrane lasted for some twenty years after his death. During that time, Mike Brecker became in turn the main sub-influence, giving extra mileage to some of Coltrane's technical innovations. Born in Philadelphia in 1949, he was a member of one of the early jazz-rock groups, Dreams, which also included his brother Randy and drummer Billy Cobham. The Brecker Brothers had more success with their own group, which has lasted on and off to the present, while Mike was also a founder-member of Steps. His exceptional technique, flying effortlessly through the octaves, made a big impression on those coming after him. (Michael Brecker: *Michael Brecker* Impulse).

RANDY BRECKER

Born in Philadelphia in 1945, Randy Brecker's career has often moved in tandem with that of his younger brother. After leaving Dreams, both he and Billy Cobham joined Horace Silver for a while, and he also worked with Clark Terry, Duke Pearson and Larry Coryell's Eleventh House, before the two Breckers formed their popular jazz-rock group. An exciting soloist, in a style which is related to that of Freddie Hubbard, Randy has also contributed to several trumpet sections, most recently to that of the Mingus Big Band. (Randy Brecker: *In The Idiom* Denon).

BOB BROOKMEYER

The first valve-trombone specialist of modern times, Bob Brookmeyer, who was born in Kansas City in 1929, got his early jobs on piano. He notably replaced Chet Baker in Gerry Mulligan's quartet and began a long association with the saxophonist which lasted up to the Concert Jazz Band, for which Brookmeyer did some of the arranging. He then helped to found the Thad Jones-Mel Lewis rehearsal band, as trombonist and arranger, and also partnered Clark Terry in a popular quintet. His profile as a composer-arranger has increased in recent years, though he still works regularly as a trombone soloist. (Stan Getz: *Getz At The Shrine* Verve).

WILLEM BREUKER

One of the first freejazz saxophonists in Europe, Willem Breuker later typified the Dutch traits: plenty of humour allied to intricate and exceptionally well-drilled ensembles. He puts this down to the country being small and having good internal communications, so that musicians have no excuse to avoid rehearsals. Born in Amsterdam in 1944, and loud enough to hold his own on Peter Brötzmann's *Machine Gun*, he struck out in the Seventies with the medium-sized Willem Breuker Kollektief. A love of parody possibly came from Carla Bley, the group's dazzling circus-styled interplay is unmistakeable. (The Willem Breuker Kollektief: *Live At The Donaueschingen Music Festival 1975* MPS).

The Brecker Brothers: Mike (left) on tenor saxophone and Randy on trumpet.

TINA BROOKS

Harold 'Tina' Brooks, born in North Carolina in 1932, died in obscurity in 1974 having had little of a career. In June 1960, Blue Note had recorded him and Freddie Hubbard on each other's debut albums. Hubbard became a star, while Brooks never had another record issued during his lifetime. But the original album, *True Blue*, became something of a critic's choice, if only because, at a time when John Coltrane was demonizing tenor saxophonists, Brooks phrased in a languid unforced manner which sounded like nobody else. He also played on Jimmy Smith's *The Sermon*, though his drug habit effectively put him out of business. (Tina Brooks: *True Blue* Blue Note).

PETER BRÖTZMANN

After touring in a group with Peter Brötzmann in the freejazz era, Carla Bley said she ended up feeling more like a gymnast than a musician. Brötzmann, born in Germany in 1941, soon latched on to the wild saxophone sounds emanating from the U.S. and reproduced them at seemingly twice the volume. His octet recording of *Machine Gun* is Europe's answer to Coltrane's *Ascension*, an unmatchable blast of energy music now reissued with, incredibly, two rejected versions. He has since played in the Globe Unity Orchestra and, more recently, as part of Last Exit. Still pretty loud, there is more mellow warmth to his playing today. *Peter Brötzmann: Machine Gun FMP).*

CLIFFORD BROWN

Clifford Brown was the outstanding trumpet star of bebop's second generation, and a huge influence on those who came after him. Born in Delaware in 1930, his own biggest influence was Fats Navarro. They were technically and stylistically on a par, though Brown's tone was brighter, and he enjoyed producing very long, heavily tongued phrases. He came to prominence in 1953 with both Tadd Dameron and Lionel Hampton, played a memorable engagement with Art Blakey and Horace Silver the following year and then became joint leader with Max Roach of a great quintet. He was killed in a car crash in 1956. *(Clifford Brown & Max Roach: Mercury).*

LAWRENCE BROWN

Born in 1907, Lawrence Brown grew up in California, and worked there with Les Hite's band (fronted at the time by Louis Armstrong). He joined Duke Ellington in 1932, where his suave but powerful open trombone was significant in the transition from Ellington's 'Jungle Band' period to a wider and more varied series of voicings. In 1951, he left to work with Johnny Hodges, and in 1955 he became a studio musician. In 1960, he rejoined Ellington, diversifying into plunger-mute effects and featuring on old favourites like 'Rose Of The Rio Grande'. He retired from playing in 1974 and died in 1988. *(Lawrence Brown: Inspired Abandon* (incorporated into *Everybody Knows Johnny Hodges*), *Impulse).*

PETE BROWN

Although a highly regarded alto saxophonist of the swing era, Pete Brown seemed to lose his way. Born in Baltimore in 1906, he was among the first to gravitate to small groups, around New York and usually with trumpeter Frankie Newton, whose career was similarly unfulfilled. His characteristically propulsive phrasing led to the term 'jump style' being invented just for him, but his career fizzled out years before his death in 1963, so he did not benefit from the renewed interest in that kind of music. *(Joe Turner: Boss Of The Blues Atlantic).*

RAY BROWN

The art of bass playing in jazz has been revolutionized at least twice. Following on from Jimmy Blanton, Ray Brown epitomized the new breed of rhythm bassist: full of tone, perfect timing and the right choice of notes. Born in Pittsburgh in 1926, he was part of Dizzy Gillespie's orchestra for two years and then acted as musical director for Ella Fitzgerald, to whom he was married at the time. After more than a decade with the Oscar Peterson trio, he settled in Los Angeles, founded the LA Four with Bud Shank and Laurindo Almeida and more recently has led his own trio. *(Ray Brown: Seven Steps To Heaven Telarc Jazz).*

JANE BUNNETT

A Canadian, born in Toronto in 1955, Jane Bunnett studied classical piano, before a combination of tendonitis and exposure to jazz (notably Charles Mingus) launched her transformation into a reeds all-rounder playing refreshingly different music. Casting her net wide, she has studied Monk and the soprano saxophone with Steve Lacy in Paris and gone out of

Dave Brubeck (piano) with Paul Desmond (l) leads the quartet that recorded 'Take Five'.

her way to record with Cuban musicians on their home ground. Her approach has something of the engaging quirkiness of Don Pullen, who adds lustre to some of her albums. Especially effective on flute, she can growl like Roland Kirk. (Jane Bunnett: *The Water Is Wide Evidence*).

DAVE BRUBECK

Always a favourite of the jazz audience, if less so of critics, Dave Brubeck discovered ways of improvizing at the piano which blended jazz and European effects and subsequently influenced the likes of Cecil Taylor and Keith Jarrett. Born in 1920, he first became prominent on the West Coast, and his famous quartet with Paul Desmond thrived by touring the college circuit, the first jazz group to capitalize on this large area of demand. An early experimenter with metres outside the 4/4 then almost universal in jazz, he has also, in recent years, collaborated on many concert works, often on religious themes. (Dave Brubeck: *Jazz At Oberlin* Fantasy).

KENNY BURRELL

It's not surprising that Kenny Burrell should have taken part in so many sessions alongside the Hammond organ, as he adopts an ultra-relaxed approach to the guitar that slots readily into a foot-tapping blues environment. Born in Detroit in 1931, he worked around New York in the Fifties, usually in the context of a trio or quartet, and recorded regularly on the so-called 'blowing sessions' put together by the smaller jazz labels. He also worked as a singer. Apart from some big band recordings which included arrangements by Gil Evans, he has continued to work with organists, including several reunions with Jimmy Smith, or as a part of all-star groups. (Kenny Burrell/Jack McDuff: *Crash* Prestige).

GARY BURTON

Gary Burton was one of the first vibraphonists (or vibraharpists) to use a four-mallet technique, and was also a pioneer of jazz-rock or jazz fusion. Born in Indiana in 1943, he cut his teeth in the groups of George Shearing and Stan Getz, before forming the first of his quartets. With Steve Swallow on electric bass and a succession of excellent guitarists, the delectable cocktail of jazz, country

Jazz-rock pioneer Gary Burton at the vibraphone.

music and the compositions of Mike Gibbs and Carla Bley made the group a popular favourite. After a few years intensive touring, he has since combined playing with work as an educator at Berklee college, where he had originally studied. (Gary Burton: *Hotel Hello* ECM).

Billy Butterfield

One of the trumpet stars of the later swing period, Billy Butterfield was born in Ohio in 1917 and got his first big break in the Bob Crosby band. After three years, he was tempted away by Artie Shaw (playing a famous solo on 'Stardust') before joining his clarinet rival Benny Goodman, to whom he often returned in later years. A powerful, Armstrong-influenced soloist, he worked in the studios, played Dixieland and was featured on several big band albums before enjoying renewed popularity with the World's Greatest Jazz Band in the late-Sixties, followed by regular tours and appearances at festivals. He died in 1988. (*World's Greatest Jazz Band: Extra Project*).

Jaki Byard

Born in Massachusetts in 1922, Jaki Byard was based in Boston and took a long time to reach a wider public. In the early Sixties, he was the pianist on some of Eric Dolphy's finest recordings and then both were in the Charles Mingus sextet that toured Europe in 1963. His style seems to have bypassed bop, at least in the single-line form exemplified by Bud Powell, as Byard often uses or implies stride patterns and, without sounding like him, has more in common with Thelonious Monk. (*Jaki Byard: Blues For Smoke* Candid).

Don Byas

Born in Oklahoma in 1913, Byas first worked in California, then toured with many bands before replacing Lester Young with Count Basie in 1941. After two years, he left Basie, and became a fixture on New York's 52nd Street. Byas joined Don Redman in 1946 for a tour of Europe, and he settled there for the rest of his life, dying in Amsterdam in 1972. Having taken part in early bebop sessions, he was a key player in the transition from swing and regarded himself as a modernist, though his greatest work was done at slower tempos on standard material. (*Don Byas On Blue Star*, EmArcy).

Donald Byrd

The second part of Donald Byrd's career was hardly hinted at in the first. He was born in Detroit in 1932 and played in the leading Hard Bop bands of the Fifties. During this time, he was frequently recorded, usually as a sideman in someone else's group. As his playing grew stronger, he went on to form an excellent quintet, co-led with Pepper Adams. Increasingly involved in teaching, he eventually became chairman of the Black Music department at Howard University. Then came *Black Byrd*, a jazz-funk album which sold exceptionally well and led on to several successors. (*Donald Byrd: Free Form* Blue Note).

Don Byron

Although he has played baritone in such big bands as the surviving Duke Ellington orchestra, Don Byron regards himself as a clarinet (and bass clarinet) specialist and has helped to popularize the instrument. Born in New York in 1958, and classically trained, he arranged for local Latin bands and worked his way into jazz with the likes of David Murray and, later, Ralph Peterson and Bill Frisell. His own albums are marked by their extraordinary range of styles, his tone changing from sweet to plaintive to sour as the context changes. One of his projects is a band which engagingly updates the klezmer satires of Mickey Katz. (*Don Byron: Music For Six Musicians* Elektra Nonsuch).

Don Byron, modern master of the clarinet.

King of Hi-de-hi, Cab Calloway led a great band in the Thirties.

MICHEL CAMILO

Born in the Dominican Republic in 1954, Michel Camilo came to New York in 1979, and was soon making his mark in the area of Jazz meets Latin America, a fusion that stretches at least as far back as the first Dizzy Gillespie big band – his tune 'Caribe' was played by Gillespie. A fiery pianist, always ready to whip up the temperature, Camilo's bands carry on the tradition. On the album cited, made with a biggish band including Cuban saxophonist Paquito D'Rivera, there are passages where brass and rhythm generate a kind of spontaneous interaction. (Michel Camilo: *One More Once* Columbia).

CAB CALLOWAY

A front-man who knew how to get a band moving, Cab Calloway was a larger-than-life figure in charge of an outstanding big band. Born in New York in 1907, his singing and showmanship attracted those who ran the Cotton Club, where he became the relief band for Duke Ellington. While Calloway's songs about 'Minnie The Moocher' and 'Cokey Joe' titillated the public, his band included such stars as Chu Berry, Jonah Jones and, briefly, Dizzy Gillespie, and compared with any on the circuit. His later career included consultancy work on the film *The Cotton Club*, which led to a renewed burst of fame. He died in 1994. (Cab Calloway: *Best Of The Big Bands* Columbia).

remained a member until his death, four months after Ellington's, in 1974. Carney played the baritone saxophone and, occasionally, clarinet or bass clarinet. A man of equable disposition, he fitted the role of anchor-man both musically and temperamentally in an organization never short of volatile characters. In his hands, the baritone grew from a

Harry Carney's work with Duke Ellington put the baritone saxophone on the map.

HARRY CARNEY

Born in Boston in 1910, a professional musician at age 13, Harry Carney became a member of Duke Ellington's band in 1929, and

BENNY CARTER

The only giant of pre-war jazz still in business, Benny Carter has always been a musician's musician, revered for all-round technical knowledge. Born in New York in 1907, he worked with Fletcher Henderson and other well-known bandleaders, playing the alto saxophone (and, occasionally, trumpet) and producing brilliant arrangements, especially for saxophone sections. Along with Coleman Hawkins, he was the most distinguished jazz musician to spend some years in Europe before the war. His polished and meticulously crafted playing remained in demand afterwards, when he became the first black musician to break into the lucrative field of film and television scores. (Benny Carter: *Symphony In Riffs* ASV).

Composer, arranger, multi-instrumentalist: Benny Carter and alto saxophone.

Their paths did cross again in the Fifties, when both were living in Los Angeles. Carter conducted a concert of Coleman's music and introduced him to trumpeter Bobby Bradford. He gradually moved from free jazz to more formal music, in the process ditching the saxophone to concentrate on the clarinet, on which he was a remarkable all-round virtuoso, able to produce microtones without sacrificing the instrument's bonhomie. Before his death in 1991, he had recorded his five-album major composition *Roots And Folklore*. (John Carter: *Dauwhe* Gramavision)).

RON CARTER

Ron Carter's curriculum vitae is still dominated by the Miles Davis years when, along with Herbie Hancock and Tony Williams, he re-invented the rhythm section, as a highly flexible, if still swinging, unit. Born in Michigan in 1937, he worked with Chico Hamilton and, notably, Eric Dolphy, after acquiring a music degree. Recognized as a superb all-round bassist with a clean yet robust sound, he has not sought the limelight. Heavily involved in education, his jazz gigs tend to be records and sessions, plus regular appearances on the touring circuit, often as part of an all-star package. (Ron Carter: *Telephone* Concord).

AL CASEY

Along with Teddy Bunn, Al Casey was a leading guitarist of the Thirties who tended to be eclipsed by the arrival of Charlie Christian. Born in Kentucky in 1915, he was one of the instrumental highlights of Fats Waller's Rhythm for 8 years. He then ran his own trio for a time but, as the demand for jazz dropped, he took the obvious option

BETTY CARTER

No one has taken the human voice closer to the flexibility and adventurousness of instrumental jazz than Betty Carter. She often re-phrases the lyrics of a song so that a familiar tune becomes unrecognizable, while her wordless improvisations on a theme may last as long as a saxophone solo. Born in Michigan in 1929, she took several years to become more than a cult figure but, from about the late Seventies (and coinciding with a new maturity on her part), the world finally caught up with her. She also has a remarkable ability to spot and develop talent in her accompanists. (Betty Carter: *The Audience With Betty Carter* Verve (2 CDs)).

JAMES CARTER

Potentially, at least, the most exciting saxophonist to come to the fore in the Nineties, James Carter was born in Detroit in 1969 and, at seventeen, was already part of Wynton Marsalis's quintet, replacing Branford Marsalis. He has also worked and recorded with Lester Bowie and saxophonist Julius Hemphill, so his experience includes a broad spectrum of current American jazz. Perhaps closest in style to David Murray, Carter's tenor saxophone sound is similarly fruity, and he likewise extracts whole chunks of melody from the tenor's upper reaches. Though a stupendous technician, Carter can play ballads with feeling, as on the album cited. (James Carter: *The Real Quietstorm* Atlantic).

JOHN CARTER

Born in the same town as Ornette Coleman and at about the same time (Fort Worth, 1929), John Carter chose a more orthodox musical education,

machine making low noises into a flexible and luxuriant-sounding instrument, and Carney himself never stopped working on his technique, developing the instrument's range and potential still further. (Duke Ellington: *Such Sweet Thunder*, Columbia).

Armstrong At Symphony Hall GRP/Decca).

OSCAR CELESTIN

Oscar 'Papa' Celestin was a mainstay of the New Orleans scene for over 40 years, a trumpeter who led from the front with no frills or flashy fingering. Born in 1884, he played in the Algiers Brass Band before forming his own band to play for dancers at the Tuxedo Hall. His Original Tuxedo Brass Band attracted the best local musicians, including clarinettist Paul Barnes, drummer Zutty Singleton and trumpeter Kid Shots Madison. Working and recording throughout the Twenties, he was able to enjoy renewed success, following the New Orleans revival, until his death in 1954. (Oscar 'Papa' Celestin: New Orleans Classics .Azure).

SERGE CHALOFF

Serge Chaloff was born in Boston in 1923, and died there in 1957, aged

Drummers of all persuasions loved to hear Big Sid Catlett.

New Orleans veteran, Oscar 'Papa' Celestin benefited from the jazz revival.

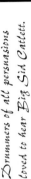

for a guitarist and played for R&B artists, among them saxophonist King Curtis. By contrast, recent interest in all areas of the music has led to the widespread acceptance he thoroughly deserves. (Al Casey: *Jumpin' With Al Black & Blue*).

PHILIP CATHERINE

Though born in London (1942), Philip Catherine's father was Belgian and he was brought up in Brussels. Hardly surprising, then, that his influences on guitar began with Django Reinhardt. Having started as a member of organist Lou Bennett's trio, he headed more towards fusion and played with Jean-Luc Ponty before forming the group Pork Pie with Charlie Mariano. A melodic player and rarely the type to go over the top, he

worked successfully with Chet Baker (in his later days), as well as freelancing around the unclassifiable European scene. (Philip Catherine: *I Remember You Criss Cross*).

SID CATLETT

Born in Indiana in 1910, 'Big' Sid Catlett became one of the most highly regarded drummers of the swing era. He also appeared on some early sessions by Charlie Parker and Dizzy Gillespie, and was equally idolized by the likes of Max Roach. Musicians praised him above all for his taste: deploying his considerable technique to musical ends, he provided the type of accompaniment they wanted on demand. In the Thirties, he worked with top bands including Fletcher Henderson's, though his most familiar recordings are probably those made during the years, shortly before his death in 1951, as a member of Louis Armstrong's All Stars. (Louis

Don Cherry with his trademark pocket trumpet.

Only 33. Learning from the solo work of Harry Carney, to Chaloff fell the task of translating the sound of the baritone saxophone into the language of bebop, retaining its distinctive flavour and depth while using dynamics frequently to imply further agility. With Woody Herman's band and related small groups from 1947 to 1949, he demonstrated the viability of this approach. In his remaining years, he made a few records which clarified his innovative role, and his best solos thereon carry great emotional impact. (Serge Chaloff Memorial: *We The People Bop* Cool'N'Blue).

PAUL CHAMBERS

Born in Pittsburgh in 1935, Paul Chambers was part of the burgeoning Detroit scene of the early Fifties, before joining the first of Miles Davis's great quintets (with John Coltrane, Red Garland and Philly Joe Jones). As their bass player, he dovetailed perfectly with Jones on the fast pieces and was just as effective when weaving around the trumpeter's ballads and mid-tempoed jaunts, while his solos looked forward to fast-fingered virtuosi of the Sixties. After leaving Davis, he continued working with Garland's replacement, Wynton Kelly, and freelanced around New York. He died in 1969. (John Coltrane: *Traneing In* Prestige).

RAY CHARLES

In his long and successful career in music, the significance of Ray Charles rests in his giving gospel-styled songs a secular message, thereby leading to a widespread acceptance of Soul. Born in Georgia in 1930, and blind from an early age, he began as a singer-pianist somewhere between Nat Cole and R&B. In the mid-Fifties, he became a cult among jazz musicians searching for roots, while expanding a popular appeal that led to a major label and major hits, based on his increasingly extravagant but always gripping vocals. Many notable performers have passed though his bands. (Ray Charles: *Blues & Jazz* Atlantic/Rhino (2 CDs)).

DON CHERRY

Oklahoma-born in 1936, Cherry met Texan Ornette Coleman in California and it was there that they first played together, in Paul Bley's quintet, in 1958. He became a cornerstone of Ornette's great quartet, and moved with the group to New York in 1960. After leaving the quartet, he worked as a leader and made many fine records. Subsequently he travelled widely, investigating many different aspects of world music, of which he became a crucial pioneer. While it was always marked by its harmonic adventurousness, and undoubtedly reflected many modern influences, Cherry's trumpet work equally recalled an earlier and perhaps more intuitive tradition of tonal variety and inflection. He died in 1995. (Don Cherry: *Brown Rice* A&M).

DOC CHEATHAM

Adolphus 'Doc' Cheatham has had one of the longest, and also one of the oddest, careers in jazz. Born in 1905, he was accompanying Bessie Smith in his native Nashville in the early Twenties, and understudied Louis Armstrong in Chicago in 1926. Cheatham was a member of several respected big and small bands in the Thirties and Forties, notably Cab Calloway's, but he then worked in Latin bands, made very few recordings, and remained little known to the jazz public until the mid Seventies. Most of his best recordings date from the last two decades. (Doc Cheatham: *At The Berne Jazz Festival* Sackville).

GEORGE CHISHOLM

As the swing era cast its benign spell over Europe, trombonist George Chisholm was making his way around the big bands, joining Ambrose in 1938. Before that, Chisholm (born Glasgow, 1915) had already been hand picked by the visiting Benny Carter to accompany him to Holland where they recorded together. A superb all-rounder in the Teagarden tradition, his considerable jazz career has been supplemented by sessions, working in the BBC's Show Band and a featured spot on television's long-running Black And White Minstrel Show, where he could display his talent for comedy. He gave up playing in the 1990s. (George Chisholm: *In A Mellow Mood* Gold Star).

CHARLIE CHRISTIAN

One of the first guitarists to use an amplifier, Charlie Christian is also celebrated as a bebop pioneer, though it was more a case of him adapting Lester Young's style to the guitar. His laid-back phrasing and an impeccable sense of swing captivated all who heard him, notably Benny Goodman, who insisted that Christian join his band. Originally from Dallas (born 1916), he settled in New York and was the guiding spirit in jam sessions at Minton's Playhouse, which legend puts as the birthplace of bop. Unable to cope with the pace of city life, he contracted tuberculosis, then pneumonia, and died in 1942. (Charlie Christian: *Solo Flight* Columbia).

SONNY CLARK

A disciple of Bud Powell, pianist Clark had the technique to get on terms with the fast runs demanded by that style, although rhythmically he departed from Powell's complexities in favour of a flowing delivery which to a degree reflected a more fluent extension of Tadd Dameron's piano work. Also like Dameron, he seemed to find a front line of two or three horns consistently congenial. Born in 1931 he toured with Buddy DeFranco before settling in New York, where he made a handful of remarkable records, featuring some fine compositions of his own, before his early death in 1963. (Sonny Clark: *Cool Struttin'*, Blue Note).

also worked with pianist Francy Boland in a jointly-led big band which included many expatriate musicians. (Dexter Gordon: *Our Man In Paris*, Blue Note).

STANLEY CLARKE

At the time when bass guitar began to muscle in on string bass territory, Stanley Clarke had a foot in each camp. Born in Philadelphia in 1951, he worked with Horace Silver, Joe Henderson and others before joining Chick Corea's Return To Forever. As the group shed its initial elfin charm and grew in power, he more often favoured the electric model over the acoustic, both on his own albums and on various jazz-rock collaborations with keyboard player George Duke. A considerable virtuoso on either bass, he can overdo the histrionics, which tends to impart a curate's-egg quality to his own albums. (Stanley Clarke: *Journey To Love* Columbia).

BUCK CLAYTON

Born in Kansas in 1911, Buck Clayton led a number of bands of his own, including one in Shanghai, before joining Count Basie in 1936. His recordings with the band reveal him as an exceptionally delicate and lyrical swing-era trumpeter, with that typical Southwest rhythmic insouciance. Often using mutes, he was at his most sympathetic in small group sessions with such fellow spirits as Lester Young and Billie Holiday. Clayton later became one of the most recorded survivors from the Thirties, before health problems forced him to give up the trumpet and make more use of his arranging talents. He died in 1991. (Buck Clayton & Buddy Tate: *Buck & Buddy* Swingsville).

JIMMY CLEVELAND

Trombonist Jimmy Cleveland (born 1926) was widely admired for his slippery technique, emulating the speed, if not quite the sound, of J.J. Johnson. Born in Tennessee, he played in the Lionel Hampton orchestra that eventually included Clifford Brown and toured Europe: he appeared both on Hampton's records and on those recorded illegally by Brown, Gigi Gryce and the others. Apart from another trip across the Atlantic, with Quincy Jones's *Free And Easy* band in 1959, he has been heavily involved in the studios and confines his live playing to local sessions and big-band get-togethers. (Gigi Gryce: *Nica's Tempo* Denon).

BILLY COBHAM

Born in Panama in 1944 and brought up in New York, Billy Cobham first attracted attention with Horace Silver, but made his biggest impact a few years later when drumming for the Mahavishnu Orchestra (along with John McLaughlin, he had participated

KENNY CLARKE

Widely recognized as the progenitor of modern jazz drumming, Kenny Clarke (1914-1985) built on the work of Sid Catlett and Jo Jones to clarify a method which perfectly matched emerging musical needs, carrying the beat on flowing open cymbal and using snare and bass drums to propose counter-rhythms. One of the Minton's Playhouse pioneers of the early 1940s, he worked subsequently with everybody who was anybody in bebop. After leaving the Modern Jazz Quartet, which he co-founded, he moved to Paris, forming a trio with Bud Powell, then an organ-combo with Lou Bennett. From 1960 to 1973, he

Buck Clayton, once a stalwart of the Count Basie band.

in the legendary Miles Davis electric sessions in 1969-70). After leaving Mahavishnu, he formed a similar jazz-rock group which, at first, included the Brecker Brothers. Cobham settled in Switzerland some years ago, and he enjoys the chance to play in different environments. He also teaches and conducts workshops, sometimes co-operating with UNICEF. (Billy Cobham: *The Best of Billy Cobham* Atlantic).

TONY COE

Tony Coe, born in Kent in 1934, is widely recognized beyond Britain as a world-class jazz musician. Never easy to pigeonhole, his career takes in the Humphrey Lyttelton band, where he replaced Bruce Turner in the mid-Fifties, a long stint with the international Kenny Clarke-Francy Boland big band, and the avant garde of both jazz and classical music, as both player and composer. However, it's as a sumptuously robust soloist on the tenor saxophone, sounding like an updated Paul Gonsalves, and as a clarinettist, with a spiky modern lilt, that Coe attracts most admiration. (Tony Coe: *Some Other Autumn* Hep).

AL COHN

A New Yorker (born 1925), Al Cohn played with several big bands in the Forties, notably Woody Herman's Second Herd. Starting with 'The Goof And I', which Herman turned into a jazz standard, he eventually became a much in-demand composer-arranger for sessions and recording projects of all kinds. For many years his main jazz activity was in an often-revived partnership with Zoot Sims. Apart from the contrast between the two tenor saxophonists (Cohn having the beefier sound), the group benefited greatly from Cohn's ability to organ-ize. Before his death in 1988, he often worked with his son Joe, a guitarist. (Al Cohn And Zoot Sims: *Body & Soul* Muse).

COZY COLE

Born in New Jersey in 1906, William 'Cozy' Cole played with Benny Carter, and later spent four years with Cab Calloway, but his reputation rests, just as much, on his drumming for smaller groups, beginning with Stuff Smith's Onyx Club sextet in the late Thirties. He gravitated to radio and theatre bands, before spending three years with Louis Armstrong's All Stars. In the Fifties, his record of 'Topsy' became a hit, and he also enjoyed success, later, with Jonah Jones, an ex-colleague from the Thirties. A keen student of the drums, Cole, who died in 1981, once ran a drum school with Gene Krupa. (Louis Armstrong: *The California Concerts* GRP/MCA (4 CDs)).

NAT 'KING' COLE

For the public at large, the enormous success of Nat 'King' Cole as a singer totally overshadowed his earlier career. He was a major pianist, influ-

Great jazz pianist who became a vocal idol: Nat 'King' Cole.

encing many at the end of the swing era and the beginning of bop. Born in Alabama in 1917, Cole became one of the most proficient disciples of Earl Hines, with a distinctively light, skipping approach to the keyboard. He began to sing while leading his drum-less trio, a most admired group, blending his jazz musician's feel for rhythm with a voice which remains utterly unique. From then, up to his death in 1965, he was a superstar, though he would still accompany his songs on stage and throw in a springy solo. (Nat 'King' Cole: *Hit That Jive Jack* MCA).

BILL COLEMAN

A swing-era trumpeter whose engagingly fluid style pointed towards bebop. Bill Coleman was born in Kentucky in 1904. He worked with the big bands of Benny Carter and Teddy Hill, and recorded with Fats Waller. In 1935, he settled in Paris, working with American bandleader Willie Lewis and appearing on some classic sides with Dickie Wells, as well as spending time in India and Egypt. After a productive stay in New York, he returned to France in 1948 and was based there until his death in 1981. Like Armstrong, Allen, Eldridge – and Gillespie – he was a trumpet-leader who enjoyed singing. (Bill Coleman: *Bill Coleman Meets Guy Lafitte* Black Lion).

GEORGE COLEMAN

A contemporary of Booker Little's in Memphis, where he was born in 1935, George Coleman joined Max Roach, along with Little, in 1958. After a spell with trombonist Slide Hampton, Coleman became a member of the new trailblazing Miles Davis quintet, and remained until he was replaced by Wayne Shorter. He has worked with Elvin Jones, Cedar Walton, toured as a single fronting local rhythm sections and, occasion-

ally, run an ambitious octet. From the beginning a formidable tenor saxophonist with a distinctive light and pure sound, he can emulate the jet-propelled chord-hopping of Coltrane's middle period and make it seem personal. (George Coleman: *At Yoshi's* Evidence).

STEVE COLEMAN

An alto saxophonist from Chicago (born 1956), Steve Coleman has always been exposed to a spread of music, from Chicago blues to Cecil Taylor, with whom he worked in New York. He was a key member of several Dave Holland groups, recording with him and also with David Murray's big band. Since then, he has launched a movement to blend the complexity of jazz improvizing with street rhythms, from funk to hip hop and rap. Giving his system the acronym M-Base, he inspired others to follow, including saxophonist Greg Osby and trumpeter Graham Haynes, and has encouraged similar movements in such centres as San Francisco and London. (Steve Coleman: *Rhythm In Mind* Novus).

JOHNNY COLES

Never in the limelight for very long, trumpeter Johnny Coles has worked with a string of prestigious bandleaders, including Duke Ellington, Count Basie, Ray Charles and Gil Evans, for whom he was probably the next best thing to Miles Davis. Born in New Jersey in 1926, he was already something of an R&B veteran when he joined Evans, taking some typically poised, mellow-toned solos on 'La Nevada', 'Sunken Treasure' and other classic sides, and also recording a few gems under his own name. More recently, he was a good choice for Damaronia, a band devoted to the

music of Tadd Dameron. (Johnny Coles: *New Morning* Criss Cross).

BUDDY COLLETTE

Very much a West Coast musician, William 'Buddy' Collette was born in Los Angeles in 1921. A friend of Charles Mingus, he also played with Lucky Thompson and Benny Carter and, around 1950, became one of the first black musicians to work regularly in the studios. Later, he was part of the original Chico Hamilton quintet. Collette, who plays clarinet and flute as well as saxophone, has rarely toured since, being content to freelance locally and do some teaching. A gifted all-rounder, his calm and measured style contrasts with that of Eric Dolphy, his most notable successor in Hamilton's group. (Chico Hamilton: *A Nice Day* Contemporary).

EDDIE CONDON

Eddie Condon was a rhythm guitarist, but his real contribution was as an

Alto saxophonist Steve Coleman has pointed modern jazz in new directions.

organizer and personality. Born in Indiana in 1905, he fell in with the circle of young white jazz musicians in Chicago and was co-leader, on one of the early sessions, of McKenzie and Condon's Chicagoans. He moved to New York in 1928, and recorded with, among others, Louis Armstrong and Fats Waller. Articulate and a noted wit, not least about his heavy drinking, Condon turned into a public figure. He organized a series of broadcast jam sessions at New York Town Hall, and then opened a club in New York which became a home for his sort of jazz. He died in 1973. (Eddie Condon *The Original Decca Recordings* MCA).

CHICK COREA

As a young pianist (born in 1941 in Massachusetts), Chick Corea worked with the best: Stan Getz and then Miles Davis, where he replaced Herbie Hancock and became the first to work in public with Davis playing electric keyboard. His own fusion group, Return To Forever, began with an enticing brand of Latin jazz featuring the vocal-percussion team of Flora Purim and Airto Moreira, but the music soon grew heavier and rather less distinctive. In recent years, Corea has reverted more often to the piano, on which he is one of the most gifted of his generation. (Chick Corea: *Now He Sings, Now He Sobs* Blue Note).

MARILYN CRISPELL

Featured prominently in Anthony Braxton's groups, Marilyn Crispell is a virtuoso pianist, influenced technically by Cecil Taylor but with her own musical ambience. Born in Philadelphia in 1947, she studied at the New England conservatory and first recorded with Braxton in 1981, subsequently appearing with him at many of his concerts. Among several recordings under her name for the Leo label are a hymn to Gaia and a solo tribute to Coltrane, her other big jazz influence (a further link is her musical partnership with Coltrane's former bassist, Reggie Workman), that includes some of his tunes. (Marilyn Crispell: *The Kitchen Concerts* Leo).

SONNY CRISS

Once linked to the emerging bebop scene on the West Coast, Sonny Criss was a fine alto saxophonist who never quite broke through. Born in Memphis in 1927, his early playing incorporated some Parker-type phrases though his tone and general style belonged more to the swing era. In the Fifties, he worked with Buddy Rich, and then benefited to an extent when a renewed interest in bebop led to records and tours abroad. Things were looking better, but the threat of illness led to his suicide in 1977. (Sonny Criss: *Portrait of Sonny Criss* Prestige).

BOB CROSBY

Bob Crosby (1913-1993), brother of Bing, was the archetypal front man, the only bandleader of the swing era hired by his own musicians. The band was a co-operative, made up of young white players who disliked the regimentation of orthodox swing and hankered after the freedom of the Twenties – this when the Bunk Johnson saga and the New Orleans Revival were stirring. Crosby's band included excellent musicians, notably trumpeters Yank Lawson and Billy Butterfield, clarinettist Irving Fazola, tenor saxophonist Eddie Miller and pianists Bob Zurke and Jess Stacy. Various bands led thereafter by Lawson and bassist Bob Haggart continued the Crosby ethos. (Bob Crosby: *South Rampart Street Parade* MCA).

ISRAEL CROSBY

A bassist whose light, skipping style was ahead of its time, Israel Crosby (born 1919) was most often found at the heart of Ahmad Jamal's popular trio. Long before that, he had played with Albert Ammons at the well-known Club de Lisa in his native Chicago, worked in the bands of both the Henderson brothers and had a minor record hit, 'Blues For Israel', under Gene Krupa's name. He joined Jamal in 1951, after several years of studio work, and appeared on his most influential records. Shortly before his death in 1962, he was a member of George Shearing's quintet. (Ahmad Jamal: *At The Pershing* Chess).

ANDREW CYRILLE

As the drummer who worked regularly with Cecil Taylor in the years after Sunny Murray left, Andrew Cyrille has continued to expand on the music developed during the Sixties, though he has worked successfully with musicians of all styles. Born in Brooklyn in 1939, his early leaders included Illinois Jacquet and Rahsaan Roland Kirk. Since then, he has worked with, among others, Carla Bley, Muhal Richard Abrams and David Murray. In addition to his percussion duets, he once formed a trio with Milford Graves and Rashied Ali, and he has recorded in a foursome with Graves, Don Moye and Kenny Clarke. (Andrew Cyrille: *My Friend Louis* DIW).

Pianist, keyboard player and band leader, Chick Corea.

TADD DAMERON

Composer, bandleader and pianist, Tadd Dameron (1917-1965) was one of the creative figures of the bop era, writing for Gillespie's big band and working with small groups frequently featuring Fats Navarro. After the Paris Jazz Fair of 1949, he lived in France for a while. In 1953, he formed a nine-piece band including Clifford Brown for a season in Atlantic City. Rarely working in public afterwards, he nonetheless recorded a quartet date with John Coltrane that outlines some of his most beautiful compositions, as well as a big-band session which reprised some of his better-known works. His relatively small recorded legacy deserves serious attention. (Tadd Dameron With John Coltrane: *Mating Call* Prestige).

Tadd Dameron wrote many great tunes in the Forties and Fifties.

EDDIE DANIELS

Somewhat late in the day, Eddie Daniels seems the logical successor to the bandleading clarinet maestro of the Thirties. Born in New York in 1941, he first attracted attention as a stalwart of the Thad Jones-Mel Lewis band, in which he played mainly tenor saxophone. Since then, it's the clarinet that has grabbed most attention. Classically trained, his technique is considerable, but what especially grabs listeners is the lush, reedy tone he produces when tune and tempo are right, something that had virtually disappeared with Artie Shaw. (Eddie Daniels: *Breakthrough* GRP).

---

fine bass player, as co-leader of an excellent new big band. (John Dankworth: *The Roulette Years* Roulette).

The young saxophonist John Dankworth helped introduce bebop to the U.K.

JOHN DANKWORTH

Born in London in 1927, alto saxophonist John Dankworth became one of the early stalwarts of bebop in the U.K. and, via his Seven, introduced many to the music. In the Fifties, he formed a big band which lasted off and on for twenty years. Dankworth often replaced the saxophone section by a four-piece front line (trumpet, etc) and the rest of his writing was equally ingenious, if sometimes over-influenced by his other work writing film music. Since then, he has acted as musical director for his wife Cleo Laine and has joined his son Alec, a

KENNY DAVERN

Kenny Davern is the most gifted traditional jazz clarinettist in the world today. His music derives from the early stars of New Orleans and Chicago – Jimmy Noone, Pee Wee Russell and Irving Fazola among them – but he has also recorded with Steve Lacy and expressed admiration for Ornette Coleman. Born in Long Island in 1935, he played with Jack Teagarden, and appeared on one of the last recordings by Eddie Condon. In the mid Seventies, his Soprano Summit quintet (co-led with Bob Wilber) became popular. He has since

concentrated on clarinet. (Kenny Davern: *Stretchin' Out Jazzology*).

ANTHONY DAVIS

Anthony Davis played piano for a time with Anthony Braxton, and it's possible that they shared a reaction against the immediate past, which put all the emphasis upon spontaneity. Both are conspicuous composers: Davis, for instance, has written an opera, *Malcolm X*, and a violin concerto, and this kind of discipline extends to most of what he does. Born in New Jersey in 1951, he has collaborated with all the like-minded musicians of his generation. His best work includes an excellent trio, with James Newton and cellist Abdul Wadud, and various pieces by the larger group Epi-steme. (Anthony Davis: *Hemispheres* Granavision).

EDDIE 'LOCKJAW' DAVIS

A tough and assertive tenor saxophonist specializing in jerky, staccato phrases, Lockjaw Davis could not be pigeonholed. Born in New York in 1922, he first impressed the jazz world at large during several spells with Count Basie, notably the 'Atomic' band, which featured some trenchant recorded solos. Often rasping at the head of organ trios, he had a rewarding partnership with Johnny Griffin, in the classic tradition of a fast and light tenor pitted against a big 'heavy'. As with Illinois Jacquet, Davis was a swing-era stylist often best heard in more modern contexts. He died in 1986. (Eddie Lockjaw Davis: *Save Your Love For Me* RCA Bluebird).

RICHARD DAVIS

Some exceptionally gifted jazz musicians don't have the highest public profile. Richard Davis has deservedly won polls as a bassist, but in recent years session and orchestral work and teaching commitments have dominated – as he once said, the steady jazz gigs are with bands that gigged with local musicians but even then chose popular pianists (Don Shirley) or a singer like Sarah Vaughan for regular work. He is still best recordings and for many years anchored the Thad Jones-Mel Lewis band. Still among the best all-rounders on his instrument. (Eric Dolphy: *Out To Lunch* Blue Note). Born in Chicago in 1930, he associated with some of Eric Dolphy's

WILD BILL DAVISON

William Davison, born in Ohio in 1906, played the trumpet with a panache that fitted his nickname, ever prepared to throw in growls or shakes to add expressiveness. As a colleague of Eddie Condon since Chicago, on and off, he was a fixture in Condon's for many years after the war, and tended to be typecast as a Dixieland front man, though he was rather more versatile and in fact recorded successfully with strings. Very popular with jazz crowds everywhere, he toured regularly almost up to his death in 1989. (Eddie Condon: *Ringside At Condon's* Savoy).

BUDDY DEFRANCO

Born in New Jersey in 1923, Boniface 'Buddy' DeFranco arrived at the tail end of the clarinet age: he played the alto saxophone in big bands during the Forties, ending up as Tommy Dorsey's featured clarinet soloist. His fulsome technique led to his acceptance as the first bebop clarinettist, notably when he led a quartet including Art Blakey and Kenny Drew. When his instrument became unfashionable, other than in a Dixieland context, he spent several years fronting a re-created Glenn Miller orchestra. Recently, he has often appeared in partnership with Terry Gibbs. (Buddy DeFranco: *Chip Off The Old Bop* Concord).

JACK DEJOHNETTE

Though his reputation has been made on drums, Jack DeJohnette also trained as a pianist in Chicago, where he was born in 1942. After freelancing around New York, he was part of the popular Charles Lloyd quartet,

and later replaced Tony Williams in Miles Davis's band (where he was soon joined by Lloyd's former pianist Keith Jarrett), when Davis was moving towards rock rhythms. Since then DeJohnette, among the most gifted and versatile of all drummers, has shone in many contexts, notably as part of Jarrett's 'standards' trio and at the head of his own Special Edition. (Jack DeJohnette: *Earth Walk* Blue Note).

BARBARA DENNERLEIN

The all-action attack of Barbara Dennerlein, born in Munich in 1964, has taken the Hammond organ out of the laid-back bluesy corner where it is so often found. Having customized her instrument with the latest technology, she produces a pingy bass sound as her feet skim across the pedals, so that she occasionally lets the pedals carry the tune. Stylistically varied and often breathtaking to watch, her busy style makes her less effective at interweaving the organ with guitar in the traditional manner, so it's best to hear her either unaccompanied or with strong horn players for company. (Barbara Dennerlein: *That's Me* Enja).

WILBUR DE PARIS

Born in Indiana in 1900, Wilbur de Paris played in big-band trombone sections during the Thirties, including those of Benny Carter, Luis Russell and The Blue Rhythm Band. After the war, he collaborated with his younger brother, trumpeter Sydney de Paris, and formed his New Orleans band that, taking advantage of the revival but performing unusual material and in no sense out to please purists, foreshadowed the more catholic

revivalist bands of the future. The band gained a big following during a long residency at Jimmy Ryan's in New York, and the attention continued when de Paris moved on to other clubs. He died in 1973. (Wilbur de Paris: *At Symphony Hall* Atlantic).

PAUL DESMOND

For many years, Paul Desmond was the alto saxophonist whose piping tones and ultra-casual phrasing introduced the tunes played by Dave Brubeck's quartet. Desmond never built a strong career identity away from Brubeck, probably because he wasn't very concerned to do so. Born in San Francisco in 1924, he was part of Brubeck's octet in the late Forties and after a brief hiatus he rejoined, remaining for 16 years, almost until his death in 1977. The ultimate cool musician, his style and phrasing bore

Among younger organists, Barbara Dennerlein has done most to push the Hammond in new directions.

VIC DICKENSON

some resemblance to early Stan Getz, though he was more devious and enjoyed milking the high notes, rather like Pee Wee Russell. (Paul Desmond: *East Of The Sun*, Discovery).

Vic Dickenson was a beneficiary of the broader perspective taken by record companies when they gave swing-era survivors the chance to be heard. Born in Ohio in 1906, he worked in the bands of Bennie Moten and Claude Hopkins, then, in 1940, replaced Benny Morton with Count Basie. After the war, he gravitated to Dixieland gigs around New York, and a series of albums with Buck Clayton, Ruby Braff and others kept him in demand until his death in 1984. A splendid improvizer, whose unhurried phrasing and amiably gruff tone reflected his personality, his sense of trombone humour was drier than anyone's. (Vic Dickenson: *Showcase*, Vanguard (2 CDs)).

BABY DODDS

The younger brother of Johnny Dodds, and a fellow-member of King Oliver's band in Chicago, Warren 'Baby' Dodds can claim to be the 'father of jazz drumming as we know it. Born in 1898, he added to his inherently-relaxed New Orleans beat an interest in exploiting every part of the drum kit. After several years working with his brother, he was caught up in the New Orleans revival and took part in sessions with Bunk Johnson and others, also recording some fascinating drum solos that have an almost African tinge. He died in 1959. (Bunk Johnson: *1944*, American Music).

JOHNNY DODDS

The most gifted of the New Orleans clarinettists in the forceful blues-

based tradition (as opposed to the more supple and melodic Creoles), Johnny Dodds (1892-1940) recorded prolifically in Chicago in the Twenties. He was a member of the classic King Oliver Creole Jazz Band along with his brother Baby Dodds, and appeared on all the famous records. Apart from the Louis Armstrong Hot Fives and Hot Sevens, he also recorded with Jelly Roll Morton at his peak and with bands he led himself. Dodds continued to work throughout the Thirties, but did not record again until shortly before his death in 1940. (Johnny Dodds: *Johnny Dodds 1926-28* JSP).

ERIC DOLPHY

Outstanding on all his instruments, Eric Dolphy is shown here playing bass clarinet.

Eric Dolphy, born in Los Angeles in 1928, was a giant of the Sixties, the first musician to affect the course of jazz on three instruments. Then the most progressive flautist yet known, he virtually introduced the bass clarinet to the mainstream. On alto saxophone, his bounding runs, zig-zagging across gaping intervals, have influenced musicians as different as Anthony Braxton and Michael Hashim. Recordings under his name ranged from free jazz to more conservative material. Some of his best solos were as a member of a Charles Mingus ensemble, and he had a short-lived but rewarding partnership with trumpeter Booker Little. He died while touring Europe in 1964. (Eric Dolphy: *Far Cry* Prestige).

LOU DONALDSON

Born in North Carolina in 1926, alto saxophonist Lou Donaldson has demonstrated unswerving dedication to the preservation of Charlie Parker's music and methods. After some

classic work for Blue Note in the early Fifties, he then took these complexities into broader popular culture. Importantly, he attempted not to dilute, but to emphasize the soundness of these structures, by setting them against Hammond organs, boogaloo rhythms, and indeed anything against which he found himself juxtaposed. Sometimes this worked, sometimes the backings rendered the exercise tedious, but, equally, there can be no questioning Donaldson's commitment to the idea. (Lou Donaldson: *Quartet/Quintet/Sextet* Blue Note).

KENNY DORHAM

Kenny Dorham (1924-1972) remains undervalued as a bop trumpeter, sandwiched between Gillespie and Davis. He worked in Eckstine's and Gillespie's big bands and, later, with Charlie Parker (1948-49), the Jazz Messengers (1954) and Max Roach (1956-58). His smooth tone and ability to sustain ideas and consistency throughout elegant and lengthy solos demanded close attention from the listener. Briefly, in 1955, he led his own group, the Jazz Prophets. In the 1960s, he formed an association with Joe Henderson that developed a more robust approach. Responsible for many fine compositions that should be played more often, he occasionally sang too. (Kenny Dorham: *Round Midnight At The Cafe Bohemia* Blue Note).

TOMMY DORSEY

Known as 'The Sentimental Gentleman Of Swing', due to his smooth-toned trombone playing, Dorsey (1905-1956) was also a hard-headed businessman and bandleader. Forming his band after splitting up with his brother Jimmy, he became one of the most successful leaders of the next decade. Though the band's output often reflected commercial considerations, it did at least include the early work of Frank Sinatra. Nevertheless, the presence of soloists like Bunny Berigan and, later, Charlie Shavers and Buddy DeFranco, plus the arrangements of Eddie Sauter and Sy Oliver, guaranteed a leavening of some of the finest swing-band music. (Tommy Dorsey: *Yes Indeed* Bluebird).

KENNY DREW

Born in New York in 1928, Kenny Drew took some years to fulfil his promise on piano. Like Charlie Parker, he had to travel for gigs, spending time in California where jazz was an underground activity. In the Sixties, he moved to Europe, soon settling in Copenhagen (where he died in 1993).

HARRY EDISON

A survivor of the Count Basie band, Harry 'Sweets' Edison joined in 1938, after Basie came to New York. Born in Ohio in 1915, Edison had passed through various bands before joining Basie, where his trumpet solos contrasted so well with Buck Clayton's – a cool, classic stylist whereas Edison, equally relaxed, spread the notes around. Afterwards, he found a home in the studios, notably as accompanist to Frank Sinatra on several famous records that would not be the same without his elliptical phrases, often muted, behind the vocals. Still in demand, he struck up a useful (and contrasting) partnership with Eddie Lockjaw Davis before the latter's death. (Harry Edison & Eddie Davis: *Jawbreakers* Riverside.).

that set him apart from the many stylists then springing up. His son, Kenny Jr. is an equally outstanding pianist. (Kenny Drew: *Recollections* Timeless.).

PAQUITO D'RIVERA

The group Irakere, formed by Arturo Sandoval, Chucho Valdes and Paquito D'Rivera in 1967, helped to put Cuba on the jazz map in its own right, rather than just as an important influence on the US-based Latin American music. D'Rivera, born in 1948 and a virtuoso reeds player from an early age, defected to the States in 1980, subsequently working both under his own name and with McCoy Tyner and Dizzy Gillespie. He performs with typical Cuban bravura on all his instruments, though he can coax a reedy tone from the clarinet during the occasional laidback passage. (Paquito D'Rivera: *Tico Tico* Chesky).

Among the stars to emerge from Cuba: reeds virtuoso Paquito D'Rivera.

BILLY ECKSTINE

Vocalist and occasional trumpeter, Billy Eckstine was born in Pittsburgh in 1914. Engaged as a singer with Earl Hines in 1939, he formed in 1944 what became known as the first bebop band: essentially swing-orientated, it included Parker and Gillespie, plus Art Blakey, Miles Davis and other future stars. When this venture ended in 1947, Eckstine concentrated on singing, and became a notable figure in popular music up to his death in 1993. Although his rich baritone voice was sometimes employed on routine material, his harmonic grasp and sense of time, derived from his earlier enthusiasm for experiment, made for highly personal and enjoyable performances. (Billy Eckstine: *No Cover, No Minimum* Roulette).

Pittsburgh (1911), he worked with several big bands and briefly led one himself. In his later years, he often teamed up with Coleman Hawkins. The best solos – highly mobile, full of passion and beautifully crafted – come from either side of 1940, and from the early Fifties. He died in 1989. (Roy Eldridge: *Heckler's Hop* Hep).

DON ELLIS

Academically trained, Don Ellis (1934-1978) was a tireless experimentalist, seeking to use serial techniques within jazz structures. In the mid-1960s, in Los Angeles, he formed an orchestra, which he used to develop his fascination with odd time signatures and with Indian and European classical music. Ellis designed a four-valve trumpet to allow him to play quarter-tones, though his style seemed to derive as much from Harry James and Maynard Ferguson as from anyone else. His orchestra achieved critical success, but pointed in a direction which, subsequently, few others have wanted to follow. Yet all his work has interest, and the breadth of his aspirations should be appreciated. (Don Ellis: *New Ideas New Jazz*).

PETER ERSKINE

Musicians tend to get labelled. Peter Erskine, born in New Jersey in 1954, played with Weather Report for four years – the first to use a drum machine on one of their records – and then joined Steps Ahead. His drumming with both exemplified the power-rock style admirably, but since then he has moved in more varied directions which often involve acoustic jazz. Apart from his own groups, for which he produces excellent material, he is also part of important bands of various sizes involving Kenny Wheeler, Miroslav Vitous and others. (Peter Erskine: *Sweet Soul Novus*).

The volatile Roy Eldridge, a trumpet influence in the Thirties.

TEDDY EDWARDS

Teddy Edwards, born in Mississippi in 1924, moved to Los Angeles in the Forties, at the time Charlie Parker was there, and played tenor saxophone with Howard McGhee. He also recorded one of the first two-tenor duels,

alongside Dexter Gordon, and later preceded Harold Land in the Roach-Brown quintet. Increasingly admired locally, he has worked steadily since then, appearing on several records as a sideman and under his own name. Often bracketed with Gordon and Wardell Gray, and now recognized as being on their level, he has more of a soulful tenor sound. (Teddy Edwards And Howard McGhee: *Together Again* Contemporary).

ROY ELDRIDGE

Nicknamed 'Little Jazz', Roy Eldridge expressed in his playing the aggressive attitude one often finds in men short in stature. A natural romantic, he could overreach himself, but on form he was as good as anyone, as well as being the most influential trumpeter in the era between Armstrong and Gillespie, upon whom he was the major influence. Born in

ROBIN EUBANKS

Robin plays trombone, essentially in a post-J.J. Johnson style but capable of fitting into any context, as befits someone whose career takes in Stevie Wonder, M-Base and the Jazz Messengers. More recently, he has worked with the bands of McCoy Tyner and Don Grolnick, and he often links up with Steve Turre in groups of two or more trombones. (Robin Eubanks: *Different Perspectives* JMT).

Part of a very talented musical family from Philadelphia (born 1955), Robin Eubanks came to prominence after his younger brother Kevin, a brilliant guitarist who is still looking for a role.

BILL EVANS

In a famous comparison, pianist Lalo Schifrin likened Oscar Peterson to Liszt, Bill Evans to Chopin. A reflective and delicate mood, imposed via a classical touch and oblique sense of rhythm, in place of headlong attack, was Evans's most distinctive contribution, something which completely changed the course of jazz piano.

Born in Illinois (1929), he was part of Miles Davis's *Kind Of Blue* sextet and then concentrated on his own trio. The most celebrated version included Scott La Faro and Paul Motian, and set new standards for group interplay, as opposed to the traditional piano-plus-rhythm, which still apply fifteen years after Evans's death. The tunes he wrote are increasingly played. (Bill Evans: *Portrait In Jazz* Riverside).

Bill Evans added a fresh lyrical sensibility to the art of playing jazz at the piano.

IRVING FAZOLA

Born in New Orleans in 1912, Irving Fazola (real name Prestopnik) worked as a clarinet player in many bands before finding his most congenial musical home with Bob Crosby. Undervalued today because he was no leader, he had a mellifluous sound and made the instrument seem very simple to play. His temperament lost him many jobs, though at the end he did work steadily back in New Orleans, until his death in 1949. (*Bob Crosby And His Bobcats Vol. 1* Swaggie).

MAYNARD FERGUSON

Canada's gift to trumpet pyrotechnics, and proficient also on a number of other brass instruments, Ferguson was born in 1928. After brief periods with Boyd Raeburn and Charlie Barnet, he played with Stan Kenton from 1951 to 1953. Here, his exceptional high-register playing was fully exploited, during Kenton's most ambitious period, notably in the eponymous solo feature written for him by Shorty Rogers. Ferguson later formed his own big band, with arrangers such as Don Sebesky and Slide Hampton, and young musicians like Willie Maiden, Joe Farrell and Jaki Byard. It produced music which at its best invites comparisons with the Thad Jones-Mel Lewis Orchestra. (*Maynard Ferguson: Message From Newport* Roulette).

ELLA FITZGERALD

Brought up in Yonkers, a suburb of New York, Ella Fitzgerald (born 1917) joined the Chick Webb band at 16 and soon became its major attraction, especially after her first hit 'A-Tisket, A-Tasket'. At this stage, her voice had not attained the astonishing creamy richness of her maturity, but she

GIL EVANS

A Canadian, born in 1912, Gil Evans was an obscure bandleader in the Thirties, before joining Claude Thornhill as an arranger and becoming one of the great orchestrators of our time. In place of scoring for sections, he developed an impressionistic approach similar to Ellington's, but totally different in its effect, built around deep brass sounds which included french horn and tuba. His most celebrated writing was for Miles Davis, from the *Birth Of The Cool* band to *Miles Ahead* and other orchestral masterpieces of the late-Fifties, and, later, for his own bands. He died in 1988. (*Gil Evans: Out Of The Cool* Impulse).

TAL FARLOW

Tal Farlow's career has not followed the usual pattern because, for several years, he earned his living as a sign-writer and rarely played in public. Born in North Carolina in 1921, he made his mark in Red Norvo's popular vibes-guitar-bass trio and, before and after retirement, he tends to form similar ones of his own. Giving up around 1960, he returned in the following decade to regular part-time playing and touring. A technically superb guitarist whose rapid-fire picking influenced some rock guitarists, Farlow's sheer uniqueness compensates for times when too many notes get in the way. (*Tal Farlow: Second Set* Xanadu).

ART FARMER

Art Farmer came up with one of the most personal trumpet styles of the Fifties, imparting a clouded, slightly wistful aura which owes something to the work of Miles Davis, while sounding quite unlike him. Born in Iowa (1928), he played in the Lionel Hampton band alongside Clifford Brown and later worked with both Horace Silver and Gerry Mulligan before forming the Jazztet with tenor saxophonist Benny Golson. A switch to the softer flugelhorn took some bite away, but he has been at his best since discovering a hybrid called the flumpet. Farmer settled in Vienna in 1968, but he continues to tour widely. (*Art Farmer: Portrait Of Art Farmer* Contemporary).

Gil Evans arranged for Miles Davis and then led his own band.

Ella Fitzgerald recorded the best songs by American tunesmiths.

TOMMY FLANAGAN

Tommy Flanagan was born in 1930, one of several distinguished pianists from Detroit, all of whom blended bop lines with the poise and beautiful touch of someone like Teddy Wilson. In the Fifties, these virtues made Flanagan one of the most heavily recorded piano players in New York. He spent most of the next decade or so unobtrusively accompanying singers Tony Bennett and, especially, Ella Fitzgerald, but then made the brave decision to try his luck on his own. Since then, he has produced an excellent series of duo and trio recordings. (Tommy Flanagan: *Eclypso* Enja).

FRANK FOSTER

Born in Ohio in 1928, Frank Foster joined Count Basie's band in 1953, and stayed for ten years. Apart from his tenor saxophone solos, he wrote the evergreen 'Shiny Stockings' and other pieces for the band, and developed the skills that enabled him to work as a freelance arranger. During the next decade, his only regular touring job was as one of the two tenors in Elvin Jones's quartet, while he became an occasional member of the Thad Jones-Mel Lewis band. Initially underrated, his hard-swinging style, influenced by Sonny Stitt, has matured over the years. Recently, he has been the leader of

already displayed a sense of time and swing. The material from her later career changed gradually from swingers to show tunes, notably the series of songs by Gershwin, Porter and others that are probably her masterpieces. Until illness intervened, she toured regularly and was a favourite with audiences throughout the world. (Ella Fitzgerald: *The Original American Recordings* MCA (2 CDs)).

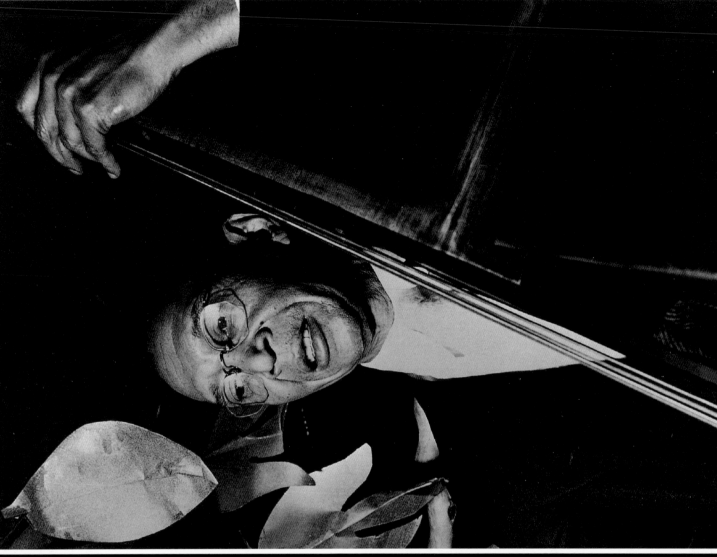

the surviving Basie band. (Frank Foster: *Shiny Stockings* Denon).

POPS FOSTER

One of the first and greatest New Orleans bassists, George 'Pops' Foster, born in Louisiana in 1892, worked with all the famous names and was a regular on the riverboats. Moving to New York, he was part of the superb Luis Russell rhythm section and stayed during the time the band was taken over by Louis Armstrong. After the war, he was a beneficiary of the New Orleans revival and never looked back, working with Sidney Bechet and, later, with Earl Hines. His playing was all about providing a swinging, springy beat, and none did it better. (Louis Armstrong: *Volume 2 1932-40* Classics).

BUD FREEMAN

Born in Chicago in 1906, Bud Freeman soon hit upon a way of playing tenor saxophone that, at least tonally, resembled what Lester Young did later – probably due to the impact of Frank Trumbauer. He was drawn into the Eddie Condon circle, and with Condon first recorded the number – 'The Eel', a slippery piece of saxophone wizardry – that became his speciality. Apart from stints with Tommy Dorsey and Benny Goodman, he worked mainly with small groups up to his death in 1991, including The World's Greatest Jazz Band. One of jazz's most urbane figures (speaking with almost an upper-class British accent), the style was the man. (Bud Freeman: *Something To Remember You By* Black Lion).

CHICO FREEMAN

Earl 'Chico' Freeman is the son of Von Freeman, a tenor saxophone legend in Chicago, where Chico was born in 1949. Growing up in the progressive Sixties, he studied with Muhal Richard Abrams, joined the AACM, acquired a music degree, and later played with Sam Rivers and Sun Ra. Beginning, perhaps, with a stint as Elvin Jones's featured saxophonist, he has edged closer to the mainstream in touring bands like The Leaders, while simultaneously running a group called Brainstorm, that uses amplification in increasingly creative ways. (Chico Freeman: *Destiny's Dance* Contemporary).

BILL FRISELL

The atmospherics produced by Bill Frisell have put him among the most revered of post-McLaughlin guitarists, an instance of space replacing pace (his early influence was Jim Hall). Though born in Baltimore, Frisell grew up in Colorado and there is a delightful open-country feel to his music. Fitting into the Mike Gibbs band and the Liberation Music Orchestra, his most regular context apart from his own small groups has been the trio run by Paul Motian. Although his style revolves around the evocative deployment of sound, he prefers older equipment that provides instant control through knobs rather than buttons. (Bill Frisell: *This Land* Elektra Musician).

SLIM GAILLARD

Bulee 'Slim' Gaillard does rather defy classification. Born in Cuba in 1911, he began as an all-round vaudeville artist and then teamed with bassist Slam Stewart in a remarkable and widely popular duo, where Slim played guitar but, more importantly sang his 'vout' routines on such imperishables as 'Cement Mixer', 'Matzoh Balls' and the famous 'Flat Foot Floogie'. That was a very hard act to follow, but he enjoyed a very successful final decade as an international celebrity on the jazz circuit. He died in 1991. (Slim Gaillard: *Laughin' In Rhythm*

Happiness is a thing called vout. The inimitable Slim Gaillard.

JAN GARBAREK

One could argue that Norwegian Jan Garbarek is, especially in Europe, the most popular jazz saxophonist of them all. Born in 1947, he was inspired originally by John Coltrane and often worked with George Russell during Russell's stay in Norway. From a style and group concept akin to Coltrane's, he developed something far more original and personal: an exquisite craftsman, his tone became infinitely pliable in the cool, clean idiom he favours. His strongest improvizing in a jazz context is found with the likes of Keith Jarrett or Miroslav Vitous. By contrast, he participated in the ultimate cross-over success by joining the Hilliard singers in a best-selling recording of plainsong. (Jan Garbarek: *Places* ECM).

The trio of Slava Ganelin caused a stir in the Eighties.

VYACHESLAV GANELIN

The Ganelin Trio, from the former Soviet Union, caused a deserved sensation in the Eighties, mostly through recordings smuggled out and issued on the Leo label. These, and their later live appearances, confirmed Vyacheslav Ganelin (born 1944) as a leading strategist of improvized music, imposing an identity upon the group that derived from a very diverse and flexible approach to structured material – as John Lewis had done with the MJQ. To push the analogy, the contrast between Ganelin's calm at the piano and saxophonist Vladimir Chekasin's agitated lines reminded one of Lewis and Milt Jackson. Ganelin has since continued his career in Israel. (Ganelin Trio: *Catalogue:Live In East Germany* Leo).

RED GARLAND

A pianist who was once in the right place at the right time, William 'Red' Garland (born Dallas, 1923) joined Miles Davis at the start of the group with John Coltrane and Philly Joe Jones. Davis based the style of that group on his liking for Ahmad Jamal's trio, which involved a 2/4 bounce at medium tempo and lots of pianistic block chords. This may have been why Garland adopted the latter, as his single-note phrases, especially on his own albums and at speed, were more boppish than Jamal's. He led a trio for a while, but then his career stuttered up to his death in 1984. (Red Garland: *Red In Blues-ville* Prestige).

ERROLL GARNER

Erroll Garner was one of the most idiosyncratic pianists in jazz history. Born in Pittsburgh (1921) and a self-taught performer who never learned to read a note of music, Garner came up with a two-handed-orchestral style, built around regular chording in his left hand while his right sometimes lagged deliciously behind the beat. His habit when performing live of giving wild, iconoclastic introductions, which bore little relation to the tune, has crept back into jazz via Sonny Rollins. From the Fifties until his death in 1977, he rarely worked with a group other than his trio and became an exceptionally popular concert artist. (Erroll Garner: *Concert By The Sea* Columbia).

Erroll Garner launched many an extravagant introduction.

KENNY GARRETT

An alto saxophonist with abundant flair and technique, he starred in the band Out Of The Blue before joining Blakey, but, since his time with Davis he has performed in more fusion-type contexts under his own name. (Kenny Garrett: *Black Hope* Warner).

Born in Detroit in 1960, Kenny Garrett attended two enviable finishing schools: Art Blakey's Jazz Messengers and then Miles Davis's group, where he took a handful of telling solos on Davis's later records.

HERB GELLER

After a stint of playing with big bands, Herb Geller (born 1928) became a busy session musician around his native Los Angeles. A hard-swinging boppish style combined with a sweetish sound made him the hottest of the allegedly cool altoists on the Coast – not surprisingly, they named one of his albums *Fire In The West*. Since the early Sixties he has been based in Europe, working in big bands and radio bands, making the occasional tour and, though his sound has changed, playing with the same fire. (Herb Geller: *That Geller Feller* Fresh Sound).

MIKE GIBBS

From the beginning, Mike Gibbs has been a genuinely distinctive composer/arranger on the jazz scene (plus films and much else). Born in Zimbabwe in 1937, he studied at Berklee and had his tunes played by fellow-student Gary Burton and (through Burton) Stan Getz. Since then, he has lived in the U.K., with some spells in the U.S., and every so often composed for a big band. He uses rock rhythms to power all but his most liturgical themes and constructs a swirl of sound out of separate tonal layers for an emotional impact recognizably his own – where Gil Evans aimed at a mellow, contemplative effect, Gibbs is more ecstatic. (Mike Gibbs: *The Only Chrome Waterfall Orchestra* Ah Um).

GIORGIO GASLINI

Pianist, composer and bandleader, Giorgio Gaslini's talents extend across the musical spectrum, from conducting symphony orchestras to supplying popular movie music; from operatic composition to brilliant solo piano dissections of the compositions of Thelonious Monk. Gaslini, born in Milan in 1929, was a child prodigy, and he gave his first recital at 13. His recent interpretations of Schumann for jazz piano trio and of Albert Ayler themes for solo piano confirm him as a highly creative mature artist whose talents, whilst acknowledged in Italy, deserve wider recognition on the world stage. (Giorgio Gaslini: *Plays Monk* Soul Note).

TERRY GIBBS

Born in New York in 1924, Terry Gibbs's career began on 52nd Street. When Chubby Jackson recruited him in 1947 for a tour of Sweden, with a group committed to spreading the gospel of bebop, it became clear that Gibbs was a vibes player of some substance, with the energy of Lionel Hampton but with a style which had already absorbed modern idioms. After a notable period with Woody Herman's 'Four Brothers' band (1948-49), he began to find studio work, also organizing excellent part-time big bands as well as small groups, frequently in partnership with Buddy DeFranco. (Terry Gibbs: *The Big Cat* Contemporary).

JIMMY GIUFFRE

Reeds player Jimmy Giuffre, born in Dallas (1921) wrote 'Four Brothers' for Woody Herman, then made his mark with a succession of trios. After testing what he called 'jazz with a non-pulsating beat', he has generally worked without a drummer and is linked above all to playing clarinet in two groups. With Jim Hall on guitar, his trio scored a big hit with 'The Train And The River' (as featured in the film *Jazz On A Summer's Day*). Less folksy and more into freedom, his next trio, featuring Paul Bley and Steve Swallow, was critically admired but ahead of public taste. They recently came together again for a record and a tour. (Jimmy Giuffre/Paul Bley/Steve Swallow *1961* ECM (2 CDs)).

BENNY GOLSON

From Philadelphia, born in 1929, Benny Golson studied music as a child, and later at Howard University. However, it was in the R&B band of Bull Moose Jackson that he met Tadd Dameron, who had great impact on his composing; Dameron's sense of melody can be discerned in such Golson compositions as 'I Remember Clifford' and 'Stablemates'. As a tenor player, he brought a fascinating if sometimes unfocused reworking of Ben Webster's style into a hard-bop

DEXTER GORDON

Born in 1923 in Los Angeles, Dexter Gordon was regarded as the first tenor saxophonist to adapt Lester

milieu in the later 1950s. Following years in the studios, he returned to jazz in 1980, proving that his tenor style had matured considerably in the interim. (Benny Golson: *Groovin' With Golson* New Jazz).

EDDIE GOMEZ

Originally from Puerto Rico (born 1944), Eddie Gomez grew up in New York and played bass both with Marian McPartland and on some early free-jazz albums. He then had a long stint in Bill Evans's trio, in which his skittish solos, with their tight, popping sound, followed the tradition laid down by Scott La Faro. Since then, he has been mainly a session and recording artist, though he did work with Steps Ahead and has continued to put together excellent groups more or less in the fusion mould, while sticking to the acoustic bass. (Eddie Gomez *Next Future* Stretch).

PAUL GONSALVES

A fixture in Ellington's saxophone section from 1950 until his death in 1974, Paul Gonsalves, born in Boston in 1920, was one of those excellent musicians who are admired rather than fashionable. He had previously worked with Count Basie and Dizzy Gillespie, but Ellington brought him on, writing pieces to feature him and, on a notable occasion, letting him loose for umpteen choruses at the Newport Jazz Festival, where he stopped the show. His sound came essentially from the Hawkins-Byas school, though it was the way he swept through unusual intervals at speed that attracted followers, including Tony Coe and David Murray. (Paul Gonsalves: *Gettin' Together* Jazzland).

Young's style to bop. His influence could be seen in the playing of Stan Getz and, especially, John Coltrane, but because he was off the scene for much of the Fifties, it took a while for people to notice. A very tall man with physique to match, he produced a hard, strong tone which had none of the furry edges linked to the Hawkins school. Shortly before his death in 1990, he took the role of the musical protagonist in the film *Round Midnight*. His finest recordings date from the Sixties. (Dexter Gordon: *Go!* Blue Note).

Late in life, the charismatic Dexter Gordon made a hit as a film star.

STEPHANE GRAPPELLI

Grappelli is not only one of the first European jazz musicians, he has also proved one of the most enduring. Born in 1908, he first came to fame as Django Reinhardt's violin-playing partner in the Quintet of the Hot Club of France. His is a very Gallic type of jazz, quite unbluesy, but full of zest

and melodic sparkle. He also pos-sessed the musical sophistication to integrate the harmonic developments that came after bop, which renewed his style to the extent that, rare for jazz, his best work probably came after his sixtieth birthday, along with deserved international acclaim. (Stephane Grappelli: *Live In London* Black Lion).

MILFORD GRAVES

A remarkably self-contained artist, drummer Milford Graves came to prominence in the Sixties and has continued to promote the concepts of African and non-European music. Born in New York in 1941, he appeared on many free-jazz recorded classics, including duets with both Don Pullen and fellow-drummer Sunny Murray. A considerable technician, he has increasingly performed in percus-sion groups or given solo recitals, though he has recorded with David Murray, a collaboration which was the subject of a fascinating film documen-tary built around their contrasting attitudes. (Milford Graves: *Percussion Ensemble* ESP).

GLEN GRAY

The Casa Loma Orchestra was one of the best white bands of the Thirties. In swing terms, it was also the earliest, preceding Goodman's, and the others that later rode the swing bandwagon. The leader was Glen Gray (born Illinois, 1906), a saxophonist who, like several others in the band, had worked previously for Jean Goldkette. Few of the names mean much today, but the band featured excellent swing arrangements by guitarist Gene Gifford, and managed to get the high-profile gigs available to white bands (e.g. radio programmes) without diluting the jazz. Gray, who stayed in charge until the Forties, died in 1963. (*Casa Loma Orchestra 1930-34* Jazz Archives).

WARDELL GRAY

Stylistically, one could call Wardell Gray a transitional figure, a tenor saxophonist clearly influenced by Lester Young while gravitating towards bebop. He managed the rare feat of being totally convincing no matter which style held the upper hand, and, for the same reason as Zoot Sims, was greatly admired for those unflappable qualities that always deliver the goods. Born in Oklahoma, he worked with Count Basie and Tadd Dameron and, as the faster man with the lighter sound, had ongoing tenor jousts with Dexter Gordon. Eventually based on the West Coast, he was only thirty-four when he died, while working in Las Vegas in 1955. (Wardell Gray: *Easy Swing* Swingtime).

BENNIE GREEN

A trombonist of the bebop generation with a swing-era style, Bennie Green (born Chicago, 1923) straddled both idioms from the time he was part of the transitional Earl Hines band. He later worked with Charlie Ventura's populist 'Bop For The People' sextet and was a part of the four-trombone outfit that led eventually to Jay & Kai. Much admired for his smooth phrasing and easy swing, he tended to lead groups that veered towards R&B. After a brief stint with Duke Ellington, he worked out of the lime-light in Las Vegas until his death in 1977. (Dennis, Green, Johnson, Winding: *Four Trombones* Prestige).

BENNY GREEN

One of many pianists whose career has been enhanced by a spell accompanying Betty Carter, Benny Green was born in New York in 1963, but grew up in California. He spent two years with Blakey's Messengers and has since led his own trio, while also working with Ray Brown. An excellent pianist, as his track record shows, he has increasingly revived some of the chunky phrases and block chord routines first developed by the likes of Erroll Garner, Ahmad Jamal, Red Garland and Bobby Timmons. (Benny Green: *Lineage* Blue Note).

FREDDIE GREEN

Born in South Carolina in 1911, Freddie Green was a guitarist who rarely if ever took a solo. He was revered for his role alongside Count Basie, which began in 1937 and lasted until Basie's death. Along with bassist Walter Page and drummer Jo Jones, he constituted the ideal rhythm section and, as the only survivor when Basie re-formed in 1952, he kept the beat steady irre-spective of what might be happening elsewhere. He died in 1987, his sin-gular talent in demand to the end.

Lars Gullin, Swedish star of the baritone saxophone.

(Count Basie: *Verve Jazz Masters 2* Verve).

URBIE GREEN

Much appreciated by fellow-trombonists, Urbie Green provides another example of a career pursued away from the spotlight. Born in Alabama in 1926, he played in Gene Krupa's trombone section at 20, and then had spells with Woody Herman and Benny Goodman. One of the supreme technicians, following the smooth, effortless path first laid down by Teagarden, Green tried everything from fronting a big band to electric rock, but he has generally worked as a studio musician and teacher, making occasional appearances at gigs and festivals. (Buck Clayton: *Jam Sessions From The Vaults* Columbia).

SONNY GREER

New Jersey-born Sonny Greer (1895-1982) joined Duke Ellington in 1920 and remained with the band until 1951. He played with Johnny Hodges's band, and then worked around New York from 1956 until his death. A highly idiosyncratic stylist with Ellington, sitting behind a huge kit, Greer was in some ways as much a decorative percussionist as a drummer. However, this did not mean that he failed to enhance the music; indeed none of the drummers who followed him ever truly matched his imagination. Often under-recorded on Ellington's studio tracks, his work is best appreciated via the many live recordings of the band. (Duke Ellington: *The Great Chicago Concerts* Limelight).

STEVE GROSSMAN

A couple of gigs in the early Seventies have, until recently, stood out in Steve Grossman's career. Born in New York in 1951, he played soprano in an early Miles Davis fusion band, and then spent some years as front-line soloist with drummer Elvin Jones. Both the fusion link and, through Jones, suggestions of following in John Coltrane's footsteps are misleading, in that he sounds more of a gruff-toned, longer-lined version of recent times. He now generally works as a single or with his own quartet, giving the standard repertory his very personal attention. (Steve Grossman: *In New York* Dreyfus).

JOHNNY GRIFFIN

Born in Chicago in 1928, Johnny Griffin stormed into New York in 1958 ready and willing to take on all the established tenor giants. If he did not have the conceptual depth of a John Coltrane, his high-energy approach underpinned a distinctive style and infectious enthusiasm for his music. After working for a time with the Jazz Messengers and with Monk, in 1960 he formed a quintet alongside the equally extrovert tenor-player Eddie 'Lockjaw' Davis, a well-balanced partnership of contrasts. In 1963, he based himself in Europe, where he has remained energetic and active. (Johnny Griffin: *A Blowing Session* Blue Note).

MARTY GROSZ

Born in Berlin in 1930 (his father is George Grosz), Marty Grosz was a product of the jazz revival, where he took the Eddie Condon role of strumming in the rhythm section. Since then, he has benefited from another revival, in collaboration with others and, latterly, under his own name, building a considerable following for his repertory of unlikely songs, sung with a grainy drawl, and his witty, propulsive solos on acoustic guitar. He often goes for unusual line-ups that exclude drums and produce a kind of chamber jazz. (Marty Grosz: *Thanks J&M*).

GEORGE GRUNTZ

One of the top European bandleaders of recent times, George Gruntz (born 1932) comes from Switzerland and was the original pianist in Phil Woods's European Rhythm Machine. He subsequently directed the Berlin Jazz Festival for many years, while running his own projects. The most famous of these, which he now runs as his Concert Jazz Band, started as a big-band collaboration in the Seventies and often includes major American musicians. As a composer, he has similar all-round interests to the likes of Mike Westbrook and Mathias Rüegg. (George Gruntz: *The New York Sessions* Enja).

LARS GULLIN

Sweden was ahead of most European countries in welcoming and recording with Americans after the last war. As a result, they produced many impressive jazz players, of whom Lars Gullin was arguably the best. Born in 1928, he was much in demand to record with visitors, including Clifford Brown and Chet Baker, and was highly ranked by most Americans. Specializing in the baritone saxophone, his style was lighter and cooler even than Gerry Mulligan's, and he could float effortlessly between registers. Unfortunately, the effects of drug addiction made him inactive as a player for some years before his death in 1976. (*Lars Gullin Vol. 1* Dragon).

TRILOK GURTU

A notable performer in the area where jazz opens out to other musics, Trilok Gurtu was born in India in 1951 and progressed from tabla playing to all-round percussion. After starting in jazz-rock, he played on Charlie Mariano's first Indian-influenced record and had key roles in the quartet Oregon and in John McLaughlin's trio before forming his own group. A complete original in jazz, *Trilok Gurtu from India, one of the most original percussionists in world music.*

terms, incorporating a miniature drum kit along with the tabla and other percussion instruments, he nevertheless swings hard when the need arises. (Trilok Gurtu: *Bad Habits Die Hard* CMP).

BARRY GUY

Barry Guy exemplifies the modern musician who crosses musical boundaries with ease. In his case, he has built a reputation as both player and composer in modern classical music, while being an important part of the free-jazz scene. Born in London in 1947, he was part of John Stevens's Spontaneous Music Ensemble, and also often worked with pianist Howard Riley. Apart from playing bass, which he does with phenomenal dexterity, he is best known for founding the London Jazz Composer's Orchestra, among the first of its kind to codify the new music (as opposed to having twenty players freaking out). It still re-groups regularly. (London Jazz Composers Orchestra: *Portraits* Intakt (2 CDs)).

BOBBY HACKETT

Bobby Hackett's beautiful tone, long, elegantly embellished lines and polished phrasing made him a favourite of trumpet-players, from Louis Armstrong to Miles Davis. When he originally appeared on the Thirties jazz scene (he had been born in Rhode Island in 1915), he was seen as a second Beiderbecke and was usually found playing with the likes of Eddie Condon. But his tastes ran more to Louis Armstrong, and his finest records were made in the company of Jack Teagarden and Vic Dickenson. In the Fifties he also had big-selling recordings with strings, under the name of the comedian Jackie Gleason, and regularly accompanied Tony Bennett. He died in 1976. (Bobby Hackett: *Coast Concert/Jazz Ultimate* Dormouse).

CHARLIE HADEN

Born in Iowa in 1937, Charlie Haden was brought up in Missouri, surrounded by music because his parents were famous on the Country circuit.

The pensive playing of Jim Hall has influenced many guitarists

Living in Los Angeles, he gravitated towards Ornette Coleman, making the Five Spot gig and playing on most of Coleman's seminal early records. His favourite bassists were those who gave music depth, and his solos are, accordingly, measured rather than dazzling. Among his own projects, his Liberation Music Orchestra, highlighting causes from the Spanish Civil War onwards, the Colemanish Old And New Dreams, trios with Paul Motian and the semi-nostalgic Quartet West are especially outstanding. (Charlie Haden: *The Ballad Of The Fallen* ECM).

AL HAIG

Al Haig played with most of the best musicians in the first decade of bebop, notably during his stint as pianist in Charlie Parker's quintet, his part in the Miles Davis 'cool' recordings and as one of the favourite accompanists of Stan Getz, during the period when Getz's playing was at its coolest. Born in New Jersey in 1924, Haig appeared on several records in the Forties but later dropped out of the spotlight, sometimes working as a bar pianist. When the bebop pioneers were hunted

Sonorous bassist and successful leader, Charlie Haden.

down in the Seventies, he came back with all his old skill and grace, and in fact sounded better than ever. He died in 1982. (Al Haig: *Ornithology* Progressive).

EDMOND HALL

Edmond Hall was the leading New Orleans clarinettist in the Johnny Dodds tradition. Born in 1901, he played alongside trumpeters such as Buddy Petit, Chris Kelly and Lee Collins before making the move to New York. After touring with the big band of Claude Hopkins, Hall worked around New York in various contexts, becoming identified with Dixieland after the revival and joining Eddie Condon. He then took his compatriot Barney Bigard's place with Louis Armstrong. A fiery tone on top of abundant technique made Hall, who died in 1967, the nearest thing to Bechet and always compelling to hear. (Edmond Hall: *In Copenhagen* Storyville).

JIM HALL

With his limpid, melodic approach and keen sense of timing and space, Jim Hall (born in Buffalo in 1930) could claim to be among the most original guitarists to appear between Charlie Christian and the advent of rock. On the West Coast in the mid Fifties, he started out with the cool Chico Hamilton Quintet, then the Jimmy Giuffre Trio. He moved to New York, and in 1961 Sonny Rollins picked him for his first 'post-layoff' quartet. After a musically rewarding partnership with Art Farmer, Hall has usually worked in trios and duos, or by himself. (Bill Evans and Jim Hall: *Undercurrent* Blue Note).

CHICO HAMILTON

Born in Los Angeles in 1921, Foreststorm 'Chico' Hamilton combined the occasional tour with working in the studios. He was the drummer on some of the famous Gerry Mulligan quartet records, though to this day he is best remembered for the quintet he led for several years, featuring flute, cello and guitar. If the resultant music was sometimes excessively twee, it probably made life much easier for those chamber/jazz groups that followed, as well as giving early exposure to such talents as Jim Hall, Eric Dolphy and Arthur Blythe. A busy studio composer, he occasionally takes a group on tour. (Chico Hamilton: *Gongs East* Discovery).

SCOTT HAMILTON

After Ruby Braff, the tenor saxophonist Scott Hamilton was the next prominent musician from a younger generation to seek inspiration from the swing era. Born in Rhode Island in 1954, he appeared in New York in 1976, the heyday of fusion, and sounded like a cross between Ben Webster and Zoot Sims. He has matured since then, developing into a distinctive and accomplished performer within the same basic style. Very popular in the U.K., where he often tours either as a single or, occasionally, linked up with such like-minded tourists as Warren Vache. (Scott Hamilton: *Live At Brecon Jazz Festival* Concord).

LIONEL HAMPTON

Lionel Hampton, then a drummer and pianist, introduced a brand new instrument to jazz around 1930 when he discovered the vibraphone, the electric variant of the xylophone. Born in Louisville in 1908, he became a member of the Benny Goodman Quartet in the Thirties, and a prolific recording artist under his own name. In 1940, Hampton launched a big band of his own, which he has run, on and off, until the present day. As one of the original extrovert performers, possessed of enormous stamina and always ready to march his musicians round the auditorium, Hampton was ahead of his time, though, when not swinging infectiously away, he is capable of rhapsodic ballad interpretation. (Lionel Hampton: *Stardust* MCA).

HERBIE HANCOCK

Herbie Hancock's transformation from studious sideman to near-megastar was a highlight of the Seventies. Born in Chicago in 1940, he came to prominence in Miles Davis's quintet, as part of the renowned rhythm section, and stayed for five years. He then formed a sextet which developed, quite ingeniously, the more contemplative elements of Davis's electric recordings, in which he had participated, but it did not draw the crowds. His next group, the Headhunters, adapted the funk formula developed by Sly Stone and even had a hit single. Since then, Hancock has switched between electric rock projects and those featuring his lyrical and highly influential

Herbie Hancock. From lyrical pianist with Miles Davis to jazz-funk superstar.

piano style. (Herbie Hancock: *Maiden Voyage* Blue Note).

CRAIG HANDY

You have to be different to win a Charlie Parker scholarship to university and end up studying psychology, but Craig Handy came from a musical background and could already play several instruments before concentrating on the tenor saxophone. Born in California in 1962, he has worked with many big names, including drummers Art Blakey, Elvin Jones and, most recently, Roy Haynes, with whom he has made some excellent records. Whatever the context, he seems to have plenty in reserve. Often underpinned by humour, his ideas unravel logically, so the whole solo makes sense, while his tone is warm and nicely rounded. (Craig Handy: *Three For All + One* Arabesque).

W.C. HANDY

In no sense a jazz musician, William Christopher Handy codified some of the material that led to the form of jazz as we know it. Born in Alabama in 1873, he soon realized that minstrelsy offered a rare chance for a black musician to make good money. He eventually led a touring minstrel band and later set up his own orchestra. Known as the Father Of The Blues, he wrote down musical snatches heard on his travels from various sources and turned them into compositions. The results, often in several strains that included a twelve-bar blues (as in his St. Louis Blues) were among the first tunes to which jazz musicians gave the full treatment. (WC Handy: *Father Of The Blues* DRG).

W. C. Handy was famous for his compositions built around blues themes.

ROY HARGROVE

Still in his twenties, Roy Hargrove was one of those pushed to the front during the Eighties. Unlike some who can be said to look back to bebop, he really does seem an instinctive classicist. On ballads and blues, especially, he just lays back and lets the phrases roll off his warm-toned trumpet, sounding like neither Miles Davis nor Clifford Brown. Born in Dallas in 1969, he was encouraged by Wynton Marsalis and soon got his own recording contract. While he undoubtedly became a leader too soon, the benefits are now paying off as his stage performances grow measurably more assured. (Roy Hargrove: *Family* Verve).

TOM HARRELL

Born in Illinois in 1946, Tom Harrell first came to general notice as Horace Silver's trumpeter for much of the Seventies. He later had an equally long stay with Phil Woods, before becoming an in-demand freelancer. His career has not been helped by being diagnosed schizophrenic, but in any context he ranks among the top contemporary trumpeters, playing long lines in a style something of a cross between Art Farmer and Woody Shaw and full of unexpected twists. (Tom Harrell: *Visions* Contemporary).

JOE HARRIOTT

Brought up in Jamaica, where he was born in 1928, Joe Harriott came to Britain in 1951 and immediately became recognized as a passionate alto saxophonist of the Parker School. In the Sixties, he developed a kind of free-form jazz which, though possibly given impetus by Ornette Coleman's work, undoubtedly bore Harriott's personal stamp. He later organized the first collaboration between jazz and Indian music through Indo-Jazz Fusions, adding sitar and tabla and playing compositions by violinist John Mayer – whatever its actual merits, the music undoubtedly inspired Harriott to play at his very best. An important pioneer, tragically ahead of his time, he died in 1973. (Joe Harriott: *Swings High Cadillac*).

BARRY HARRIS

From the musical hothouse of Detroit, where he was born in 1929, Barry Harris became recognized in his home town as a pianist of outstanding talent. Moving to New York in 1961, he extended his reputation for a deep understanding of the great bop pianists and composers with his ability to interpret their ideas clearly and freshly, examine their styles and compositions with affection and admiration and, indeed, to teach both musicians and audiences a greater appreciation of this music. Although he has worked in many small bands, Harris is at his best in a trio with bass and drums. (Barry Harris: *Live in Tokyo* Xanadu).

BILL HARRIS

A sense of fun was never far from Bill Harris (1916-1973), although he looked as stern as a bank manager. He studied many instruments before deciding on trombone; equally in his career he worked with many bands in many settings, but will be best remembered for what he did with Woody Herman. A featured soloist in the First Herd, he also graced the 'Four Brothers' band, then returned intermittently until 1959. Both gentle and powerful, reflective and laconic by turns, he took an exuberant tradition, put it into a modern context, and arguably influenced a generation of free-jazz players on the instrument. (*Bill Harris And Friends* Fantasy).

CRAIG HARRIS

Born in New York in 1954, trombonist Craig Harris has often been associated with Sun Ra. His own groups generally exploit the rip-roaring potential of his instrument to good, disciplined effect. Harris chose to name one of them Tailgater's Tales (referring to the way Kid Ory and other pioneers made room for their slides at the back of the wagon), indicating his feel for tradition, which he enthusiastically combines with funkier and more abstract sounds of more recent origin. (Craig Harris: *Black Bone* Soul Note).

EDDIE HARRIS

During an unusual career, Eddie Harris has often lost the allegiance of jazz fans, the first occasion resulting from a big hit early on (the theme from *Exodus*). Born in Chicago in 1936, he was rightly regarded as one of the city's upcoming tenor saxophonists. Then, in the Seventies, he was among the first to play an electric saxophone, replaying his solos on stage via a tape loop – in an accomplished manner that had got beyond being experimental. He also teamed up with soul pianist Les McCann. When he plays straight, one realizes just how good he is: a distinctively light sound, bags of technique and plenty of ideas. (Eddie Harris: *Artist's Choice* Atlantic (2 CDs)).

JIMMY HARRISON

An important figure in the development of the trombone, Jimmy Harrison was born in Kentucky in 1900. After touring with minstrel shows, he worked with several bands around New York, including Ellington's, before joining Fletcher Henderson in 1927, where he stayed for three years before illness forced him to retire. His range, strong and authoritative sound and sense of time made the perfect contrast to the playing of his good friend and fellow pioneer, Jack Teagarden. (Fletcher Henderson: *A Study In Frustration* Columbia).

Young star of the trumpet, Roy Hargrove.

DONALD HARRISON

Linked with New Orleans contemporary Terence Blanchard from the time they both joined the Jazz Messengers, Donald Harrison later teamed with Blanchard in a co-led quintet. Born in 1960, he had worked previously with Roy Haynes and Jack McDuff, and performed with the kind of assurance expected of former pupils of Ellis Marsalis. An alto-saxophonist, he is among the less strident of his generation, though he has plenty of panache, and has been adventurous enough to record with New Orleans Indians. (Donald Harrison: *Indian Blues* Candid).

MICHAEL HASHIM

Some musicians cut right through barriers between styles and schools,

Michael Hashim, born in New York in 1966, launched himself several years ago with the Widespread Depression Orchestra, reviving mainly Thirties material. He has since worked with Roy Eldridge and Sonny Greer and his repertory has not changed very much. However, Hashim, an alto saxophonist who now often works as a single, kicks just as hard when he switches to soprano, pitting the wide sweeps of Eric Dolphy against the smoother swing phrases he probably started with and throwing in chunks of bebop for good measure. (Michael Hashim: *Transatlantic Airs* 33 Records).

HAMPTON HAWES

Among the earliest bebop pianists to emerge around Los Angeles, where he was born in 1928, Hampton Hawes played with Parker during his visit there and claimed that Bird was his biggest influence. He participated in the so-called West Coast movement, making excellent recordings with Shorty Rogers, and then formed a very well-received trio. Gaoled for drug offences, Hawes came back in the Sixties, making several records in the U.S. and abroad. These reflected more recent piano trends, not always successfully, and it's his earlier, long-lined and crisply attacking style with bluesy undertones for which he is remembered. (Hampton Hawes: *The Trio Vol 1* Contemporary).

TUBBY HAYES

A prodigy, who featured both vibes and flute, Edward 'Tubby' Hayes was essentially a tenor saxophone player whose career was cut off in its prime. Born in London in 1935, he had worked for several bandleaders and led his own group by the time he was twenty. After a long and productive two-tenor partnership with Ronnie Scott, he formed a quartet, ran an excellent big band and was in demand across the Atlantic and in Europe. Unfortunately, he underwent heart surgery and, though he continued playing until his death in 1973, could no longer spin out those flowing lines. His best work from the mid-Sixties combined technique, swing and imagination. (Tubby Hayes: *For Members Only* MasterMix).

ROY HAYNES

A kind of godfather of post-bop drumming, Roy Haynes was plucked from Boston at the age of twenty (he was born in Massachusetts in 1925), to join Luis Russell in New York. He became the regular drummer for Lester Young and, later, Charlie Parker. In the Sixties, he often replaced Elvin Jones in Coltrane's quartet and he has since worked successfully with such top musicians of the younger generation as Pat Metheny. He describes his crisp, open style as one where the rhythms are smooth and easy to play with. An imaginative leader of, first, the fusion-type Hip Ensemble and more recently of a quartet. (Roy Haynes: *Home-coming* Evidence).

JIMMY HEATH

Born in Philadelphia in 1926, the brother of the MJQ's Percy and of drummer Al, Jimmy Heath joined Dizzy Gillespie's big band in 1949, having already written and arranged for one of his own. A tenor saxophonist who probably influenced his compatriot John Coltrane, he worked with and/or wrote for most of the leading musicians in the Fifties and he has continued to combine the two functions, at one time in the Heath Brothers group. A fine soloist, his writing has generally overshadowed his playing. Miles Davis recorded his 'For Miles And Miles' and 'Ginger-bread Boy', and later hired his son, Mtume, as percussionist. (Jimmy Heath: *Nice People* Riverside).

MARK HELIAS

A frequent colleague of Ray Anderson and Gerry Hemingway, notably in the trio BassDrumBone, Mark Helias has also worked with Anthony Braxton, Anthony Davis and those associated with them, and made excellent recordings with Ed Blackwell. Born in New Jersey in 1950, he has composed for and played in symphony orchestras and has a wide performing experience which reveals itself in his jazzier pieces. As a bassist in that context, he is among the best of his generation. (Mark Helias: *Desert Blue* Enja).

GERRY HEMINGWAY

Often the drummer with Anthony Braxton, Gerry Hemingway had earlier played with trombonist George Lewis and like-minded musicians while he was studying in New Haven, also his birthplace (born 1955). Adept at combining with the bass player in producing patterns independent of what the front line is doing – a prerequisite of recent Braxton groups – Hemingway is equally skilled in a more orthodox role, combining the two in his own quintet and in com-

Respected by his peers, Joe Henderson found a wider audience in the Nineties.

Saxophonist and Chief Herdsman, Woody Herman.

bination with other performers. (Gerry Hemingway *Demon Chaser* hat ART).

FLETCHER HENDERSON

Fletcher Henderson led the first jazz orchestra. Born in 1897 in Georgia, he drifted into music and, by 1924, found himself leading a star-studded big band, a job for which he was temperamentally unsuited. The odd aspect of a career rich in irony is that his finest hour came after the decade that put him in the history books, when he was finally forced to write his own arrangements. Paring these to the bone, he revealed a remarkable flair for simple riffs that swung right off the page. Adapting these for the Benny Goodman band, Henderson became the godfather of the swing age. He died in 1952. (Fletcher Henderson: *Tidal Wave* MCA).

JOE HENDERSON

In the Sixties, the tenor saxophone was dominated by two giants: Rollins and Coltrane. Joe Henderson (who was born in 1937) took a little from each, often adopting a gentler, more mellow approach, and a softer tone. Under his own name, he made excellent recordings for the Blue Note label and worked with a variety of bands, while being prepared to tour the world and suffer the vagaries of unknown rhythm sections. Long recognized as one of the best around, he has finally won public acclaim for a series of concept albums, of which the first was dedicated to Billy Strayhorn. (Joe Henderson: *Inner Urge* Blue Note).

JON HENDRICKS

Vocalese is the term used for the art of putting words to jazz solos: early classics included King Pleasure's 'Moody's Mood For Love', Annie Ross's 'Twisted' and Eddie Jefferson's 'Workshop'. Jon Hendricks, born in Ohio in 1921, made his early reputation in this field, notably in the trio with Dave Lambert and Annie Ross that specialized in singing hardened jazz fans came a decade Hendricks's lyrics to complete Basie performances, plus other well-known jazz tunes. Since then, he has continued, and expanded, one of his projects being a group featuring his wife and daughter. Outside vocalese, some of his rhyming routines seem to foreshadow rap, formally if not textually. (Jon Hendricks: *Freddie Freeloader* Denon).

WOODY HERMAN

Born in 1913 in Milwaukee, Woody Herman's bandleading career began in 1936, though his big success with later through his fiery First Herd, including Flip Phillips, Bill Harris and Dave Tough. Two years on, the so-called 'Four Brothers' band, named for the smooth sound of its saxophone section of three tenors and a baritone, enjoyed equal critical success. Almost up to his death in 1987, he continued to lead orchestras, generally composed of unknown college graduates plus one or two

veterans, all of which exuded that Herman fire. (Woody Herman: *Keeper Of The Flame* Capitol).

VINCENT HERRING

Vincent Herring, born in Kentucky in 1964, played with Lionel Hampton and Horace Silver among others. He came into his own when he concentrated on alto saxophone and, it could be said, took the Cannonball Adderley role in the quintet led by Nat Adderley. Skilled at brinkmanship, he kept his fervent, rasping sound and declamatory solos from going over the top, while his more economical style was sufficiently different from

Cannonball's for there to be no copyright problems. He has continued to grow since leaving the quintet. (Vincent Herring: *Folklore* Limelight).

J.C. HIGGINBOTHAM

Born in Georgia in 1906, Jack Higginbotham came to New York in the late Twenties and joined the excellent band of Luis Russell. Along with Red Allen, he was the major figure, his trombone solos irresistibly fast and furiously swinging. He then worked in several swing bands, rejoining Russell during the time when Louis Armstrong headed the band. Like many of his generation, he tended after the war to slip into Dixieland, and most aficionados feel that, not helped by the amount he drank, he was never the same musician. He died in 1973. (*Henry 'Red' Allen And His Orchestra -1935-36* Classics).

and local gigs before making his record debut in New York in 1962. The performances that followed must be acknowledged to be amongst the finest of a generally productive era. Following a steady output to 1969 his recordings, though never drying up, became more sporadic, as he interspersed teaching in a variety of settings with concert and club appearances. Alluding to the great bop pianists, although with a personal freedom of expression, his work is well worth seeking out. (Andrew Hill: *Point Of Departure* Blue Note).

EARL HINES

Earl Hines, born in Pennsylvania (1903), was the first pianist to transcend the ragtime idiom. His bass patterns were irregular and his right hand seemed to plunge about at will – except that his timing and swing never faltered. With Louis Armstrong in Chicago, he produced easily the most galvanic moments in recorded jazz to that time, their 'Weatherbird Rag' duet defying analysis even today. He then led a big band which, at one stage in the Forties, employed both Dizzy Gillespie and Charlie Parker. After the war, he joined Armstrong's All-Stars for a time and then worked mainly with a trio until his death in 1983. His real forte was unaccompanied piano. (Earl Hines: *Tour De Force* Black Lion).

TERUMASA HINO

Among the more recent Japanese musicians to make an international impact, Terumasa Hino was born in Tokyo in 1942 and, as a budding trumpeter, studied the work of musicians from Armstrong to Hubbard. A regular in the U.S. in the Seventies, he has worked with Gil Evans, Elvin Jones and Dave Liebman, appears at many festivals and often records under his own name. Closer to Miles Davis, his other favourite, than to Armstrong, he has a winningly broad tone and abundant technique. (Terumasa Hino: *Live At The Warsaw Jazz Festival* Jazzmen).

MILT HINTON

A remarkable survivor from the swing age, bassist Milt Hinton, born in Mississippi in 1910, even worked with Freddie Keppard, though in retrospect his most famous trumpet colleague was Dizzy Gillespie, when

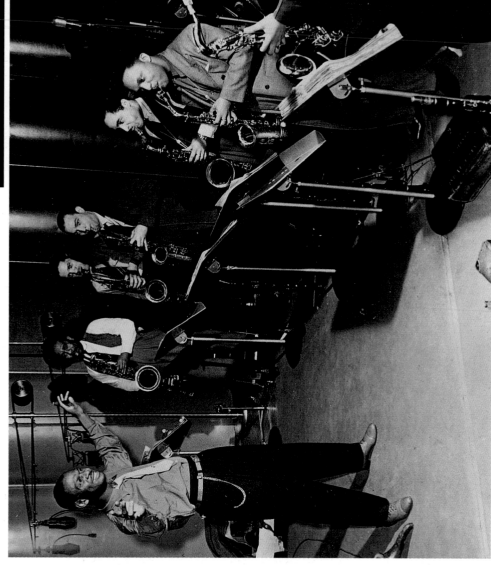

Earl 'Fatha' Hines conducting his orchestra during a 1940 session.

BILLY HIGGINS

Billy Higgins's career began familiarly: born in Los Angeles in 1936, he first rode the rhythm-and-blues circuit with Amos Milburn. Then, joining a band led by Don Cherry, he came into contact with Ornette Coleman and worked with him from 1958 to 1960. The classic Atlantic records from this period define Higgins's contribution: relatively straightforward, anchoring the complexities of the music – not too far removed, in this avant-garde setting, from the manner of Kenny Clarke. From 1961, when he gigged with Monk in San Francisco, Higgins became more in-demand in the recording studios, to the point where his recorded output may begin to rival Shelly Manne's. (Ornette Coleman *The Shape Of Jazz To Come* Atlantic).

ANDREW HILL

A strikingly original pianist and composer, Andrew Hill was born in Chicago in 1937, and mixed academic study they were both with Cab Calloway. He flirted with Dixieland after the war, but instead chose the studios, where his brilliance and ultrareliability on bass were much in demand (he was rumoured to have three instruments continually on the move between sessions). Hinton still plays and records, often with young admirers, and has built a subsidiary career through the photographs he has taken during his years on the scene. (Milt Hinton: *Laughing At Life* Columbia).

AL HIRT

Born in New Orleans in 1922, and classically trained, Al Hirt played with several big bands before his series of hits in the Sixties. Often associated with clarinettist Pete Fountain, another New Orleans Dixieland star, Hirt on his own recorded 'Java', a big seller, as well as more jazz-oriented material, including some with orchestral accompaniment. Still active in New Orleans and always admired by other trumpeters for his ability, he has not always catered for purists, but his best work has plenty of fire. (Al Hirt: *Our Man In New Orleans* Novus).

ART HODES

Art Hodes had an extraordinary life. Born in Russia in 1904, he absorbed the jazz scene in Chicago and, later, in New York, ran a magazine *The Jazz Record* in addition to his work as a pianist, which included some classic Blue Note recordings. Part of his later career was spent combining playing with writing and lecturing and even having a television programme. As a pianist, he showed a great affinity for the blues, interpreted with true dignity; at the same time, he played very effective stride piano in which the feeling overcame any lapses in technique. He was an active performer up to his death in 1993. (Art Hodes: *Sessions At Blue Note* Dormouse).

JOHNNY HODGES

Hodges modelled himself on the imperious New Orleans master, Sidney Bechet, who gave him lessons. Up to the Forties, Hodges played Bechet's instrument, the difficult soprano saxophone, though

Blues and Morton tunes came easily to Art Hodes.

he will for ever be associated with the alto, and for his place in Duke Ellington's orchestra. Born in Massachusetts (1907), he joined Ellington in 1928 and stayed until his death in 1970, apart from the period 1951 to 1955, when he led an Ellington-style small group of his own. In his younger days, he could swing forcefully at fast tempo, though one remembers mainly the luxuriant, rhapsodic solo features of later years. (Johnny Hodges: *Back To Back/Side By Side* Verve (2 CDs)).

Johnny Hodges, a cornerstone for years of the Ellington band.

DAVE HOLLAND

Dave Holland was one of the first European musicians to become an accepted star of the American jazz circuit. Born in the West Midlands in 1946, he was spotted playing bass by

South African pianist and composer Abdullah Ibrahim.

Miles Davis at Ronnie Scott's Club in London. Shortly afterwards, he joined Davis, who was not only in the process of changing his personnel but was also planning the sessions that would lead to *In A Silent Way*. Holland subsequently worked with Anthony Braxton and Sam Rivers, and later formed a group that once included both Kenny Wheeler and Steve Coleman, giving it unusual emotional range. As leader and all-star sideman, he remains in demand. (Dave Holland: *The Razor's Edge* ECM).

RICHARD HOLMES

Known as 'Groove', Richard Holmes was born in New Jersey in 1931 and, at some point, switched from piano to Hammond organ. He recorded with the soul pianist Les McCann, who discovered him, and he eventually had something of a hit with Erroll Garner's tune 'Misty'. Holmes deserved his nickname: while having reserves of technique he was, in the context of the organ-guitar-drums trio, among the least egocentric of organists and one most prepared to make the other musicians sound good. He gave guitarists space to surge through, his timing was great and his own solos were often shot through with humour. He died in 1991. (Richard 'Groove' Holmes: *Groovin' With Jug* Capitol).

ELMO HOPE

Growing up with Thelonious Monk and Bud Powell in New York, where he was born in 1923, Elmo Hope ranks alongside them as a pianist and composer. On tour for some years with the R&B band of Joe Morris, he did not make jazz records until 1953, displaying a many-noted Powellish style, though with a lighter touch. Later solos are more relaxed and distinctive harmonically, notably on two outstanding albums from 1959, towards the end of a stay in Los

Angeles, both packed with his excellent tunes. He returned to New York, but was dogged by ill health and died in 1967. Overdue a revival. (*Elmo Hope Trio* Contemporary).

FREDDIE HUBBARD

One of a crop of very talented trumpeters to emerge in the late Fifties, Freddie Hubbard took Lee Morgan's place in the Jazz Messengers and influenced many trumpet players who came after. Born in Indianapolis in 1938, he came to New York and did all the right things: apart from the Messengers, he got a Blue Note contract and recorded with Eric Dolphy and with Ornette Coleman (on the *Free Jazz* album). While not quite succeeding in devising a group concept truly his own, he developed into a splendid soloist whose sound – hot and spicy, with a dash of vibrato – is a considerable trademark. (Freddie Hubbard: *Backlash* Blue Note).

Curtis Amy and Charles LLoyd before arriving in New York in 1960. He became a Blue Note recording artist during that label's documentation of many free jazz players; his music from the period 1965-68 gave a clear indication of an outstanding and original musician, able to take the vibraharp into a completely fresh musical dimension. Later, Hutcherson formed his own group, adding the marimba and taking a more conventional approach within which the delicacy of detail transcended the standard repertoire, to create, frequently, robust music. (Bobby Hutcherson: *In The Vanguard* Landmark).

DANIEL HUMAIR

The advantage for a European drummer of having the chance to accompany Americans is shown by the career of Daniel Humair. Born in Geneva in 1938, from the late-Fifties he was working in Paris behind all the best visitors, developing the kind of swinging skills that enabled him to cater for musicians as different as ex-Ellington trumpeter Ray Nance and Eric Dolphy. He has continued to do so while working regularly with French and Swiss musicians, including Martial Solal, trumpeter Franco Ambrosetti and bassist Henri Texier. (Daniel Humair: *Edges* Label Bleu).

BOBBY HUTCHERSON

Born in Los Angeles in 1941, Hutcherson worked in California with

numerous re-creations and scholarly recitals, both solo and as part of a group, formed the Perfect Jazz Repertory Quintet and lectured on jazz history. His own style is unclassifiable swing. (Ruby Braff: *Younger Than Swingtime* Concord).

ABDULLAH IBRAHIM

The increasingly familiar Ellington-Monk piano lineage claims one of its more unusual and most distinguished adherents in the South African Abdullah Ibrahim, once known as Dollar Brand. Born in Cape Town in 1934, he followed his former trumpet colleague Hugh Masekela in moving to Europe. Ellington heard him in Zurich and was sufficiently impressed to encourage him, not least to try his luck in the U.S. Now one of the bigger stars on the circuit, Ibrahim has his own approach to playing and composing that reflects, with considerable emotional depth, the moods and melodies of his former homeland (he has gone back frequently since the end of apartheid). (Abdullah Ibrahim: *African Piano* Japo).

DICK HYMAN

In the Forties, Dick Hyman was as likely to be playing bebop piano as anything else, not unexpected in someone born in New York in 1927. He then worked with Red Norvo and Benny Goodman before displaying his interest in the chronology of jazz, with special reference to the piano. Over the years, he has taken part in

CHUBBY JACKSON

Born Greig Stewart Jackson on Long Island in 1918, 'Chubby' played with a number of bands before joining Woody Herman in 1943. As well as playing a five-string bass of his own design, he was an enthusiastic talent-scout, responsible for introducing Lennie Tristano, among others, to New York audiences. He played again with Herman intermittently from 1948, also leading his own short-lived big band. From the 1950s on, he worked mainly in small groups and, occasionally, non-musically, in television. Although often overlooked, his work on many sessions, under his own name during the 1940s, deserves serious investigation.

Once with Ornette Coleman, Ronald Shannon Jackson now leads his own Decoding Society.

MILT JACKSON

Nothing in Milt Jackson's vast body of work can be indicated as his 'masterpiece'. This does him a disservice. As both the quality and consistency of his improvizing, especially on blues and ballads, and the elegant sound he draws from the vibraharp become over-familiar, so the subtlety of his work gets overlooked. Born in Detroit in 1923, he worked with Gillespie and, notably, on record with Thelonious Monk, before founding the Modern Jazz Quartet in 1952 and remaining with them through their various incarnations. This work is widely and deservedly recognized: sometimes a more extrovert performer may be identified on recordings elsewhere. (Milt Jackson: *Bags & Trane*, Atlantic 7567-81348-2).

QUENTIN JACKSON

Born in Ohio in 1909, Quentin 'Butter' Jackson could claim to have played with bands that span the musical eras between Zack White, with whom he started in 1930, and Charles Mingus, with whom he worked in 1962. In between, he spent eleven years with Ellington (1948-1959), taking solos on trombone with a broad open tone as well as working with plunger-mute. His feature on 'Sonnet For Sister Kate' from the *Such Sweet Thunder* suite is certainly a high point, but his ability to mix it with Mingus at his most ferociously creative is equal proof of his versatility. He died in 1976. (Charles Mingus: *The Black Saint And The Sinner Lady*, Impulse).

RONALD SHANNON JACKSON

Musicians from Fort Worth, Texas, tend to gravitate to its most famous son. Shannon Jackson, who was born in 1940, joined Ornette Coleman in the early days of Prime Time and displayed the polyrhythmic force one has learned to expect from his drumming. Following a gig with ex-Prime Timer James Ulmer, his own Decoding Society invested jazz-rock with heavy funk undertones and set the pattern for his crackling percussion alongside Sonny Sharrock, Bill Laswel and Peter Brötzmann in Last Exit and Bill Frisell in Power Tools. (Last Exit: *Last Exit* Enemy).

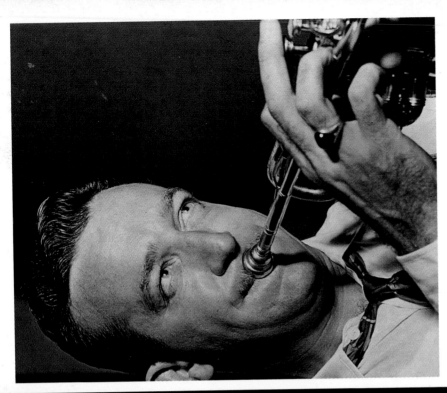

ILLINOIS JACQUET

Tenor saxophonist Illinois Jacquet blew himself into jazz history in 1942, with the solo he played on Lionel Hampton's recording of 'Flying Home', one of the first improvised solos to subsequently become part of the arrangement, both in Hampton's band and whenever Jacquet played it elsewhere, notably during his long partnership with organist Milt Buckner. Though born in Louisiana (1922), Jacquet exemplifies the 'Texas tenor', with his rich tone, bluesiness and no-nonsense approach. A showman and extrovert, he is also a highly skilled interpreter of ballads and blues and has lately organized a big band with some success. (Illinois Jacquet: *Flying Home* Verve).

AHMAD JAMAL

One of the first post-bop pianists to do something different, Ahmad Jamal influenced Miles Davis to the extent that Davis adapted his routines wholesale and encouraged pianists to copy him. Born in Pittsburgh in 1930, and possibly influenced by his compatriot Erroll Garner, he chose catchy tunes and dispensed with the usual practice of harmonic improvization. Instead, he offered solos based on contrast, both melodically and in the use of dynamics, often underpinned by the precise 2/4 rhythm that Davis borrowed. Jamal initially impressed the general public more than the jazz audience, though he has long since broken through to the latter. (Ahmad Jamal: *Ahmad's Blues* Impulse).

After 'Flying Home', Illinois Jacquet has never lost his rapport with audiences.

HARRY JAMES

Harry James was born into a circus family in 1916, and some of his commercial successes reflect such razzmatazz. Yet, when he worked with Benny Goodman (1937-38), it was clear that his bold trumpet style was securely founded in the roots of jazz. In 1939 he formed his own band. By the early 1940s, it had built up a huge following, and James was occasionally tempted to play too many cloying ballads. Cutting down to an octet later, he regained form, and in the 1960s he reorganized his big band. He died while leading this outfit in Las Vegas in 1983. (Harry James: *Yes Indeed* ASV).

A star with Goodman and with his own band; Harry James.

Art Blakey (1965-66), Charles Lloyd (1966-69) and Miles Davis (1970-71), his career has been self-sufficient and varied. He has run two outstanding and contrasting quartets – one American, the other European – re-invented the improvized piano recital and, more recently, played show tunes and jazz standards at the head of a trio. The somewhat folksy lyricism imparted, at times, during more reflective solos has had a huge influence on younger pianists. (Keith Jarrett: *Belonging* ECM).

BUDD JOHNSON

A Texas tenorman who had a smoother sound than the one usually linked to the territory, Budd Johnson (born Dallas, 1910) worked with the top local bands before a long stint in Chicago with Earl Hines. Something of a background figure, he was part of

KEITH JARRETT

Jarrett, born in Pennsylvania in 1945, is one of the most gifted talents of the past thirty years, immensely popular worldwide while still revered by musicians. Apart from spells with

the early bebop scene as an arranger for Hines and Billy Eckstine, and was sufficiently in vogue with those who matter to take the tenor solo on 'La Nevada', one of the great Gil Evans tracks. Sounding like Lester Young without (it seems) actually being influenced by him, Johnson, who died in 1984, was probably at his peak in the Sixties. (Budd Johnson: *Let's Swing Swingville*).

BUNK JOHNSON

The story of Bunk Johnson's comeback is the stuff of romance. Born in New Orleans in 1889, he was once Buddy Bolden's second trumpeter. Unlike some emigrants, he did not subsequently have luck on his travels until much later, when people interested in possible New Orleans survivors started looking for him. A cussed man who still enjoyed his drink, Johnson went along with their ideas. One problem was that they wanted blues and spirituals whereas Johnson, when he finally chose a band, picked musicians to read music and play rags. By the time he died in 1949, he had done enough to prove the fuss was worth it. (Bunk Johnson: *Brass Band and Dance Band American Music*).

JAMES P. JOHNSON

From 1910 onwards, James P Johnson was a leading member of the Harlem school of so-called stride pianists. Essentially ragtime, their music had a harder, big-city edge and space for improvization. He also accompanied blues singers and, in the Forties, worked and recorded with revivalist bands. Johnson, the main influence on Fats Waller, was a prolific and important composer. His 'Carolina Shout' is a classic post-ragtime piano speciality, and he also wrote songs for Broadway shows, though his more extended pieces, like those of many black composers,

rarely got performed. Born in New Jersey in 1894, he died in 1955. (James P Johnson: *Snowy Morning Blues* MCA).

J.J. JOHNSON

Born in Indianapolis in 1924, J.J. Johnson developed a staccato, linear style on an instrument noted for smears and slurs, thereby translating bebop to the slide trombone. The difference was not in speed so much as in his tone; firm and round, rather like that of a French-horn, and with exceptional fullness in the higher registers (comparable to Miles Davis's trumpet c. 1960). His partnership with fellow-trombonist Kai Winding is still remembered, though Johnson, a skilled orchestrator, gave up trombone for film/TV scores in the Seventies and has only recently resumed playing and recording. (J.J. Johnson: *The Eminent J.J. Johnson* Blue Note (2 CDs)).

ELVIN JONES

Born in Pontiac, Michigan (1927), the youngest of three musical brothers (Hank and Thad were the others), Elvin Jones built a considerable reputation gigging around New York

Spearhead of the New Orleans revival, Bunk Johnson first recorded in his sixties.

A master of polyrhythms and always compelling to watch: Elvin Jones at the drums.

and developing an original drumming style. Basing it on the elements of bebop, he considerably expanded the polyrhythmic aspects, frequently maintaining the cymbal beat by implication rather than statement. In 1960, he joined John Coltrane's quartet, where his style and stamina fuelled some of Coltrane's greatest extended improvisations. He left Coltrane in 1966, to join, improbably, Duke Ellington (for a brief period). Subsequently he has taken various small groups on the road with considerable success. (John Coltrane:

Live At Birdland, Impulse MCAD-33109).

HANK JONES

Hank Jones is arguably the father of Detroit pianists, possessing a rippling touch and with a foot in both the bebop and the swing camps. The eldest of the distinguished Jones brothers (born in Mississippi in 1918), and very much a musician's musician, he has worked with virtually everybody, from Charlie Parker to Ella Fitzgerald, and made innumerable records, especially during the Fifties as a house pianist for Savoy. His career has deservedly taken off in recent years, with regular trips round the international touring circuit and

recordings with everybody from Abbey Lincoln to African musicians. (Hank Jones: *The Oracle* Emarcy).

JO JONES

A swing-era colossus, Jo Jones (1911-1985) was reunited with his old boss Walter Page when they became the bass/drums team which, with guitarist Freddie Green, fuelled the Count Basie band in its legendary first edition. Renowned for his light, dancing beat, derived from cymbals rather than the bass-drum, Jones can be seen as a forefather of modern jazz. After Basie, he had less chance to demonstrate his talents until the 'mainstream revival' gave him the chance to work with musicians match-

ing his skill and imagination. Improvements in recording technique then offered a chance to hear him at his best. (*The Jo Jones Special*, Vanguard).

JONAH JONES

After an orthodox beginning for a jazz trumpeter, Jonah Jones struck lucky. Born in Kentucky in 1908, he left the big bands to join Stuff Smith in a music-cum-knockabout duo that proved very popular. Then it was back to bands, though again with show-manship, his boss being Cab Calloway. In 1955, while working at the Embers club, he made a record which caught on, mainly because of the gently bouncing beat. More of the same followed, and Jones never looked back. At best a commanding swing-era stylist, his playing and singing on these later albums are infectious in their own way. (Jonah Jones: Muted Jazz Capitol).

PHILLY JOE JONES

So-called to distinguish him from (Kansas City) Jo Jones, Philly Joe (1923-1985) worked with various musicians before achieving his greatest prominence with Miles Davis in the period from 1955 to 1958. Although regarded as central to hard-bop, he studied in his early years with Cozy Cole, and this reflection of an earlier era can also be detected in his playing. Philly Joe was unarguably one of the great masters of snare-drum technique: his solos frequently revolve around that single piece of equipment. A later-period achievement was the formation of a group dedicated to sustaining the excellent compositions of Tadd Dameron. (Philly Joe Jones: Blues For Dracula, Riverside).

QUINCY JONES

The career of Quincy Jones extends beyond jazz in the narrower sense, but that is where he began. Born in Chicago in 1933, he joined Lionel Hampton at nineteen, sitting alongside such excellent trumpeters as Benny Bailey and, later, Art Farmer and Clifford Brown. His strength lay on the compositional side; he was becoming Gillespie's musical director for a time, then formed his own band, while producing arrangements for the likes of Basie and Ray Charles. He has since taken off as a record producer and composer of film music, but his writing for groups big and small during the Fifties was innovative and ranks with that of anyone. (Quincy Jones: This Is How I Feel About Jazz Impulse).

THAD JONES

A favourite trumpeter of Charles Mingus (for whom he recorded), Thad Jones (born Pontiac, 1923), spent several years with Count Basie, where he also wrote for the band, before becoming a session player and writer. With drummer Mel Lewis, he formed a big band which played in public weekly, at New York's Village Vanguard. Many contributed at the start, though Jones eventually did almost all the writing and, in collaboration with Lewis, developed the stop-starts and tempo changes that set the style and influenced many bands that came after. After a move to Denmark, where he wrote for the radio big band, he died in 1986.

Jonah Jones worked with Cab Calloway and Stuff Smith.

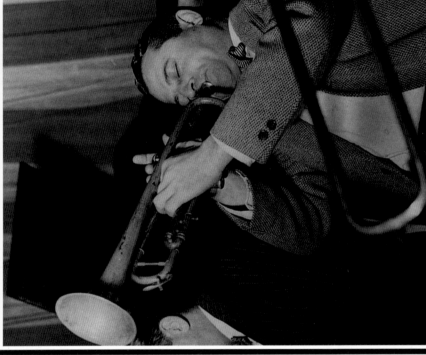

Max Kaminsky worked with all the top traditionalists.

(Thad Jones: *The Fabulous Thad Jones* Debut).

SCOTT JOPLIN

If W.C. Handy gave birth to the blues, Scott Joplin did the same for ragtime. Born in Texas in 1868, he became a saloon pianist in St. Louis, where he developed the ability to write down the tunes he and others played, and mould them into formal compositions. In 1899, his new rag, already turned down once, was heard by Joseph Stark, who forthwith published it. With the money he made from 'Maple Leaf Rag', Joplin was able to leave the circuit and devote his life to composition. His finest rags, and the opera *Treemonisha* (eventually performed and recorded in 1975), date from these latter years. He died in 1917. (Joshua Rifkin: *Piano Rags* Elektra/Nonsuch).

DUKE JORDAN

Born in New York in 1922, pianist Irving 'Duke' Jordan is known above all for his presence in Charlie Parker's quintet (before Al Haig and John Lewis). Although not a flashy technician, his timing enabled him to cope with the fast tempos, and his singing touch enlivened anything else. His career has tended to move in fits and starts, but he made a few splendid albums in the hard-bop era. Since then, he has been recorded mainly in Europe, where he lives. An underrated writer of tunes, his 'Scotch Blues' and, especially, 'Jordu' are standards. (Duke Jordan: *Trio And Quintet* Denon).

LOUIS JORDAN

In his own way a pioneer, a clear forerunner of rock 'n' roll, Louis Jordan (born Arkansas, 1908) played alto saxophone and sang with Chick Webb's band before branching out with his Tympany Five. It became hugely popular and, by the end of the war, Jordan had already appeared in films and recorded such classics as 'Five Guys Named Moe' (the song of the musical), 'Caldonia', with 'Choo Choo Ch'Boogie' coming just afterwards. When the hits eventually dried up, he rejoined the jazz circuit and gave a lot of pleasure until his death in 1975. But it's his stuff with the Tympany Five, packed with humour, that really counts. (Louis Jordan: *Best Of Louis Jordan* MCA).

SHEILA JORDAN

One of the most fascinating singers of the post-bop era, Sheila Jordan was born in Detroit in 1928. She moved to New York in 1951, studying with Lennie Tristano and working in clubs. In 1962 she made a spectacular recorded debut for Blue Note, at that time diversifying – albeit briefly – into vocalese. These performances revealed a subtle sense of texture and time, remarkable interpretive skills and exceptional control, enabling her to work with minimal accompaniment. Since then, Jordan has worked in both America and Europe, and her occasional records are well worth hearing. (Sheila Jordan: *Lost And Found* Muse).

STANLEY JORDAN

The hype surrounding Stanley Jordan has tended to polarize reactions. Born in Chicago in 1959, he hit upon the method of prodding the strings on his guitar instead of picking them; also, he adopted the ten-fingered approach of a pianist. A few others had done it, but they were free improvizers, while Jordan plays well-known tunes. Although his swing occasionally falters when he plays solo, he has worked at the system enough to exploit its advantages, such as playing parallel runs or introducing walking bass lines. In his chosen field, a true original. (Stanley Jordan: *Stolen Moments* Blue Note).

JULIAN JOSEPH

Since breaking through on the British jazz scene, the foresight shown by Julian Joseph in planning his career has been almost as impressive as his piano playing. Born in London in 1966, he won a scholarship to Berklee, and during his time there played in Branford Marsalis's quartet. Part of an emerging scene back home, he signed with a major label and has since undertaken various projects, including composing for his big band, which played at the London Proms, and organizing a series of recitals with such guests as Eddie Daniels and Johnny Griffin. A virtuoso soloist in any context, he also writes durable themes. (Julian Joseph: *Reality* East West).

MAX KAMINSKY

Fans praise Max Kaminsky, especially for the way he led the traditional jazz ensemble. Born in Massachusetts in 1908, his career developed professionally along the lines one could predict: Chicago, big bands, revivalism, Dixieland. He found jobs with Tommy Dorsey and Artie Shaw, and then, during the revival, had a very rewarding partnership with Sidney Bechet, on record and in concert. You can always rate a trumpeter in this idiom by the breaks on 'Bugle Call Rag' which Kaminsky, with Art Hodes, eases through expertly in the Armstrong manner. He became an established star of Dixieland clubs like Eddie Condon's and, later, Jimmy Ryan's, before his death in 1994. (Eddie Condon *1942-43* Classics).

GEOFF KEEZER

An unknown teenager when he joined the Jazz Messengers, though

WYNTON KELLY

previously the winner of an award for young talent, Geoff Keezer should develop into one of the more distinctive pianists in an area where there is massive competition. Born in Wisconsin in 1970, his albums show that he has plenty of technique and can write respectable jazz originals. What seems especially promising is that he comes from a tradition that may have started with Earl Hines, and takes in those flashy two-fisted stylists who force their improvizations into corners, so they can break free with one exhilarating bound. (Geoff Keezer: *World Music DIW*).

Some commentators expressed surprise when Kelly replaced Bill Evans in Miles Davis's quintet in 1959, comparing Kelly's more percussive, extrovert lines with Evans's intricacies. However, Davis liked the piano to offer contrast to the intensity of the horns and, given that the trumpeter was entering a period when his playing became more powerful, Kelly's uncomplicated approach offered variety within the group. Leaving Davis in 1963, Kelly then gigged around New York. He recorded frequently as a leader, but can be heard rarely as an invaluable member of various rhythm sections. Born in Jamaica in 1931, he died in 1971. (Hank Mobley: *Soul Station Blue Note*).

STAN KENTON

A controversial bandleader, Stan Kenton (1912-1979) put the word progressive in the jazz lexicon, and once proclaimed, "We don't know where we are going, but we are going somewhere." In his heyday, from the midForties to the midFifties, he was always willing to blend with elements of both Latin and European music. Forecasts that jazz was heading for the concert halls did not please

traditionalists, though he has since been proved undeniably (if partially) correct. The quirks – screaming brass, over-plummy trombones and portentous titles – tended to get in the way of the good points, which are now increasingly acknowledged. (Stan Kenton: *The Best Of Stan Kenton Capitol*).

FREDDIE KEPPARD

One of the legendary New Orleans kings of the trumpet, Freddie Keppard was born in 1890 and at 16 was already running an orchestra. He left in 1914, initially on a theatre tour,

and is supposed to have turned down the chance to make the first jazz record, afraid of people stealing his material. Reports suggest that he played classic lead trumpet: direct and very powerful, with well-timed breaks and elaborate use of a variety of mutes. A heavy drinker, he was considered past his best by the time he did record. He died in 1933. (*The Complete Freddie Keppard King Jazz*).

BARNEY KESSEL

Born in Muskogee, Oklahoma in 1923, Barney Kessel worked in the Los Angeles studios during the

Forties, where he was handily placed to appear on Charlie Parker's 'Relaxin' At Camarillo' date. Already a confident stylist who, following his mentor Charlie Christian, made sure he swung hard before he did anything else, Kessel became a prolific recording artist, though his gigs, apart from a stint with Oscar Peterson, tended to be local ones. In the Sixties and after, he toured much more frequently, and was a regular on the festival circuit. (Barney Kessel: *Straight Ahead Contemporary*).

Stan Kenton gave the big band a new sound.

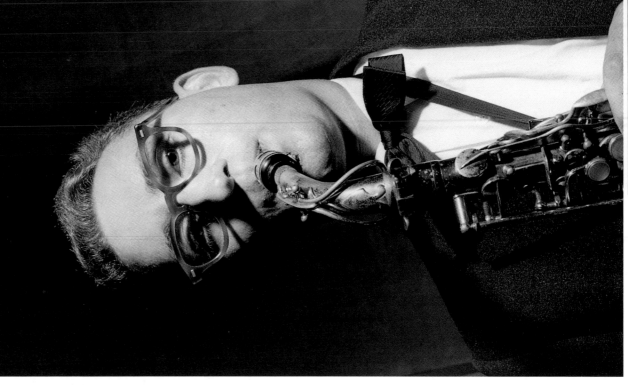

DAVE KIKOSKI

Born in New Jersey in 1961, Dave Kikoski was encouraged by his father, a part-time musician, who had him play piano on his gigs. He studied at Berklee, and later became a member of several groups, notably the quartets of Bob Berg and Roy Haynes (with whom he has worked for several years). He has also been involved in various Latin-jazz projects. Roughly in the Herbie Hancock tradition, his hard-swinging style is particularly well represented on albums by Roy Haynes. (Dave Kikoski: *Dave Kikoski* Epicure).

PETER KING

Photographs all over the British press of Peter King playing Charlie Parker's soon-to-be-auctioned saxophone hinted, perhaps unwittingly, at the way King is pigeonholed by local fans. Born in Surrey in 1940, he did make his initial impact as a teenage alto player in the Parker mould, fronting rhythm sections in London clubs and then working under many leaders, including visiting Americans. While often called up by bebop revival projects, he tends to try different things with his own groups: stylistically, with his even-paced phrasing and rounded tone, backed by an exceptionally robust technique, he is, if anything, closer to Phil Woods than to Parker. (Peter King: *Tamburello* Miles Music).

JOHN KIRBY

With few exceptions, the swing era meant big bands. John Kirby, born in Maryland in 1908, played bass with Fletcher Henderson, Chick Webb and others, but he is best known by far for his sextet at New York's Onyx Club in the late Thirties. A front line of trumpet, clarinet and saxophones, plus rhythm, and Kirby's wife, Maxine Sullivan, handling the vocals, were given slick arrangements, which were often written by trumpeter Charlie Shavers, and always comprehensively rehearsed. The sextet's records also sold very well, and they had a big following on the radio. Kirby, who died in 1952, may have been the forerunner of such groups as the MJQ (John Kirby: *John Kirby Sextet 1939–41* Columbia (2 CDs)).

ANDY KIRK

Born in Kentucky in 1898, tuba player Andy Kirk eventually joined the Dark Clouds Of Joy led by Terrence Holder, a gifted trumpeter but personally somewhat erratic. Before long Kirk, as he put it, fell heir to the band. Renamed the (Twelve) Clouds Of Joy, the band moved to Kansas City. Kirk drew on some of the best younger talent, such as Mary Lou Williams, a splendid pianist and soon their chief arranger, and tenor saxophonist Dick Wilson. None matched the drawing power of Pha Terrell, one of those svelte near-falsetto crooners so popular at the time. Kirk, who died in 1992, later ran an agency and did the occasional gig. (Andy Kirk: *Mary's Idea* MCA).

RAHSAAN ROLAND KIRK

While you may sometimes find a saxophonist blowing on two instruments at once, Rahsaan Roland Kirk, born in Ohio in 1936, played manzello and stritch simultaneously with his tenor-saxophone, on which he was truly a virtuoso, even after a stroke left him with virtually one arm. He also played the flute and frequently blasted off on a whistle. All this from someone totally blind. Unique seems an inadequate description and, in truth, there has never been anyone remotely like him. Understandably in demand as a leader, Kirk also made telling contributions to records by Charles Mingus, and perhaps his sideman potential might have been exploited more often. He died in 1977. (Roland Kirk: *The Inflated Tear* Atlantic).

KENNY KIRKLAND

Kenny Kirkland had a varied career before becoming part of the Marsalis story. Born in New York in 1955, he worked with violinist Michal Urbaniak and later with Terumasa Hino. From the start, he was the pianist in the quintet led by Wynton Marsalis with brother Branford on saxophones. After the brothers split, he became part of Branford's quartet along with Robert Hurst and Jeff Watts. A brilliant all-rounder, from hard-swinging jazz to electric groups, he has appeared on albums by John Scofield, Chico Freeman, Carla Bley and many others. (Branford Marsalis: *Crazy People Music* Columbia).

Lee Konitz – an individual voice on the alto saxophone in big bands and small groups alike.

First as a mainstay of Benny Goodman's band, and then with his own, Gene Krupa set the pattern for drum showmanship.

JIMMY KNEPPER

A trombone player whose silvery tone and relaxed phrases illuminate any context, Jimmy Knepper was born in Los Angeles in 1927 and worked his way through several name bands before joining Charles Mingus in 1957. He played on some of Mingus's finest albums, including *East Coasting* and *Tijuana Moods*, though they later had a well-publicized row when Mingus lost his temper and slapped Knepper in the mouth, breaking a front tooth. As a New York session player, he was often part of the Thad Jones-Mel Lewis band, and he continues to be in demand. One of the great stylists of recent years. (Jimmy Knepper: *I Dream Too Much* Soul Note).

LEE KONITZ

In the Forties, alto saxophonist Lee Konitz (born in Chicago in 1927) drew attention because his undeniably post-war style – oblique phrasing and diaphanous tone – owed seemingly little to Charlie Parker. He worked with both Miles Davis and Stan Kenton, as well as Lennie Tristano (his former teacher) and such fellow-alumni as Warne Marsh. Of all the Tristanoites, Konitz later became the most independent, in that he was often backed by proper drummers and collaborated with musicians of different backgrounds on both sides of the Atlantic. His sound has grown more vinegary and less disembodied, but he remains cussedly individual. (Lee Konitz: *Subconscious Lee* Prestige).

GENE KRUPA

In many ways the antithesis of his contemporary, Dave Tough, Krupa developed a flamboyant solo routine, modelled on that of Earl Hines, somewhat initiating, whilst with Benny Goodman, a crowd-rousing 'drum act', which subsequently became a constituent of almost every big band (and small band) appearance. This aspect has led to a lack of attention being paid both to his more restrained work, and to the excellent big bands he led between 1939 and 1951. Born in Chicago in 1909, he became a fine technician, influenced by classic New Orleans styles, and he retained, throughout his life, a serious and scientific interest in all forms of percussion. He died in 1973. (Gene Krupa: *Drummin' Man* Charly).

BILLY KYLE

Pianist Billy Kyle came to prominence in John Kirby's Onyx Club sextet, where his leaping attack, somewhat modelled on that of Earl Hines, added plenty of zest. Born in Philadelphia in 1914, he also recorded with the sextet's clarinettist, Buster Bailey, and with Red Norvo and Rex Stewart. His career never got going after the war until, following a long spell of work in Broadway pit bands, he joined Louis Armstrong's All Stars, where he remained until his death in 1966. Apart from the Kirby period, Kyle was underrated by the jazz public, though highly regarded within the business. (Louis Armstrong: *Satch Plays Fats* CBS).

Now based in Europe, Steve Lacy was the first musician of modern times to specialize on the soprano saxophone.

STEVE LACY

A New-Yorker, born 1934, Steve Lacy's recorded output would command many feet of shelving. Originally inspired by Sidney Bechet, he has ventured into free jazz, performing and recording with many musicians in many varied settings. This ability to integrate into open-ended contexts has allowed him to work in Europe with particular distinction. Throughout, however, his allegiance to the soprano saxophone (before Coltrane brought back the instrument) and his consistent exploration of the compositions of Thelonious Monk remain perpetual threads. No matter how 'far-out' the setting, the purity and density of his playing indicates how solidly rooted in jazz and how invaluable to its future his work has become. (Steve Lacy: *Morning Joy* hat Art).

TOMMY LADNIER

Another New Orleans trumpeter who left for Chicago, Tommy Ladnier, born in 1900, worked with King Oliver's band post-Armstrong as well as recording with Lovie Austin and backing several singers. In the Thirties, he made some fine records with his friend, Sydney Bechet, but did not live to benefit from the New Orleans revival, dying in 1939. Ladnier was a trumpeter in the classic mould: an excellent lead player, he also took no-nonsense solos and imparted plenty of feeling. (*The Legendary Sidney Bechet* RCA Bluebird (4 CDs)).

SCOTT LAFARO

A highly imaginative bassist with an exceptional technique, original style and strong melodic sense, LaFaro was born in Newark, N.J. in 1936. In 1955 he toured with Buddy Morrow, ending up in Los Angeles, where he settled, before returning to New York in 1959. There, he joined Bill Evans, and, with him, produced his greatest work. Together with drummer Paul Motian, they redefined the language of the piano-led trio in a series of stunningly beautiful performances and recordings within which bass and drums accompaniment developed wide-ranging improvisational commentary. Sadly, LaFaro's life was cut short in an automobile accident in 1961. (Bill Evans Trio: *Waltz For Debbie* Riverside).

BIRELI LAGRENE

Of all the gypsy successors to Django Reinhardt, Bireli Lagrene has made the biggest impact. Born in France in 1966, he started very young and was playing in public as a teenager. Having performed and recorded in several Reinhardt-type contexts, he broadened his range to include electric guitar (once trading musical punches with Jaco Pastorius), which he plays with the same frothy exuberance. Even when in full cry on top of a rocking beat, he never seems to be straining for effect. A singular talent. (Bireli Lagrene: *Standards* Blue Note).

HAROLD LAND

Born in Texas in 1928, Land spent his early years in San Diego before moving to Los Angeles, where, in 1954, he became a member of the legendary Clifford Brown-Max Roach quintet. With a lean sound and original ideas, Land should have become more widely known, but he has, instead, remained somewhat in the background. Later, Land worked with the bassist Curtis Counce, teamed up on several occasions with Bobby Hutcherson and co-led a group with trumpeter Blue Mitchell in the 1970s. As leader of a quintet with Elmo Hope and trumpeter Dupree Bolton, he was responsible in 1959 for one of the defining recordings of California bebop. (Harold Land: *The Fox* Contemporary).

EDDIE LANG

One of the first ranking guitar soloists in jazz, Eddie Lang, whose real name was Salvatore Massaro, was born in Philadelphia in 1902. Often featured on record with Joe Venuti, he also worked with Mound City Blue Blowers (whose leader, singer Red McKenzie, blew into a comb and paper), Jean Goldkette, the Dorsey brothers and Paul Whiteman. One of his best sessions was made with fellow-guitarist Lonnie Johnson, a rare instance for the time of white and black musicians recording together (Lang was billed under the pseudonym Blind Willie Dunn). He died during an operation in 1933. (Eddie Lang: *A Handful Of Riffs* ASV).

YUSEF LATEEF

Born William Evans in Tennessee in 1920, Yusef Lateef will always be seen as a graduate of Detroit's forcing-house in the 1950s. Playing tenor and flute, sometimes oboe and bassoon, as well as indigenous Middle-Eastern instruments, he was a pioneering, if largely isolated, figure in an attempt to relate jazz to other cultures. Nevertheless, his powerful tenor style and warm flute sound remained rooted in the mainstream of jazz – the two strands of his music, in fact, rarely interconnected. In his seventies, Lateef has increasingly returned to the tenor. A fascinating musician. (Yusef Lateef: *Tenors* YAL).

GEORGE LEWIS

Apart from Bunk Johnson, the main discovery associated with the New Orleans revival was George Lewis. A clarinettist, born in 1900, he worked with famous names such as Buddy Petit and Chris Kelly and, in the Twenties, was one of those who did not seek his fortune elsewhere. Having once played in a band with Bunk Johnson, their coming together in the Forties might have seemed natural. In fact, Johnson preferred schooled musicians whereas Lewis played moving blues clarinet in the Dodds tradition. After they split up, Lewis had quite a successful career up to his death in 1968, lionized by revivalist fans in many countries. (George Lewis: *Trios And Bands* American Music).

GEORGE LEWIS

Born in Chicago in 1952, George Lewis was of the generation to benefit from the AACM, being taught by Richard Muhal Abrams. A trombonist who has developed an awesome technique, he can and does play in any style, and he even did a brief stint with Count Basie. Part of many of Anthony Braxton's projects, he has worked with free improvizers from Europe, including Evan Parker and Derek Bailey, and conducted bassist Barry Guy's London Jazz Composer's Orchestra. He has also incorporated computers into his music. (George Lewis: *Shadowgraph 5* Black Saint).

JOHN LEWIS

The most cherished jazz musicians are those who introduce a fresh sensibility. With his limpid touch and ultra-precise phrasing, John Lewis did just that, with Charlie Parker, Miles Davis and, since the early Fifties, as pianist-director of the Modern Jazz Quartet. He has been a significant composer for larger ensembles, reflecting his persistent interest in European classical music, and some of his tunes, notably 'Django' and 'Afternoon in Paris', have joined the standard repertory. But it's as composer/arranger for the MJQ, and the brains behind their complex interplay, plus of course for his piano solos, contrasting so well with Milt he is most renowned. (Modern Jazz Quartet: *Concorde* Prestige).

MEADE LUX LEWIS

Even more than his Chicago colleague, Albert Ammons, Meade Lux Lewis became identified with the fashion for eight-to-the-bar boogie that swept the world at the end of the Thirties. Born in 1905, his record of 'Honky Tonk Train Blues' from 1927, though ignored by most jazz fans at the time, was eventually picked up by the indefati-

Like Bunk Johnson, George Lewis flourished, late in life, during the jazz revival.

During the Thirties, pianist Meade Lux Lewis became part of the boogie-woogie craze.

DAVE LIEBMAN

Born in New York in 1946, Dave Liebman first came to prominence with Elvin Jones. He subsequently worked with Miles Davis and ran several groups of his own, the most admired probably being the one including John Scofield and Terumasa Hino. Mostly identified with the more unclassifiable (and more interesting) end of fusion, he is admired especially for his exceptional brilliance on the soprano saxophone, which has affected many younger musicians. As a trained teacher, he has long been involved in jazz education and is founder/artistic director of the International Association of Jazz Schools. (Dave Liebman: *Setting The Standard* Red).

ABBEY LINCOLN

One of the most dramatically different vocal personalities in jazz, Abbey Lincoln came to prominence in the late Fifties. Born in Chicago in 1930 and named Anna Mae Wooldridge, she launched her career as a night-club singer under the name Gaby Lee. Often collaborating with Max Roach (they were married for several years), she then specialized in songs on social and political issues, as on her album *Straight Ahead* and Roach's *Freedom Now Suite*. Now based in Europe, and singing the occasional standard, she still features songs of what she calls social awareness, many of which she writes herself. Her trademark is heavy irony, laced with humour. (Abbey Lincoln: *Devil's Got Your Tongue* Verve).

BOOKER LITTLE

Born in Memphis in 1938, Booker Little died in 1961. Avoiding the

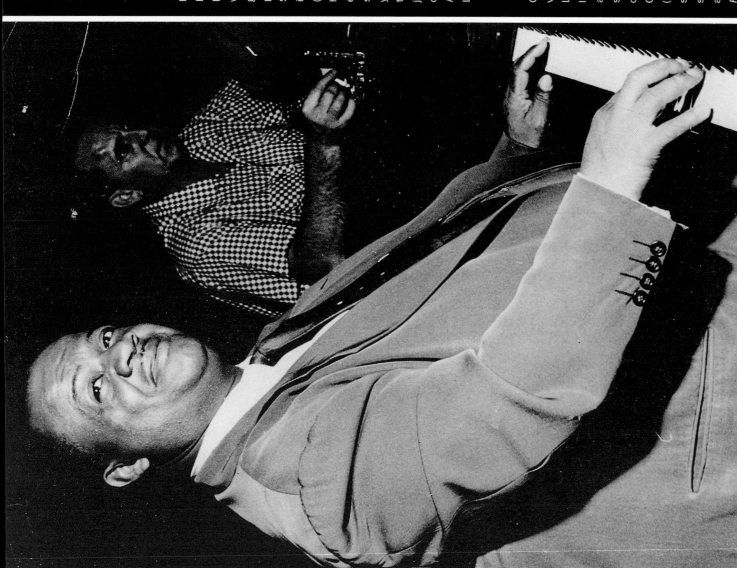

gable John Hammond, who had him re-record the number and teamed him with Ammons and Pete Johnson. 'Honky Tonk' is deservedly a classic, but Lewis was an all-rounder who, one imagines, would have preferred to be known as such. At least he managed to work steadily up to his death in 1964. (Meade Lux Lewis *1927-29* Classics).

MEL LEWIS

Mel Lewis was born in Buffalo in 1929. Best-known for his work at the drums with big bands, he could be equally articulate with small groups. Joining Stan Kenton in 1954, his accomplished playing, using a wide range of dynamics, made the band swing without being driven. In 1965,

he founded the legendary Village Vanguard Monday Night Orchestra with Thad Jones, beginning a virtually endless residence at that club. After Jones left, Lewis retained the band. The strength of its library ensured that the organization survived Lewis's own death in 1990. (The Thad Jones-Mel Lewis Orchestra *Basle, 1969* TCB).

Humphrey Lyttelton (right) gets a little unsolicited help from Eddie Condon.

familiar R&B circuit, he studied trumpet at Chicago Conservatory before joining Max Roach for two stints with the band, 1958-59 and 1960-61. His pure tone, fast execution, ability to elaborate long lines and, in the piano-less Roach band, find the space to drift away from chord-changes, quickly demonstrated his true originality. Later he co-led a quintet with Eric Dolphy, where the two adventurous horn-players seemed perfectly matched. His life was short and his contribution to jazz therefore curtailed, but he influenced other trumpeters, and the musicians he worked with enabled a clear indication of promise to be fulfilled. (Max Roach: *Percussion Bitter Sweet*, Impulse).

JOE LOVANO

Almost surreptitiously, Joe Lovano became the tenor saxophone name on everyone's lips in the early Nineties. Born in Cleveland in 1952, he played in a Woody Herman Herd for three years, then with the Jones-Lewis band. His big break probably came with Paul Motian's long-standing trio: both he and Bill Frisell were passed over initially, but, as Motian said later, people suddenly realized how good they were. He played in John Scofield's high-profile quartet, by which time the change of status was complete – and justified, because he has a commanding presence and a forthright style that makes sense out of a broad spread of material from bebop tunes to the freest forms. (Joe Lovano: *From The Soul* Blue Note).

JIMMIE LUNCEFORD

In the late Thirties, Jimmie Lunceford led the most distinctive of the swing bands, stylistically, apart from Duke Ellington's. Well-drilled in showmanship gestures (synchronized trumpet-waving, etc.), the music was rehearsed just as scrupulously and, led by the great Willie Smith, there has never been a finer saxophone section. Instead of mixing rifftunes and blues, the band played various sorts of popular ditties, often transformed into dazzlingly kaleidoscopic routines by chief arranger Sy Oliver, two superb examples being 'Annie Laurie' and 'Lonesome Road'. In its later period especially, you see where Stan Kenton may have been influenced. Born in Mississippi in 1902, Lunceford died in 1947. (Jimmie Lunceford *Rhythm Is Groovin'* Black Lion).

HUMPHREY LYTTELTON

One of the pillars of revivalism in Britain, Humphrey Lyttelton's trumpet playing has barely changed: a classic style, based on a strong tone, spiced with just enough vibrato, and effortless timing. He has, though, changed the context, continually renewing his bands and using a variety of arrangers. Born in Berkshire in 1921, he played with the pioneering George Webb Dixielanders before forming his own band that at first became a standard bearer for New Orleans jazz. Over the years, a saxophone or two was added (to the disgust of some diehards) and Lyttelton has often hired musicians with modernist reputations. A media personality, notably on radio, he has written brilliantly on early jazz. (Humphrey Lyttelton: *Movin' And Groovin'* Black Lion).

CECIL McBEE

Employed as bassist by many participators – of all persuasions – in the jazz of the Sixties and thereafter, Cecil McBee's list of credits includes Jackie McLean, Charles Lloyd, Alice Coltrane, Pharoah Sanders and Sonny Rollins. Born in Oklahoma in 1935, he has often played in Chico Freeman's acoustic groups, in which his clean tone and powerful swing get plenty of exposure. Through Freeman and his links with Arthur Blythe and with pianist Kirk Lightsey, he was a natural choice as bassist for the all-star The Leaders. (Arthur Blythe: *Calling Card* Enja).

CHRISTIAN McBRIDE

Of the younger bass players, Christian McBride is praised particularly by those of whatever generation who cherish the instrument's rhythmic role. That's underlined by a bass trio on his debut leader album where McBride, born in Philadelphia in 1972, is joined by Ray Brown and Milt Hinton. Already a seasoned tourist, he has done the circuit with the likes of Freddie Hubbard, Benny Green and Joshua Redman. Now leading his own group in public, he does everything from bowed passages, articulated at speed, to light, dancing solos, to pumping the beat out, as steady as a rock. (Christian McBride: *Number Two Express* Verve).

STEVE McCALL

A founder-member of Chicago's Association for the Advancement of Creative Musicians, drummer Steve McCall was born there in 1933. He was generally found with musicians connected with or sympathetic to the AACM: during a spell in Paris, he played with both Roscoe Mitchell and

Christian McBride has won several accolades from his peers.

...Anthony Braxton. His best-known work in this field was as part of Air, the trio formed in the mid-Seventies that included Henry Threadgill and bassist Fred Hopkins. Reacting to the others, he produced mellow timbres and controlled rhythms in a way that made him the Chicago equivalent of Ed Blackwell. He died in 1989. (Air: *Live Air Black Saint*).

BOBBY McFERRIN

An original performer who has enormously expanded the possibilities of wordless singing, Bobby McFerrin was born in New York in 1950. Discovered by Jon Hendricks, he soon became the most discussed new vocalist. As well as interacting with musicians, he gave solo recitals that proved his command of an audience. Sometimes he sings fairly straight, but people come to hear him beat time on his chest while his voice alternates rapidly between falsetto and low notes (close your eyes and there are two singers). He can reproduce the rasp of Louis Armstrong or the sheen of Nat King Cole. In the Eighties, he had a big hit, 'Don't Worry, Be Happy'. (Bobby McFerrin: *The Voice* Elektra).

JACK McDUFF

Among those pianists to follow Jimmy Smith's lead and change to organ, Jack McDuff was born in Illinois in 1926 and got his first jobs around Chicago. As a leader, he was frequently recorded by Prestige in the Sixties, notably with his then-current guitarist, George Benson. In later years, he had a cross-over hit with 'Electric Surfboard' before catching the trend back to basic jazz and funk. Always swinging and relaxed in his use of the organ's power, he is said to aim for a Count Basie sound – he sometimes wears a Basie-style cap, and his preferred nickname has changed from 'Brother' to 'Captain Jack'. (Jack McDuff: *Another Real Good 'un Muse*).

HOWARD McGHEE

Not a bebop trumpeter in the narrow sense, Howard McGhee was among the pacesetters who came up in the mid-Forties. Born in Oklahoma in 1918, he was featured on his own composition, 'McGhee Special', with the Andy Kirk band, and he influenced the work of his section colleague, Fats Navarro. On many bebop sessions, McGhee displayed a driving, extrovert style, midway between those of Eldridge and Navarro. In the Sixties, and up to his death in 1987, his approach grew more measured. Never the most consistent musician, his best work had real individuality. (Howard McGhee: *Maggie's Back In Town Contemporary*).

CHRIS McGREGOR

British jazz owes much to pianist Chris McGregor and the musicians who came with him from South Africa. His father taught in a mission school and McGregor, born in 1936, was soon studying European classics by day and playing jazz at night. His Blue Notes fell foul of the apartheid system and settled in Britain in the mid-Sixties, forming bands which eventually came together as the Brotherhood Of Breath, remarkable for McGregor's use of African dance rhythms, for collectively-generated counterpoint, powered by the springy rhythms of drummer Louis Moholo, and for volcanic solos, notably by saxophonist Dudu Pukwana. After moving to Europe, McGregor died in 1990. (The Brotherhood Of Breath: *Live At Willisau Ogun*).

DAVE McKENNA

Dave McKenna claims to prefer playing without accompaniment, which he does with absolute confidence. Born in Rhode Island in 1930, he worked mainly in small groups, including Charlie Ventura's and, later, Bobby Hackett's. Apparently, it was going to live in Cape Cod, where jobs are available for bar pianists, that persuaded him to develop his methods. Instead of stride patterns, he generally offers variants of the walking bass, often filtering them into what the right hand is playing, so that each hand is almost fighting the other. Using mainly standard songs, he often links these together according to the subject matter of the lyrics. (Dave McKenna: *Easy Street Concord*).

JOHN McLAUGHLIN

Born in Yorkshire in 1942, John McLaughlin played with the more adventurous groups in British R&B, and acquired a taste for Indian music, before moving to New York in 1969. A participant in the first Miles Davis electric sessions, he also joined Tony Williams's Lifetime, a group contain-

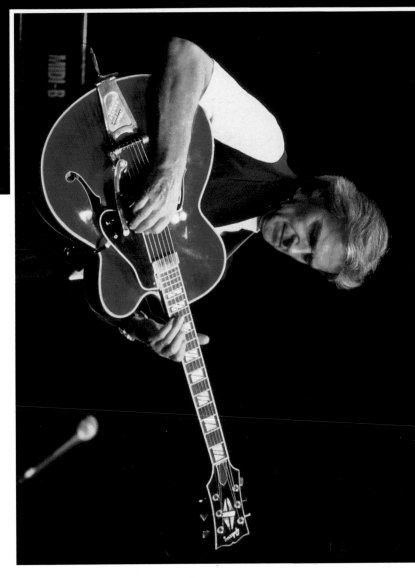

Guitarist John McLaughlin became an international success.

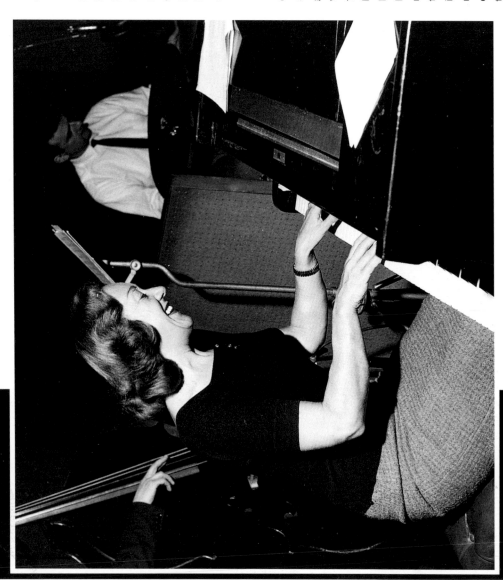

A smiling Marian McPartland at the piano.

her husband and a keen interpreter of Broadway songs, her best-known work has been either solo or at the head of a trio. Her articles on jazz have been published and she is a regular broadcaster: many of her dialogues with musicians have been issued. (Marian McPartland: *Live At Maybeck Recital Room Vol. 9* Concord).

CHARLES McPHERSON

Charles McPherson has been associated in different ways with two giants. Born in Missouri in 1939, he worked on and off for Charles Mingus for twelve years, Dannie Richmond being the other constant in the Mingus group. Alternating with Eric Dolphy in the early years, at least on record, McPherson offered Mingus the same passionate commitment, if in a less radical form. Praised by many for his flowing, Parker-like lines on alto saxophone, he contributed to the soundtrack of the film Bird, based on Parker's life. Occasionally involved in bebop revival projects, he frequently tours as a single. (Charles McPherson: *First Flight Out* Arabesque).

ing the elements which later made McLaughlin's Mahavishnu Orchestra so successful. A superb guitarist, his *Extrapolation* album, recorded just before he left Britain, is still revered. With Mahavishnu, and later, critics and audiences sometimes found his playing rather strident and gratuitously fast, but he has also produced work of great subtlety, outstanding for the harmonic and rhythmic awareness it demonstrates. (Mahavishnu Orchestra: *The Inner Mounting Flame* Columbia).

JACKIE McLEAN

Of the post-Parker altoists, Jackie McLean came up with a style that delivered Parker's bluesiness via a full, strong tone, as though Dexter Gordon had changed up a saxophone. Born in 1932, he worked and recorded with Art Blakey, Charles Mingus

and Miles Davis and, later, influenced by both John Coltrane and Ornette Coleman, made records which reflected the free-jazz ethos of the Sixties. In some ways a more complex soloist today, at least technically, it's the fearsomely direct approach of his classic period, and his withering sound, that so many younger saxophonists have latched on to. (Jackie McLean: *New Soil* Blue Note).

JIMMY McPARTLAND

In many respects the archetypal Chicagoan, one of the so-called Austin High School Gang, trumpeter Jimmy McPartland was an unabashed admirer of Bix Beiderbecke. Born in 1907, he took Beiderbecke's place in the Wolverines and then went on to appear on the 'Gang's' best-known outing, McKenzie's And Condon's Chicagoans, alongside Bud Freeman,

clarinettist Frank Teschmacher and Gene Krupa. Apart from a spell with Ben Pollack, he freelanced until the war, during which he married Marian Turner (see below). Invariably on the move, he made friends throughout the jazz world, always displaying a firm, effective lead and no-nonsense solos. He died in 1991. (Jimmy McPartland: *That Happy Dixieland Jazz* RCA).

MARIAN McPARTLAND

Born in Berkshire in 1920, Marian Turner came from a very musical family and won a scholarship to the Guildhall. During the war, she was abroad with the British forces entertaining the troops when she met Jimmy McPartland in Belgium. After they married, she worked in New York and became a regular pianist in local clubs. Stylistically more modern than

CARMEN McRAE

Widely admired in the business, Carmen McRae was never particularly well known by the public. Born in New York in 1922, she did not record until 1954. She can be as rhythmically or harmonically audacious as Mel Torme or Sarah Vaughan, though less obviously so (as a pianist, McRae sometimes accompanied herself). Among her later projects was an album of Thelonious Monk pieces, something few singers would care to attempt. The most unschmaltzy of vocalists, she never quite became the big star she deserved to be, but gathered a volume of tributes from other singers which speaks for itself. She died in

ALBERT MANGELSDORFF

In a career spanning over 40 years, Mangelsdorff (born Frankfurt, 1928) has developed a comprehensive trombone technique. He plays with the silky smoothness of a Lawrence Brown or Tommy Dorsey, or makes the gutsiest noises via various mutes. Having started as a kind of bebop player, he went on to pioneer multiphonic effects through a combination of blowing and singing. As one might expect from someone with such a breadth of expression, he is not typecast: identified with the European avant garde and a part of many such ensembles, he also records with Elvin Jones. (Albert Mangelsdorff *Three Originals* (MPS (2 CDs)).

SHELLY MANNE

Although born in New York (in 1920), Shelly Manne is forever associated with the 'West Coast sound'. He at first gained recognition locally, gigging with Coleman Hawkins and Eddie Heywood, then internationally with Stan Kenton from 1946 to 1952, when he settled in California. He achieved wide popularity with his jazzy version of 'My Fair Lady', while his regular band, Shelly Manne And His Men, provided excellent post-bop performances. Both a brilliant technician and a sensitive musician, he may be the most recorded jazz drummer ever. A reunion with Coleman Hawkins in 1962 provided more remarkable music: he was still working when he died suddenly in 1984. (Shelly Manne: *2-3-4* Impulse).

CHARLIE MARIANO

Born in Boston in 1923, Mariano studied there and worked locally before joining Stan Kenton, with whom he played alto in a forceful post-Parker manner. Once married to pianist Toshiko Akiyoshi, he lived in Japan for a time. Discovering Indian music, he studied indigenous instruments. Whilst retaining contact with his home town, he also toured in the East, eventually settling in Europe and working with most of the top musicians there, including Eberhard Weber. It is arguable that his citizen-of-the-world attitude and endless musical curiosity has led to his excellent work being overlooked. If so, this is the listener's loss. (*Toshiko-Mariano Quartet* Candid).

BRANFORD MARSALIS

The eldest of the New Orleans brothers, born in 1960, Branford Marsalis partnered Wynton in the latter's quintet. He also plays the European classics and has researched jazz styles on his instruments. But his debut album, *Scenes In The City*, suggested that he had ideas of his own, something he proved by leaving his brother's group to tour with rock star Sting, and, more recently, by including rap, a DJ and lots of sampling in his group Buckshot LeFonque. As a jazz tenor saxophonist, he comes on like an update of Warne Marsh or mid-Sixties Wayne Shorter, ticking over coolly even at speed, battling over the ferocious drive emanating from his favourite rhythm team. (*Branford Marsalis: Bloomington* Columbia).

Saxophonist Branford Marsalis has done everything from straight jazz to European classics and hip hop.

WARNE MARSH

The other saxophonist linked to Lennie Tristano, Warne Marsh continued to perform intermittently with Lee Konitz. While Konitz developed outwards, Marsh focused upon what he had always played: in the process, he invented something not only underrated at the time but locked into the future. Born in Los Angeles in 1927, he lived in California after a spell in New York, did some teaching and occasionally toured, as a single or with Konitz, up to his death in 1987. His control on the tenor saxophone, expressed via a cloudy and deceptively anonymous tone, allowed him to play exceptionally long lines where the accents came in unexpected places, while he could easily resolve the most intricate ideas. (*Warne Marsh Two Days In The Life Of Storyville*).

PAT METHENY

More than other guitaris[ts] of the rock generation, Pat Me[theny] cast his appeal among the totality of jazz fans. As a teenager in Missouri (born 1954) he began by copying Wes Montgomery; by the time he joined Gary Burton's quartet in 1974, he was already into crossover territory. Having attracted a mass audience by combining romantic tunes and virtuoso playing involving a range of electronic effects, he has since varied the mix, offering impeccably mellow-toned jazz, with more than a nod to

Pat Metheny, a crossover hit who retains the allegiance of jazz fans.

Ornette Coleman (with whom he has recorded), contrasting with work exploiting the synthesizer. (Pat Metheny: *Travels* ECM).

BUBBER MILEY

Possibly no musician made as big an impact on the formative style of Duke Ellington as James 'Bubber' Miley. Born in South Carolina in 1903, he had heard King Oliver in Chicago by the time Ellington discovered him, and had adapted Oliver's clever use of trumpet mutes and growling tones. Together with the equally gifted trombonist 'Tricky' Sam Nanton, he inspired many of the jungle sounds that have characterized the Ellington band, then and after – on 'Black And Tan Fantasy', 'Creole Love Call' and many others – and have remained an essential part of the jazz soundscape. Miley died in 1932, his role already passed over to Cootie Williams. (Duke Ellington: *Early Ellington: Complete Brunswick And Vocalion Recordings* MCA (3 CDs)).

MULGREW MILLER

One of several excellent pianists exposed worldwide as part of the latter-day Jazz Messengers (and having previously learnt the ropes by accompanying Betty Carter), Mulgrew Miller was born in Mississippi in 1955. Other important affiliations include Woody Shaw in the early Eighties and, in recent years, Tony Williams's quintet, with whom he has made some splendid records. Most often heard now at the head of a trio, or in all-star company, he has considerable technique and makes the most of a choppy, many-noted attack somewhat in the McCoy Tyner manner. (Mulgrew Miller: *The Countdown* Landmark).

ROSCOE MITCHELL

Long associated with Chicago's progressive wing, Roscoe Mitchell (born there in 1940) was an early member of the AACM and later became one of the founders of the very influential Art Ensemble of Chicago. Within the group, the contrast between the two reed players puts Joseph Jarman as the more theatrical, while Mitchell is generally cool and controlled. This is a feeling he transplants to groups led under his own name, where his compositions clinically explore musical ideas not found that regularly elsewhere. (Roscoe Mitchell: *Live At The Knitting Factory* Black Saint).

HANK MOBLEY

Hank Mobley (1930-1986) was unswerving in his dedication to the hard-bop tradition. Arguably the genre's greatest tenor player, and no mean composer, he was never side-tracked, even though he was active throughout the turmoil of the free-jazz revolution. Maintaining a supple tone and unfailing ideas, able to use rhythm as a springboard, he played with Max Roach in 1952, the Jazz Messengers (1954-56) and Miles Davis (1961-62), but mostly worked around New York. Recorded frequent-ly for Blue Note, these lucid docu-ments remain his greatest legacy. (Hank Mobley: *No Room For Squares* Blue Note).

LOUIS MOHOLO

Born in Cape Town in 1940, Louis Moholo took the drum chair in Chris McGregor's Blue Notes in the early Sixties. Because apartheid operated at the time (and McGregor was white), the group fell foul of the system, and wisely emigrated to Europe. Based in the UK, Moholo, together with bassist Johnny Dyani, toured with Steve Lacy's quartet, including a trip to South America. Since then, he has worked with McGregor's Brotherhood of Breath and put together his own groups – most recently Viva La Black, which toured South Africa post-apartheid. Only survivor of the original Blue Notes, he is a compulsively swinging drummer who lifts any ensemble, from abstract to fusion. (The Dedication Orchestra: *Spirits Rejoice Ogun*).

WES MONTGOMERY

A musician who suddenly hit the top in his mid-thirties, Wes Montgomery (born 1923) played in Lionel Hampton's orchestra, then retreated to his native Indianapolis. There, he took a day job and raised a family,

playing in local bars at night. He emerged to form a group with brothers, Monk (bass) and Buddy (vibes) and, eventually, the word got around about his unusual brilliance. As a guitarist, he combined elements of Django Reinhardt, notably his chord-ing and the singing guitar sound produced by his thumb plucking the amplified strings, with the relaxed timing of cool jazz. Up to his death in 1968, his records were very popular, even if the settings towards the end rarely stretched him. (Wes Montgomery: *The Incredible Jazz Guitar Riverside*).

TETE MONTOLIU

From Barcelona in Spain, born in 1933, Tete Montoliu studied at the local conservatory but got sucked into jazz. He recorded with such visiting musicians as Rahsaan Roland Kirk and Anthony Braxton, and became one of those pianists often chosen to accompany the likes of Ben Webster, Dexter Gordon, Lucky Thompson and George Coleman. He has worked in New York and made excellent albums under his own name. Like many blind pianists, he has an awesome tech-nique that, in his case, he uses with considerable imagination and subtle-ty, whether improvising on folk themes or jazz standards. (Tete Montoliu: *Yellow Dolphin Street* Timeless).

JAMES MOODY

A member of Dizzy Gillespie's orches-tra in the heyday of bebop, James Moody (born Georgia, 1925) became one of the first of that côterie to attract an outside audience. Based in Paris from 1948, he made records in France and Sweden that included the

first of his striking, plaintive-toned ballads on alto saxophone. Back in the U.S., he led mini-bands which mixed stomping blues with inimitable may resemble Art Pepper's, but the outcome was reversed. When Pepper returned, his playing took on a more acidulous character whereas Morgan, who went to jail a Parker disciple, emerged with a decorative style based on a smooth, creamy tone. (Frank Morgan: *Mood Indigo* Antilles).

before eventually rejoining Gillespie. He now plays mostly tenor saxophone (combining straightahead drive with throaty cries) and flute, on which he was among the pioneers. (James Moody: *Moody's Mood For Blues* Prestige).

FRANK MORGAN

A career that once appeared still-born was revived dramatically in the Eighties. Born in Minneapolis in 1933, Frank Morgan later lived in Los Angeles and appeared on a few well-received recordings. He then spent most of the next twenty years in gaol

on drugs charges until, on resuming his career, he was hailed as an out-standing alto saxophonist. His story ballads, and attracted R&B support.

LEE MORGAN

Though he used the language of Clifford Brown, Morgan spoke with the fiery accent of Roy Eldridge, adding a puckish sense of humour. Born in Philadelphia in 1938, he was spotted by Dizzy Gillespie in 1956. From 1958 to 1961 he was a Jazz Messenger, and in 1963 he had a surprise hit, 'The

A trumpet prodigy, ex-Jazz Messenger Lee Morgan's reputation has continued to grow since his death.

PAUL MOTIAN

Born in Philadelphia in 1931, Paul Motian is beyond doubt one of the most important drummers of his generation – and, luckily, very widely recorded. His method of working, subtle and textural, responding to other musicians, implying rather than stating the beat, became clear when he joined the legendary Bill Evans Trio. Although the most sympathetic of drummers in this context, having subsequently worked very effectively with Paul Bley, Keith Jarrett, Geri Allen and others, Motian's style fits easily into such orchestral settings as the New York Jazz Composers' Orchestra. In addition, Motian has for several years led at least three intriguing and contrasting post-bop groups. (Paul Motian: *Misterioso* Soul Note).

BHEKI MSELEKU

One of many musicians to come to the U.K. from South Africa, pianist Bheki Mseleku (born Durban 1955) gained experience in New York in the Seventies after playing at the Newport Jazz Festival, and subsequently worked in Europe. His approach differs from many compatriots in that the jazz input clearly derives from American practice, his style a unique amalgam of Bud Powell's and McCoy Tyner's, while his African heritage comes through in sonorous chants and incantatory phrases, perhaps reflecting a background similar to that of Abdullah Ibrahim. He is also an excellent composer, writing tunes one wishes to hear again. (Bheki Mseleku: *Timelessness* Verve).

GERRY MULLIGAN

For a period in the early fifties, Gerry Mulligan led a quartet which caught the public's imagination by giving the modern jazz of the time a Dixieland twist, while dispensing with piano accompaniment. Born in New York in

Sidewinder'. This success seemed to introduce some temporary uncertainty into his career, but he came back in a spirited way, rejoining the Messengers (1964-66). By the end of the decade he seemed fully able to deal with the breadth of his talent, but his life was cut short when he was shot dead in 1972. (Lee Morgan *Leeway* Blue Note).

SAM MORGAN

The most widely travelled of the four Morgan brothers was Al, one of many pioneer bassists from New Orleans, who later worked with Cab Calloway and even appeared in Hollywood's The Gene Krupa Story. The eldest – trumpeter Sam, born in 1887 – led a band including his other brothers on two memorable record sessions. The close-knit ensemble textures of 'Sing On', 'Bogalusa Strut' and the rest un-wound over the lithe, dancing rhythms that typify all New Orleans music, from brass bands to Fats Domino to Doctor John. Based in the city, but popular throughout the surrounding area, Morgan died in 1936. (Sam Morgan: *Papa Celestin & Sam Morgan Azure*).

JAMES MORRISON

James Morrison provides the rare example in jazz of an Australian going to the top of the international stage. Born in 1962, he played all the brass instruments from an early age and had a jazz club gig aged thirteen, playing at the Monterey festival four years later. He worked with Red Rodney, recorded at the Montreux festival and eventually formed a multi-national band. On both trumpet and trombone, he plays with great technical skill, clearly enjoying himself, and conveying the fact to his audiences. (James Morrison: *Two The Max East West*).

A youthful Gerry Mulligan caught at rehearsal in 1957.

Stripped for action: David Murray, on tenor saxophone.

1927, he had already made his mark as arranger for Gene Krupa, Claude Thornhill and Miles Davis. Right up to his death in 1995, he never did anything long enough to get bored, forming and re-forming his orchestra and working for a time with Dave Brubeck's quartet. On the baritone saxophone, he produced a fruity sound and his phrases were lighter and sunnier than anything that had emerged before. (Gerry Mulligan: The Best of Gerry Mulligan Pacific Jazz).

David MURRAY

David Murray has links with free jazz but admits to being influenced by tenor-saxophonists all the way from Coleman Hawkins to Albert Ayler, and this certainly comes across in the different contexts he favours, from his own big band all the way down to solo performances. Born in Berkeley in 1955, he was brought up in the gospel church, and that kind of fervour imbues much of his playing. Also featured on bass clarinet and soprano saxophone, he is pre-eminent among those who have used the experiences of free jazz to refresh the structures associated with earlier traditions. (David Murray: Spirituals DIW).

SUNNY MURRAY

Born in Oklahoma in 1937, James 'Sunny' Murray emerged as, in some ways, the most radical of the free-jazz drummers of the mid Sixties. Using a minimum of equipment, he created structures which had little relevance to either metre or clear rhythmic design, texturally dense while being conceptually simple. 'Melodic' he wasn't, but with groups led by Cecil Taylor, Albert Ayler or himself he offered infinite chances to select from the pick 'n' mix range of his devices. Over the years he has added a greater variety of equipment but this elemental concept has not greatly changed. (Alexander von Schlippenbach and Sunny Murray: Smoke FMP).

ZBIGNIEW NAMYSLOWSKI

The first Polish jazz musician of modern times to make waves outside Poland (born Warsaw, 1939), Zbigniew Namyslowski was versatile enough to play trombone with a Dixie-

149

Bebop trumpet star Theodore 'Fats' Navarro.

land band and modern jazz on the cello. Eventually, he found his role and took up the alto saxophone. His recordings include those by his own quartet and with fellow Poles, pianist Krzystof Komeda and violinist Michal Urbaniak (the latter now based in the U.S., where the record was made). Though there are folk elements in what he does, the straight jazz content of his headlong phrases is strong. He is a prolific composer for radio and television. (Zbigniew Namyslowski: *The Last Concert* Polonia).

FATS NAVARRO

Theodore 'Fats' Navarro was just 24 (born 1923 in Florida) when he recorded 'The Squirrel' for Blue Note. In the bebop idiom, it is an astonishingly mature performance from a young trumpeter. Though he learnt from Gillespie, and from Howard McGhee, his colleague in the Andy Kirk band, Navarro's style was more relaxed, the phrases just rolling off the trumpet, and boosted by the ample warmth of his sound. He was already the complete musician, and one struggles to imagine how good he would have become had a mixture of ill health and drug addiction not killed him within three years. (Fats Navarro /Tadd Dameron *The Complete Blue Note and Capitol Recordings* Blue Note).

PHINEAS NEWBORN JR.

An unfulfilled talent though, some years after his death in 1989, his reputation among other pianists is high. Born in Tennessee in 1931, he was part of the Memphis scene in the Fifties before making a highly publicized album in New York. A rapid-fire technique, with parallel runs played at speed, captured the attention, though some found it mechanical. Later

recordings dazzled less but seemed more thoughtful. Unfortunately, illness and injury intervened, and he was never quite the same when he came back. Two Contemporary albums under Howard McGhee's name are particularly recommended. (Phineas Newborn: *A World Of Piano* Contemporary).

JOE NEWMAN

A New Orleans trumpeter with comparatively little direct musical connection with the Crescent City, Joe Newman was a leading member of Count Basie's second great band, appearing on all the best-known albums from 1952 until leaving in the early Sixties. Born in 1922, he had worked previously with Lionel Hampton and Illinois Jacquet. During the latter part of his career, he was involved with the trust Jazz Interaction, eventually becoming President and composing pieces for their Jazz Interaction Orchestra. A fine, extrovert

swing-style trumpeter whose general approach has been compared to that of Harry Edison, Newman died in 1992 shortly after a stroke. (Joe Newman: *Hangin' Out* Concord).

FRANKIE NEWTON

Much admired, though perhaps not focused enough to forge a successful career, Frankie Newton was born in Virginia in 1906 and started off in the New York bands of Charlie Johnson and Chick Webb. Though he recorded one of the hits of the late Thirties, Maxine Sullivan's *Loch Lomond*, he did not long hold the trumpet chair in her husband John Kirby's popular sextet. Often sharing jobs with his friend, saxophonist Pete Brown, he appeared on several notable records, including Billie Holiday's *Strange Fruit*, that featured his bold tone and challenging ideas. He died in 1954, by then interested mainly in painting. (Frankie Newton: *Frankie's Jump* Affinity).

JAMES NEWTON

A flute specialist after starting on alto saxophone, James Newton was initially inspired by Eric Dolphy. Born in Los Angeles (1953), he studied for a time with Buddy Collette and moved to New York after getting his music degree. He was often associated with Anthony Davis: they appeared on each other's albums and Newton's arrangements were similarly intricate. By concentrating on the flute, he has been able to develop all kinds of effects, including those produced by using his voice to add overtones and provide harmony. (James Newton: *Luella* Gramavision).

HERBIE NICHOLS

One of the unsung heroes of jazz, Herbie Nichols was born in New York in 1919 and trained at City College. His piano style related intimately to his compositional skill; with a delicacy of touch, he worked thematically with

infinite variation of time and texture. His music therefore retained an organic sense, indicating directions without being over-prescriptive. To make a living, he frequently worked in inappropriate settings. Consequently, his small recorded output, mostly of his own material, remains encapsulated, though some of his compositions have been utilized by artists as diverse as Steve Lacy, Archie Shepp and Geri Allen. He died in 1963. (Herbie Nichols: *The Art Of Herbie Nichols* Blue Note).

RED NICHOLS

An exceptionally prolific recording artist in the Twenties, Ernest Loring 'Red' Nichols and his bands used various pseudonyms – a common practice he pushed to extremes. Born in Utah in 1905, he teamed up with the fine trombonist Miff Mole, who was usually a part of the Five Pennies (the authorized name). In the Thirties and after, Nichols worked regularly in theatres, on the air and on tour. In 1956, he recorded the soundtrack of the film, *The Five Pennies*, and was much in demand until he died in 1965. Compared, as a trumpeter, to Bix Beiderbecke, he was more generally assertive, though less lyrical. (Red Nichols: *Rhythm Of The Day* ASV).

RED NORVO

Kenneth 'Red' Norvo began as a xylophonist and it took some time before he switched to the ubiquitous vibraphone, potentially a smoother sounding instrument, on which he still managed to be choppier than most. Born in Illinois in 1908, he led one of the more unusual big bands of the Thirties, featuring songs by Mildred Bailey (then Mrs. Norvo) and scores by the brilliant Eddie Sauter. In 1950, he formed a very popular trio that had Charles Mingus (then Red Mitchell) on bass and Tal Farlow (then Jimmy Raney) on guitar. He continued to work, on and off, until the Eighties, sometimes teaming again with Farlow. (Red Norvo: *Move* Savoy).

JIMMIE NOONE

Often contrasted with Johnny Dodds, Jimmie Noone was the probably the best-regarded New Orleans clarinet player in the Creole tradition. His tone was pure, his technique supple and strong enough for him to study with a classical teacher in Chicago. Born in 1895, he gigged around Storyville before joining the migration to Chicago, where he worked at the Apex and other nightclubs. Records don't always do him justice, and he sometimes indulged a taste for oily sentimentality. The best Noone is to be found on some tracks he made in 1928, on which the formidable Earl Hines appeared. Noone died in 1944. (Jimmie Noone: *The Complete Recordings, Volume 1* Affinity (3 CDs)).

After moving to Chicago, Jimmie Noone, shown here on clarinet leading his band, became a popular figure.

ANITA O'DAY

Anita O'Day's great moment in public came in the film *Jazz On A Summer's Day*, a fair reflection of the success of her performance that day at the 1958 Newport Jazz Festival. Born in 1919 in Chicago, she became a star with Gene Krupa and, later, Stan Kenton, in whose orchestra her cool delivery and laid-back phrasing led to a new school of singers that included June Christy and Chris Connor. Sometimes over-tricksy, at her best she can effortlessly tug the heartstrings on ballads, while her timing and musicianship enable her to sail through the quicker standards. (Anita O'Day: *Anita Sings The Most* Verve).

DAVE O'HIGGINS

Born in Birmingham, England, in 1964, Dave O'Higgins taught himself on saxophones, and soon became a regular on the London scene. Among the groups he has worked with at various times, apart from his own, have been Roadside Picnic, a fusion quartet, and those led by guitarists Jim Mullen and Martin Taylor. Though he seeks to perform in different contexts, O'Higgins is unusual among the newer breed of British tenor saxophonists in that his current group puts the emphasis on such old-fashioned concepts as a driving rhythm section. Certainly, he has the imagination, technique and sense of timing to do this successfully. (Dave O'Higgins: *Beats Working For A Living* EFZ).

KING OLIVER

Joseph 'King' Oliver – a tall, dignified man who once worked as a butler – was the third in a regal succession of New Orleans cornet players, after Buddy Bolden and Freddie Keppard. Born in 1885, he worked with various bands,

Trumpeter King Oliver brought Louis Armstrong to Chicago.

including Kid Ory's, before moving to Chicago in 1919. He started his long residency at the Lincoln Gardens in 1922, where his Creole Jazz Band soon included the young Louis Armstrong. A subtle and driving lead trumpeter, he lacked the fluency to keep up with the new fashion. Struggling to survive, he became stranded in Georgia, where he worked as a pool-room attendant and died almost destitute in 1938. (King Oliver: *The Great Original Performances, Volume 1* Robert Parker).

SY OLIVER

Melvin 'Sy' Oliver was one of the most talented arrangers in jazz. Born in Michigan, he played in territory bands (including Alphonso Trent's, possibly a source of ideas) before joining the Jimmy Lunceford trumpet section in 1933. His arrangements gave the band its unique flavour. Though he composed a few numbers, his most characteristic writing was reserved for such unlikely swing vehicles as 'Annie Laurie', 'Lonesome Road' and 'Organ Grinder's Swing', the ceaseless invention of the first two contrasting with the lazy charm of the other. He carried on in that vein with Tommy Dorsey, and later as a staff arranger for, notably, Ella Fitzgerald and Louis Armstrong. He died in 1988. (Jimmy Lunceford: *For Dancers Only* MCA).

NIELS-HENNING ORSTED PEDERSON

For a teenage Danish bassist to be asked to join Count Basie's band, he has to be exceptional. That has always been the word about Niels-Henning Orsted Pederson, born 1946: as the house bassist at

Copenhagen's Montmartre, one of Europe's top jazz clubs of the time, he accompanied all the visiting Americans. He often worked in tandem with the club's regular pianist, Kenny Drew, but was better-known internationally for the time he spent with Oscar Peterson's trio. Renowned for a big sound and rock-solid beat,

he is praised less often for his brilliant solos. (Niels-Henning Orsted Pederson: *The Viking Pablo*).

KID ORY

Born in 1886, Edward 'Kid' Ory was the dean of New Orleans tailgate trombonists, so-called because, in

providing the bass-line counterpoint, the trombonist sat at the back of the cart and kept his slide out of everyone's way. In 1922, he led the first black jazz band to record (in Los Angeles, as Ory had already left New Orleans for good). He also played on the Hot Fives and Sevens, and on some Red Hot Pepper sides. After

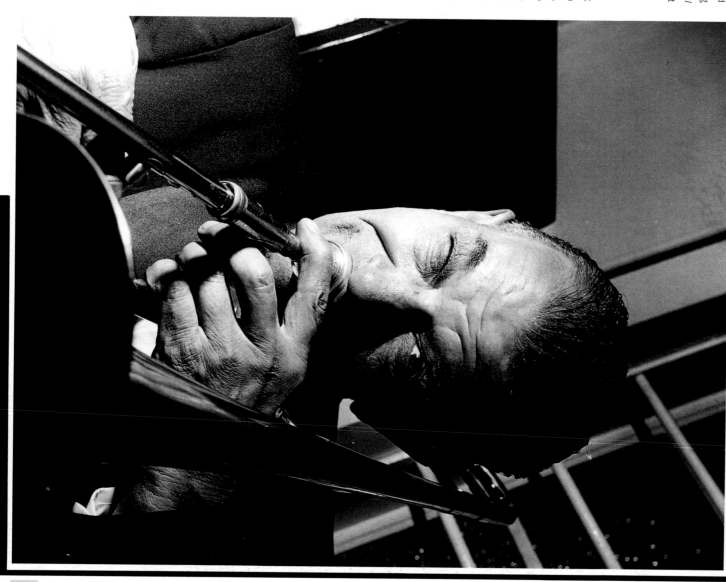

Kid Ory, once a New Orleans tailgate trombonist, who also wrote 'Ory's Creole Trombone' and 'Muskrat Ramble'.

running a chicken farm, he came back with the New Orleans revival and worked regularly until his retirement in 1966. He died in 1973. (Kid Ory: *Ory's Creole Trombone* ASV)

HOT LIPS PAGE

"Don't mess with Lips on the blues" was the advice once given, pointing to the depth of feeling trumpeter Oran 'Hot Lips' Page could extract from the 12-bar blues. He was born in Dallas in 1908 and made his way through the territory bands to join Count Basie.

Remaining in Kansas City when Basie left for New York, Page later worked with Artie Shaw but was otherwise mainly heard in a small-group context where, joined by some of the best musicians around, his declamatory Armstrong-styled trumpet and fervent vocals were given a proper context. He died in 1954. (*Hot Lips Page 1938-40* Classics).

EVAN PARKER

Born in Bristol in 1944, Evan Parker studied the saxophone in his teens

and became interested particularly in the work of John Coltrane and Eric Dolphy. Among the first British musicians to take up free improvising in the Sixties, he concentrated his efforts on the saxophone itself (he plays tenor and soprano), developing skills of circular breathing, double-tonguing and multiphonics – an extraordinarily comprehensive technique that enables him to span several octaves and to give the illusion of playing several notes at once. Long past the experimental stage, his music can be extremely melodious.

Brazilian composer Hermeto Pascoal has blended jazz improvisation with a Latin beat.

He is also heard occasionally in an orthodox jazz context. (Evan Parker : *Conic Projections* Ah Um).

HERMETO PASCOAL

An exceptionally self-contained musician, in some respects the Brazilian equivalent of Sun Ra, Hermeto Pascoal was born in 1936. He recorded on keyboards with Miles

Davis in 1970, but otherwise appears mainly in the context of his own band. His music is hard to classify. Mostly using Brazilian rhythms, it involves kaleidoscopic mood changes carried out to the letter by his sparkling and meticulously rehearsed ensemble, while percussive effects contrast with streams of melody. Apart from influencing contemporary Brazilian music, Pascoal has had a big impact on jazz in a wider context. (Hermeto Pascoal: Festa Dos Deuses Philips).

JOE PASS

Like fellow-guitarist Wes Montgomery, but for different reasons, Joe Pass took some time to be fully appreciated. Born in New Jersey in 1929, he became a drug addict, relying on commercial sessions to earn money to pay for his habit. He managed to kick it, was snapped up by Pablo and partnered all the big-name artists regularly featured on that label. In the decade before his death in 1994 he became celebrated, along with Britain's Martin Taylor, for playing the standard repertory on an amplified guitar with no accompaniment. Pass made it work by underpinning his melodic lines with a strong bass where necessary and keeping the beat alive. (Joe Pass: Virtuoso Pablo).

JACO PASTORIUS

Regarded as the most revolutionary bass guitarist of his time, Jaco Pastorius (born Pennsylvania, 1951) grew up in Florida where he played in several musical styles. His biggest impact came when he joined Weather Report in 1976 at its peak of popularity, appearing on six albums. A talented writer, he later ran his own big band. Pastorius could play as fast as anyone, but his sound was excep-

Jaco Pastorius set new levels for the bass guitarists who followed him.

tionally clean and his lines as a soloist more complex than was the norm among bass guitarists. Because his personality was somewhat unstable, he drifted out of regular work and died destitute in 1987. (Jaco Pastorius: *Jaco Pastorius* Epic).

GARY PEACOCK

A man of many interests, Gary Peacock was born in Idaho in 1935, and began playing bass whilst in the US Army in Europe. He stayed on after that, working with local musicians before eventually arriving in New York, where he played with Bill Evans, Albert Ayler, Jimmy Guiffre, Paul Bley and George Russell amongst others. Notable for a beautiful sound and solo ability, Peacock has nevertheless taken time out from music to study Oriental medicine and biology, and also to teach. Despite these interests, his reputation has allowed him to return to the jazz scene whenever he wishes to do so. (Paul Bley/Gary Peacock *Partners* Owl).

ART PEPPER

Art Pepper's career splits neatly in two, divided by a spell of on-off incarceration for drug offences. Born in California (1925), he became one of the strongest soloists on the West Coast scene, his melodic phrasing and singing sound on alto saxophone cross Lester Young with Benny Carter. After his period inside, graphically described in his no-holds-barred autobiography, he developed a more aggressively emotional style, making more use of rhythm and space and adding a vinegary edge to his tone. The best solos hit you with sledgehammer force. He died in 1982. (Art Pepper: *Meets The Rhythm Section* Contemporary).

OSCAR PETERSON

The Canadian pianist Oscar Peterson, born in 1925, brought to jazz an astonishingly fluent technique that has led to comparisons with Art Tatum. An obvious early influence was Nat King Cole (he sometimes also sings like Cole) and perhaps the most characteristic of his trios adopted the Cole formula of piano, bass and guitar. Propulsive in the rhythm section, often recorded in all-star groups as well as with a trio, some of Peterson's finest playing has been done without accompaniment, where, without copying, he captures the spirit of Tatum, while steering clear of the mechanistic phrasing so often part of his own trio performance. (Oscar Peterson: *Plus One* Emarcy MPS).

MICHEL PETRUCCIANI

Born in Montpelier, France in 1962, Michel Petrucciani was able to learn the trade in his family band before moving to Paris and, after a few years, to the US. Varying the context, he has worked as a soloist, as pianist in all-star groups, with his own trio, alongside synthesizers and as a duo with organist Eddie Louiss. Triumphing over the handicap of a bone disease that affects growth, he has

A tempestuous life did not stop Art Pepper from making great music.

become a major contemporary pianist. Seemingly a romantic at heart, he has tended lately to play standard tunes with abundant lyrical warmth. (Eddie Louiss: *Conférence de Presse Dreyfus*).

OSCAR PETTIFORD

An exact contemporary of Mingus, and equally temperamental, Oscar Pettiford, like him, played bass (and, later, the cello). Born in Oklahoma in 1922, he grew up within the environment of his family's touring band. With Duke Ellington from 1945 to 1948, his ability to further the pioneering work of Jimmy Blanton became evident in his powerful tone

and propulsive drive. His harmonic sophistication brought him into demand for work with bop musicians, where his dexterity also allowed him to contribute an intriguing solo voice. For the last two years of his life, he lived in Europe, where he died, in Copenhagen in 1960. (*The Complete Essen Jazz Festival Concert* Black Lion).

FLIP PHILLIPS

Along with Charlie Ventura, Vido Musso and Illinois Jacquet, Joseph 'Flip' Phillips belonged to a generation of bravura tenor saxophonists that flourished in the later swing big bands. Born in New York in 1915, he joined Woody Herman in 1944, at the point where that band emerged as a great jazz orchestra, and remained until 1946. Recruited to Jazz At The

Philharmonic, he toured with them for the next eleven years, establishing a reputation as a barnstorming exhibitionist that tended to obscure his wider talents. Semi-retired throughout the 1960s, he began to work again in the 1970s, and he has continued to produce some excellent work. (*Flip Phillips: A Real Swinger* Concord).

COURTNEY PINE

Before 1980, most nationally-known British jazz musicians were white. A major factor in changing this situation was saxophonist Courtney Pine, who came from nowhere to become something of an icon. Born in London in 1964, he was encouraged by drummer John Stevens, a proselytising teacher whose example perhaps inspired Pine to form an organisation designed to attract black Britons to jazz. By 1990, he had launched a big

band, made several records for a major label and worked and recorded with top Americans. A powerful soloist, his fluent technique was modelled on Coltrane's but his music increasingly explores areas of British black music. (*Courtney Pine: To The Eyes Of* Creation Island).

BEN POLLACK

One of the important bandleaders during the Twenties, Ben Pollack (born Chicago, 1903) hired most of the best white musicians at one time or another – in later years, he regretted that some became better-known after they moved on , such as Benny Goodman, Harry James, Glenn Miller and half the Bob Crosby band. An excellent drummer who hit the front with the New Orleans Rhythm Kings and whose style looked beyond Dixieland, Pollack came back in the Fifties

until ill health intervened. He died in 1971. (*Ben Pollack And His Orchestra* Sunbeam).

JEAN LUC PONTY

The French can claim the number one spot when it comes to jazz violinists. Of those coming after Stephane Grappelli, Jean Luc Ponty has made the biggest impact to date. Born in Normandy in 1942, he is classically trained, and has been in demand in the U.S. since the mid Sixties. Shortly after emigrating, he joined the Mahavishnu Orchestra at the height of its popularity, and since then he has appeared both with his own groups and in all-star contexts. He has a splendid command of the instrument and, like his compatriots, rarely exploits amplification for its own ends. (Jean Luc Ponty: *Imaginary Voyage* Atlantic).

CHRIS POTTER

Discovered by Red Rodney when the late trumpeter was playing in South Carolina, Chris Potter eventually joined Rodney's group and amply justified the glowing build-ups the trumpeter always gave him. Born in Chicago in 1970, Potter's main instruments (though he plays several others) are the alto and tenor saxophones, and he gets a pleasingly full sound from them both. As well as albums of his own, he has recorded with Rodney and with the Mingus Big Band, with which he toured Europe in 1995. (Chris Potter: *Pure Concord*).

BUD POWELL

On his earliest records with Cootie Williams's band, Bud Powell (born in New York in 1924) stood out. His

Bud Powell had dazzling gifts as a bebop pianist.

achievements subsequently confirmed his enormous talent: a soloist setting the pace for bebop pianists and a composer/theorist whose influence lives on. His touch – metallic, totally un-European, each note individually hammered even at speed – served his acute all-round imagination. Mental problems, possibly caused by being beaten over the head by New York's police, took the executive edge off his later work, though to the end (he died in 1966) one could

DON PULLEN

Don Pullen's first record, a duet with drummer Milford Graves of totally free improvisation, launched a career that, while based around structured material, regularly came up with something different. Born in Virginia in 1941, he sometimes worked as a Hammond organist around the club circuit, then joined the strongest of Charles Mingus's later groups. It included saxophonist George Adams, who became co-leader with Pullen of an excellent quartet. Pullen's style on piano, lacing his orthodox lines with oddball effects, typified his approach overall. Before his death in 1995, he led a group called African-Brazilian Connection, while his last project incorporated American Indians. (Don Pullen: *Random Thoughts* Blue Note).

Don Pullen's first record, a duet with drummer Milford Graves of totally free improvisation, launched a career that.

His life inspired the film *Round Midnight*, about an expatriate jazzman in Paris. (Bud Powell: *The Best of Bud Powell* Verve).

sense an exceptional musical mind.

IKE QUEBEC

Born in 1918 in Newark, N.J., Ike Quebec never lost his tenor-playing roots, firmly based within the fertile soil prepared by Coleman Hawkins. His longest job was with Cab Calloway (1944-51); otherwise, he led small groups in and around New York. Despite his powerful swing-based style, he took great interest in more modern concepts and could work well with them. In this, he revealed similarities with Don Byas. Quebec did much work for the Blue Note label, both as a musician and as a talent-scout, introducing many fine musicians to that company. He died in 1963. (Ike Quebec: *Blue And Sentimental* Blue Note).

JIMMY RANEY

Jimmy Raney was born in Louisville, Kentucky in 1927. His first major gig was a spell with Woody Herman; later, he joined Stan Getz, before replacing Tal Farlow in Red Norvo's trio. During the Fifties, he recorded under his own name, and worked regularly. Then his career rather petered out, but he came back strongly in the Seventies, often playing guitar duets with his son Doug, and recording with such compatible pianists as Hank Jones and Tommy Flanagan. Of those cool-school guitarists who played long,

even-toned phrases and kept the amplifier down low, Raney, who died in 1995, showed the most wit and invention. (Jimmy Raney: *Here's That Raney Day* Black & Blue).

ENRICO RAVA

Born in Trieste, Italy in 1943, Enrico Rava played Dixieland trombone in his teens, then took up the trumpet, heard Chet Baker and became interested in modern jazz. In the Sixties, he played with Gato Barbieri and toured South America as part of Steve Lacy's free improvising quartet. Since 1900, he played saxophones in

then, he has worked with bands of all sizes and in all styles, generally inclined towards the sharper end. His tone on trumpet is satisfyingly fat and warm, and his solos in any setting show plenty of imagination. (Enrico Rava: *Secrets* Soul Note).

DON REDMAN

Don Redman wins his place in the archives as the father of orchestral jazz, the man who arranged all the music on Fletcher Henderson's early records. Born in West Virginia in

Henderson's first band and established the ground rules (brass and reed section, background riffs) for the future. Redman refined his art as director of McKinney's Cotton Pickers but, a reluctant leader, did not form a band until the Thirties. His classic 'Chant Of The Weed' casts an edgy, brooding spell and shows how he got his music to hustle, pitting saxes against brass and then piling something extra on top. He later worked as an arranger up to his death in 1964. (Don Redman: *Doin' What I Please* ASV).

JOSHUA REDMAN

Joshua Redman hit the jazz scene when, aged 22, he won the Thelonious Monk International Competition. Born in California in 1969 (his father, Dewey Redman, is himself a formidable saxophonist), he began to get involved with jazz at college and, during the vacation, took part in several jam sessions around Boston. Technically assured, with unerring command of the high register, he produces a full, warm sound that is personal to the extent that others are already showing its influence, notably on ballads. Though Redman at present fits into the category of those who emphasise the tradition, he already gives enough signs of flexibility to suggest that his music will move on. (Joshua Redman: *Wish Warner*).

The exciting Buddy Rich at the Royal Command Performance of 1969.

drummer, and the most spectacular solo style, if hardly the most relaxed swing. (Buddy Rich: *No Jive* BMG/Novus).

BUDDY RICH

One of the great virtuosos of jazz, the drummer Buddy Rich was always riveting to watch. Born in Brooklyn in 1917 to a show-business couple, he evolved from an infant prodigy to playing with many of the major swing bandleaders, including Tommy Dorsey, Harry James and Artie Shaw. In the Fifties, he led mainly small groups and pushed his own singing, but for the rest of his career, until his death in 1987, he led mostly his own big band. It tended to overdo the flag-wavers, but those contexts enabled Rich to strut his stuff, displaying probably the fastest hands of any

DANNIE RICHMOND

Outside of Duke Ellington alumni, few musicians have been so identified with the work of a particular composer as Dannie Richmond, who for 20 years, on and off, was the drummer with Charles Mingus. Born in New York in 1935, he began as a saxophonist and his playing benefited, according to Mingus, because he had few received ideas about what a drummer should do. After Mingus died, he formed the group Mingus Dynasty and worked with the quartet run by ex-Mingus staffers George Adams and Don Pullen. Richmond, who died in 1988, deserved more independent recognition for his versatility, and for his driving accompaniment. (Charles Mingus: *Changes 1* Rhino).

In his twenties, Joshua Redman has already made a big impact.

Once Charlie Parker's drummer, Max Roach later became a significant composer and bandleader.

SAM RIVERS

Born in Oklahoma in 1930, Sam Rivers enjoys a high reputation among his peers, while keeping, mostly, out of the limelight. Much of his early playing was done in Boston, where he studied at the Conservatory and where at one time he had Tony Williams as his drummer. After a few months with Miles Davis (before Wayne Shorter joined) he settled in New York, where he taught music and put on events in the studios he ran with his wife. He has since written some notable pieces for big bands. Best known for his saxophone playing, Rivers is a brilliant all-rounder whose music defies close categorisation. (Sam Rivers: *Waves* Tomato).

MAX ROACH

Born in North Carolina in 1924, Max Roach made an enormous impact as Charlie Parker's regular drummer, in person and on Parker's classic Dial and Savoy recordings. A fine technician, who invented many of the rhythmic fill-ins now commonplace, he had total mastery of the top cymbal on which he implied endless variations while keeping the beat going. An important leader, first with Clifford Brown and then with his own groups (including a drum choir) some of his finest albums were made in the early Sixties, notably in the company of Eric Dolphy, Booker Little and his then-wife Abbey Lincoln. (Max Roach: *Percussion Bitter Sweet* Impulse).

SPIKE ROBINSON

Henry 'Spike' Robinson's unusual career in jazz began late. He was born in Wisconsin in 1930, and gained a following among bebop fans in Britain by making a few records there in 1951, while serving with the Navy. Back home, he got a day job in Colorado, keeping his hand in via local sessions, but otherwise not recording until the Eighties. Back in music full-time and based in Britain, he is recognised as a brilliant tenor saxophonist, combining the natural swing of Zoot Sims with some of

MARCUS ROBERTS

One of the most intriguing and original talents to be involved in the brouhaha over paying attention to past glories, Marcus Roberts first came to prominence as pianist in Wynton Marsalis's postbop group. Born in Florida in 1963, and blind from an early age, his career has to some extent parallelled that of Marsalis. Apart from his own albums, he has directed the Lincoln Center Jazz Orchestra and composed for large ensembles. An excellent pianist in any style, he is identified mainly with his personal re-creations of compositions ranging from Joplin through Gershwin to Monk. As with Marsalis playing Armstrong, stunning successes easily outweigh failures. (Marcus Roberts: *If I Could Be With You* Novus).

Warne Marsh's restlessly oblique lines. (Spike Robinson: *In Town* Hep).

RED RODNEY

Born Robert Chudnick in Philadelphia in 1927, Red Rodney's reputation took off when he joined Charlie Parker's quintet in 1949, having played with several big bands. Subsequent problems with drugs were finally put behind him in the Seventies, when he emerged, notably, as part of a two-trumpet team with Ira Sullivan. He then led his own quintet, to increasing international acclaim (helped by on-screen portrayal and off-screen playing in the film *Bird*). Rodney never lost the hard on-the-beat swing he had developed alongside Parker, while becoming a far better all-round trumpeter. He died in 1994. (Red Rodney: *Then As Now* Chesky).

SHORTY ROGERS

A stalwart of the bands of Herman and Kenton, Milton 'Shorty' Rogers then opted for the Los Angeles studios, becoming an early figurehead of West Coast jazz. Born in Massachusetts in 1924, he was an average (though recognisable) trumpet soloist, and his main impact was as a writer. Of his West Coast classics, his Giants albums used similar textures to those of Miles Davis's 'cool' nonet, but with a looser feel: his big-band album, *Cool And Crazy*, combined a relaxed beat with stratospheric section work from Maynard Ferguson, as heard previously on Kenton's 'Jolly Rogers'. He came back to full-time playing before his death in 1994. (Shorty Rogers: *Short Stops* RCA Bluebird).

ADRIAN ROLLINI

A highly gifted maverick, good enough to impress Coleman Hawkins, Adrian Rollini established the bass saxophone as a jazz instrument (though

Red Rodney transcended his bebop roots to become a considerable all-round trumpeter.

few apart from Britain's Harry Gold took it up), and he was also first to use a vibraphone. Born in New York in 1904, he made his reputation with the California Ramblers before freelance work in New York and, in 1927, a job in London, working at the Savoy and making an impact upon local musicians. He later returned to session work, then reverted to leading small groups, quartets or trios, on vibraphone, right up to his death in 1956. (Joe Venuti: *Violin Jazz* Yazoo).

WALLACE RONEY

Arriving on the scene at the same time as Wynton Marsalis, Wallace Roney (born Philadelphia, 1960) also worked with the Jazz Messengers, and went on to become one of the best trumpeters of his generation. For several years, he worked in Tony Williams's quintet, recording excellent solos with them. His other high-profile gigs have tended to be with bands looking at the past: he took the Miles Davis role in a revived quintet and actually played alongside Davis at Montreux. He was also part of singer Helen Merrill's Clifford Brown tribute album. (Wallace Roney: *Obsession* Muse).

LEON ROPPOLO

The New Orleans Rhythm Kings were one of the best bands of their time, formed in Chicago in 1921 by New Orleans exiles, including trombonist George Brunies, cornettist Paul Mares and the clarinet player Leon Roppolo. A superior and more relaxed ODJB, they were joined on a memorable session by Jelly Roll Morton, probably the first mixed-race jazz recording. Roppolo, born 1902, was an oddball: very gifted, he would play duets with the sound from telegraph wires. After a breakdown, he was put in an institution, where he led a band, and was rarely heard playing again before his death in 1943. (*New Orleans Rhythm Kings 1922-25* Milestone).

JIMMY ROWLES

Jimmy Rowles has made innumerable albums as an accompanist to Billy Holiday and others, so much so that he was pegged like Ellis Larkins as the perfect background pianist, especially for lady singers. But he is much more than this. His thistledown touch, precise timing and impish imagination make him one of the more beguiling pianists in post-war jazz. Born in Washington (1918), he spent the Fifties working in the Los Angeles television and recording studios. Since then, he has made more jazz albums, some of them on solo piano, though many still ask for his accompaniment. (Jimmy Rowles: *The Peacocks* Columbia).

GONZALO RUBALCABA

One of many exceptional musicians from Cuba (born Havana, 1963) pianist Gonzalo Rubalcaba studied at the conservatory and eventually formed his own group Proyecto, in which he often played keyboards. His career was boosted by Charlie Haden, who heard him in Cuba and appeared with at the Montreux festival of 1990. That performance was recorded (cited below) and revealed his authority in a jazz trio setting. Later albums confirm this while including other influences, not least that of his own country's music. (Gonzalo Rubalcaba: *Discovery* Blue Note).

ROSWELL RUDD

Born in 1935, Roswell Rudd played in a Dixieland band while a student at Yale. Becoming associated with experimental jazz from the 1960s, he pursued his involvement through the Jazz Composers Orchestra, the New York Art Quartet, Archie Shepp's band, the Primordial Quartet and Charlie Haden's Liberation Music Orchestra amongst others. He also worked with another ex-Dixielander, Steve Lacy, exploring Thelonious Monk's music. His early involvement maybe influenced the way in which he brought a broad approach, intimately connected to the technology of the trombone, into these avant-garde settings. (Carla Bley: *Dinner Music* Watt)

MATHIAS RUEGG

Among the glories of European jazz, one has to include the Vienna Art Orchestra. It was founded in 1977 by Mathias Ruegg, a Swiss pianist and composer (born Zurich, 1952), who collected musicians from Austria and elsewhere and, over the years, has put together a remarkable programme, much of it composed or arranged by Ruegg himself. Their music extends beyond the range encompassed by the traditional big band, but they also cover that kind of music and do so exceptionally well, as in their superb adaptations of Mingus and Ellington scores. The album chosen as representative includes both the arty material and the hard swing. (Vienna Art Orchestra: *Plays For Jean Cocteau* Amadeo).

JIMMY RUSHING

Jimmy Rushing, born in Oklahoma City in 1903, became one of the most famous big-band vocalists, being one of the constants when Walter Page's Blue Devils were taken over by Bennie Moten and then transformed into the Count Basie band. One way and another, he began to specialize in blues, which was not all that common among band singers outside the south-west, and made many great recordings, both with Basie and later, from the Fifties up to his death in 1972. A man whose bulk deserved

His many recordings with Count Basie established Jimmy Rushing as the big band's blues shouter.

GEORGE RUSSELL

Born in Cincinnati (1923), George Russell is one of the great theorists of jazz. His contribution to 'Cubana Be, Cubana Bop' for Dizzy Gillespie's bebop band (notably the introduction) announced a singular talent. Sidelined by illness for a while, he formulated his Lydian Chromatic Concept Of Tonal Organization. The practical result was to widen the choice of notes available to soloists, which led to improvising on modes and scales rather than chords, as popularised by Miles Davis. Unusually, Russell's bandleading career took off in Scandinavia during the Sixties, where he incorporated rock rhythms and wrote some major works. Since then, he has regularly put together touring bands. (George Russell: *The London Concert Label Bleu* (2 CDS)).

PEE WEE RUSSELL

Charles 'Pee Wee' Russell was a clarinettist with a highly eccentric style. In his solos of the Thirties and Forties, his clarinet grunts, shrieks, rasps and approaches the theme with a harmonic latitude unheard of at the time. Born in Missouri in 1906, Russell recorded early on with Coleman Hawkins and Henry Allen but was associated mainly with the white Chicagoans. A mainstay of Eddie Condon's groups, he sometimes worked with more modern groups in the Fifties and Sixties, as the pundits began to catch up with him: one was a pianoless quartet performing compositions by Coltrane, Monk and

the nickname of 'Mister Five By Five', he had a unique and instantly recognisable voice. (Jimmy Rushing: *Complete Vanguard Recordings Vanguard*).

DAVID SANBORN

The alto saxophonist David Sanborn has a strong, beautiful, expressive tone on his instrument. Its sound is obviously derived from the blues, which was his starting point. Born in Tampa in 1945, by his early teens he was already playing with bluesmen like Albert King. In 1967, he joined the Paul Butterfield Blues Band, then went on to play with Gil Evans, with whom he did some of his best work, and the Brecker Brothers, as well as with Stevie Wonder, David Bowie and Paul Simon. A player of great power, Sanborn is a performer who, like Johnny Hodges, is often at his best when presenting a tune. (David Sanborn: *Another Hand* Elektra Musician).

DAVID SANCHEZ

Originally from Puerto Rico (born 1968), David Sanchez has lived in the US since 1988. Along with pianist Danilo Perez, from Panama, he was encouraged by Dizzy Gillespie, with whom he recorded. At their best, his tenor saxophone solos sound rather like a contemporary Dexter Gordon. The mix of jazz with Latin rhythms in his music can be quite subtle – a two-way split with the percussion – while he also enjoys bouncing phrases against the drums like riffs erupting from one of the great mambo bands. (David Sanchez: *Sketches Of Dreams* Columbia).

PHAROAH SANDERS

Among the tenor saxophonists who emerged during the Sixties and were highly trained musician who has associated with free jazz, Farrell 'Pharoah' Sanders had especially close links with John Coltrane, and is also a considerable pianist. working in his group for a time and

Ornette Coleman. He died in 1969. (Pee Wee Russell & Coleman Hawkins: *Jazz Reunion* Candid).

Tenor sax player David Sanchez mixing jazz with Latin rhythms.

appearing on several albums. Born in Little Rock in 1940, his strong point has always been his declamatory tone – comparable to, though different from, the sound produced by his contemporary Gato Barbieri – and this has come to fore in recent years when, after a period out of the limelight – Sanders has become something of a hit with a younger audience. (Pharoah Sanders: *Tauhid* Impulse).

ARTURO SANDOVAL

Something of a wild man on the trumpet, Cuban Arturo Sandoval is a highly trained musician who has performed classical pieces in public and then formed his own group, with which he toured widely until defecting to the US in 1990. Influenced by Gillespie but with a different kind of technical bravura that goes with his bullring tone, he enjoys playing notes at tremendous speed or reproducing Miles Davis-type phrases two octaves up. (Arturo Sandoval: *Straight Ahead* Jazz House).

LOUIS SCLAVIS

One of the new wave of French musicians, Louis Sclavis was born in Lyon in 1953. An early member of the Workshop de Lyon, he has since

Born in Havana in 1949, he founded Irakere, with pianist Chucho Valdes,

A stint with Miles Davis in the Eighties helped raise the profile of guitarist John Scofield.

1927, he became part of the emerging bebop scene, and led his own group before starting a quintet with fellow tenor saxophonist Tubby Hayes. After opening his club in 1959, he continued with various groups of his own and was also part of wider European ventures such as the Kenny Clarke–Francy Boland big band. Having gone through several stylistic phases, he hit upon something of a cross between Hank Mobley and Zoot Sims that has served him extremely well. (Ronnie Scott: *Never Pat A Burning Dog Jazz House*).

BUD SHANK

A former Kenton sideman who settled in Los Angeles, Clifford 'Bud' Shank was born in Ohio in 1926 and had worked previously with Charlie Barnet's orchestra. Changing from tenor to alto saxophone, he was on several West Coast albums of the Fifties and appeared regularly with the Lighthouse All Stars, named after the club run by bassist Howard Rumsey at Hermosa Beach. Since the Seventies, he has emerged more regularly on the jazz scene, first with the LA4, on which his flute was well featured, and later with Shorty Rogers and as a single. (Bud Shank: *I Told You So* Candid).

quartet featuring Joe Lovano on saxophone. These blend bluesy funk with a kind of free jazz that often has similarities, especially on Scofield's themes, with what Ornette Coleman did in the Sixties. (John Scofield: *Time On My Hands* Blue Note).

SONNY SHARROCK

Identified early on with the Sixties avant garde as an associate of Sunny Murray and Don Cherry, Warren 'Sonny' Sharrock (born in New York, 1940) became nationally known through working with flautist Herbie Mann for several years, appearing on his album *Memphis Underground*. Sharrock's style, post-Jimi Hendrix, could involve plenty of feedback and

RONNIE SCOTT

Now better known for running one of the world's great jazz clubs, Ronnie Scott has lived the life of the British jazz musician. Born in London in

become familiar in the context of contemporary European jazz and improvised music, working for a time with Chris McGregor and recording with the top names. Among his recent groups are the Acoustic Quartet with violinist Dominique Pifarely and a clarinet trio that both improvises and plays works by Boulez and others. Sclavis is generally heard on clarinet, bass clarinet or soprano saxophone, and is a considerable virtuoso on them all. (Louis Sclavis: *Ellington On The Air* Ida).

JOHN SCOFIELD

The guitarist John Scofield, born in Ohio in 1951, gravitated to the best-known fusion leaders, replacing John Abercrombie in Billy Cobham's group and later spending time with Gary Burton and Dave Liebman, as well as running his own quartet. He achieved a major public breakthrough when he joined Miles Davis in 1982, winning deserved praise from many critics and subsequently making some well-publicised records with his own

noise, but never went over the top, as proved by his successful contributions to Mann's group. Before his death in 1994, his best-known gig was with Last Exit, and he was also among those linked to New York's avant garde club, the Knitting Factory. (Sonny Sharrock: *Guitar Enemy*).

CHARLIE SHAVERS

Not particularly well represented on record, Charlie Shavers, born in New York in 1917, was amongst the greatest of all swing trumpeters. Improvising long lines with a powerful sound, immense technical skill, fertile imagination and no little humour, he was reckoned by some to be even more gifted than his contemporary Roy Eldridge. A key figure in the popular John Kirby sextet, he then worked with Tommy Dorsey and led his own small groups, as well as backing Frank Sinatra. He was a vocalist, intermittently, and a talented composer as well. He died in 1971. (*Charlie Shavers Live Black And Blue*).

ARTIE SHAW

Artie Shaw was one of the more unusual bandleaders, repeatedly giving up the business to do other things. A perfectionist in everything, he made himself into a consummate saxophonist and, later, a clarinettist skilled enough to be compared with Benny Goodman. Born in New York in 1910, he had an remarkable ability to present a tune, so that such hits as 'Begin The Beguine' were his creations whether or not he formally wrote the arrangement. His bands were always intriguing, whether conventional or with violins attached. Shaw eventually became bored with it all, and, though occasionally conducting he has not played the clarinet in public since 1954. (*Artie Shaw: Begin The Beguine* RCA Bluebird).

WOODY SHAW

Born in North Carolina in 1944, Herman 'Woody' Shaw played on some of Eric Dolphy's last American albums, and spent a few years in Paris working with most of the notable expatriates. He also spent a couple of years with Horace Silver, co-led a group with drummer Louis Hayes and then had something of a hit with his album *The Moontrane*, featuring the tune of that name. In later years, before his death in 1989, he led his own quintet, often including Steve Turre, or appeared in all-star groups. Stylistically close to Freddie Hubbard, he developed into an original performer whose harmonic improvising influenced many younger trumpeters. (*Woody Shaw: Imagination* Muse).

GEORGE SHEARING

Leaving his native London in 1948 to settle in the U.S., George Shearing (born 1919) confounded precedent by becoming a big hit almost overnight: his quintet specialising in cool-toned unison lines played by vibes, guitar and piano produced a sound since immortalised by muzak systems. Like many blind pianists, he has a most comprehensive technique that, in

After an apprenticeship with the likes of Horace Silver, Woody Shaw made an impact on the style of trumpeters who came after him.

Work with Art Blakey, Miles Davis and Weather Report gave saxophonist/composer Wayne Shorter a pedigree second to none.

ANDY SHEPPARD

Born in Wiltshire in 1957, Andy Sheppard spent some years with the Coltrane-styled quartet Sphere, before going to Paris and playing with various French bands, among them the performance group Urban Sax. Back in the UK, he gained plenty of kudos after winning a televised jazz competition, since when his career has taken off. His own groups include an orthodox big band and smaller, more electric groups, and he has also worked with George Russell and Carla Bley. A brilliant saxophonist on both tenor and soprano, he has increasingly concentrated on writing, including work for films and television. (Andy Sheppard: *Rhythm Method* Blue Note).

WAYNE SHORTER

Praised highly by Stan Getz for his compositional skills, Wayne Shorter did write the best tunes played by two very important groups, while being no mean soloist. Born in New Jersey in 1933, he joined Art Blakey's Jazz Messengers in 1959, and ended up as musical director. In 1964, he left to do a similar job for Miles Davis. A hard-blowing tenor saxophonist, who bludgeoned seemingly shapeless phrases into solos of impeccable logic, his lines became more varied and sinewy, ultimately influencing the likes of Branford Marsalis. As co-leader of Weather Report, he began to concen-

upon especially in Europe. In recent years, his base has been in Europe, where he tours with fellow expatriates and shows off his attractively dark, Ben Websterish tone mainly on ballads and blues. (Archie Shepp: *Fire Music* Impulse).

ARCHIE SHEPP

Tenor saxophonist Archie Shepp, born in Florida (1937), appeared on an early Cecil Taylor recording, and soon became strongly identified with the radical free-jazz scene. Always handy

with a telling quote for punters and publicists, his most important contribution was programmatic, in that he would merge free-form blowing and recognisable tunes in the popular domain within a single unbroken performance, a tactic many seized

more recent years, has been heard to good advantage away from the quintet formula. He has written several quite popular jazz pieces, but the one the world knows is 'Lullaby Of Birdland'. (George Shearing: *That Shearing Sound* Telarc).

trate on soprano, on which he continues to produce an attractively keening sound. (Wayne Shorter: *Speak No Evil* Blue Note).

From 'Opus De Funk' to 'Sister Sadie', Horace Silver's tunes were identified with the Fifties, as were his witty piano solos.

HORACE SILVER

Horace Silver, born in Connecticut in 1928, was pianist in the first Jazz Messengers, where, compulsively energetic when backing a soloist, he would supplement the barrage emanating from Art Blakey's drums. He also wrote such Hard Bop classics as 'The Preacher' and 'Doodlin'', and

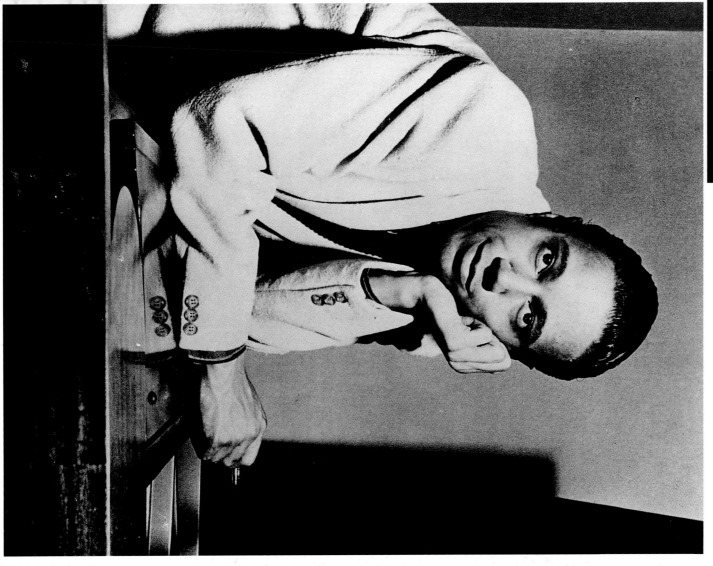

many more after forming his own quintet in 1956. Hitting the keys with a percussive touch, quoting merrily from unlikely songs and churning out accents with either hand in a manner that had some impact upon Cecil Taylor, he could also play superb blues. Since the mid-Sixties, he has simmered down and increasingly put words to his songs, enjoying something of a revival recently with his mini brass band. (Horace Silver: *Blowin' The Blues Away* Blue Note).

ZOOT SIMS

John Haley Sims, known as Zoot and born in 1925, was one of the flood of predominantly white tenor saxophonists arriving in the Forties who took Lester Young as their point of departure. He was a member of the Woody Herman saxophone section from 1947 to 1949, appearing on the famous recording of 'Four Brothers'. A quite unforced and naturally swinging style and an attractively light tone became his trademarks, best appreciated perhaps in the groups co-led with another 'ex-Brother' Al Cohn (in the tradition of two-tenor contests, Cohn had the forceful sound while Sims seemed to float). Before his death in 1985 he was touring mainly as a single. (Zoot Sims: *Suddenly It's Spring* Pablo).

ALAN SKIDMORE

Alan Skidmore's father, Jimmy Skidmore, is an established tenor saxophonist in his own right, and the two have done gigs together. Born in London in 1942, Alan worked with Alexis Korner's Blues Incorporated and later formed his own quintet with Kenny Wheeler on trumpet. In the Seventies, he worked for all the top British bands and was part of the trio SOS with John Surman and Mike Osborne – he was also part of SOH (with drummer Tony Oxley and bassist Ali Haurand). Skidmore's compulsive style, though based on Coltrane's, sounds like that of no other disciple, a reason why his various Coltrane tributes are so effective. (Alan Skidmore: *Tribute To Trane* Miles Music).

BESSIE SMITH

Blues and jazz came together commercially in the 1920s, when the

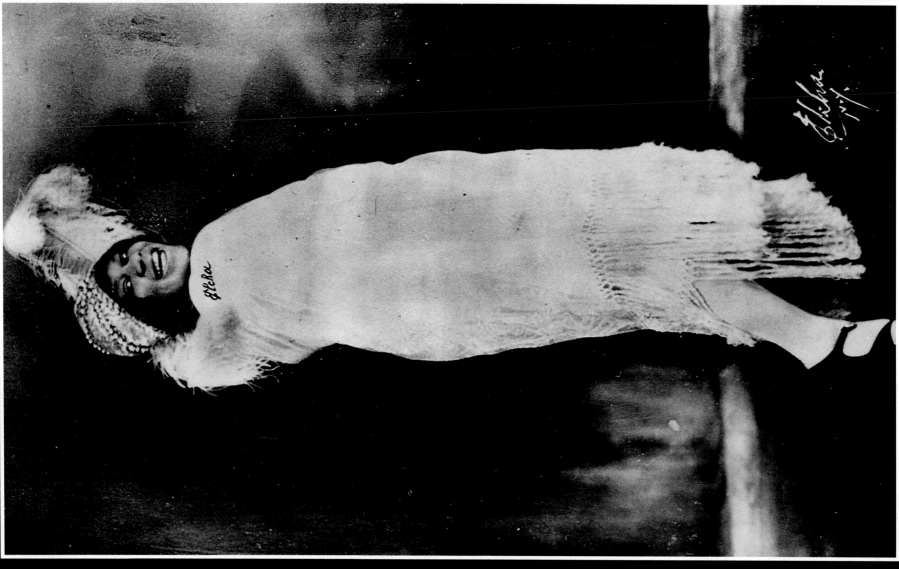

great classic blues singers often featured top jazz musicians in their recording groups. Arguably the greatest, Bessie Smith had a magnificent voice which was unusually rich and dark, and she could really bend a note. Born in Chattanooga, Tennessee, in 1895, she had her first big hit with 'Down Hearted Blues' and subsequently made impressive records with such accompanists as Louis Armstrong, James P. Johnson and cornettist Joe Smith. Her music then went out of fashion and, before she could make a comeback, she was killed in a car accident outside Clarksdale, Mississippi, in 1937. Bessie Smith: *The Complete Recordings* Columbia).

JABBO SMITH

Another musician with a career outside the norm, Cladys 'Jabbo' Smith (born Georgia, 1908) was once regarded as a rival to Louis Armstrong. He had plenty of speed and technique, and his solos, 'Decatur Street Tutti' among them, have a futuristic quality that looks forward to Dizzy Gillespie in the Forties: an undeveloped tone, but a corrosive attack using odd intervals and strange melodic ideas. His scat singing was likewise an extension of his playing. A life of excess caught up with him but, virtually unheard after 1930, he returned forty years later and, though nothing like the old trumpeter, did very well until his death in 1991. (Jabbo Smith *1929-38* Classics).

JIMMY SMITH

Pennsylvania-born in 1925, Jimmy Smith brought the Hammond organ to town when he blew into New York in

The talented and popular blues singer of the classic period, Bessie Smith's life had a tragic ending.

1956, after first establishing a reputation in Philadelphia. With a powerful blues-based style, providing his own bass lines via the foot-pedals, crowding in chords and long explosive lines with his hands, he re-wrote the book for the instrument, banishing its novelty aspects and establishing it as a mainstream instrument. Signed to Blue Note, he produced a torrent of records, often in an extended jam-session format, before moving on to bigger labels, to a degree leaving his best work behind. An incomparable performer, whose impact on popular culture generally cannot be over-estimated. (Jimmy Smith: *The Sermon* Blue Note).

MARVIN 'SMITTY' SMITH

Marvin Smith's track record puts him among the best all-round drummers on the current scene. Born in Illinois in 1961, he studied at the Berklee College and has since played with just about everybody. He was part of Dave Holland's quintet when Steve Coleman was there, and also played on some M-Base sessions. In between, he has been picked to appear on many albums, by Art Farmer, David Murray, Archie Shepp and South African pianist Bheki Mseleku, among others. (Dave Holland: *Seeds Of Time* ECM).

STUFF SMITH

Hezekiah 'Stuff' Smith pioneered creative amplification. If you bow across three strings on a violin, you produce a chord; if you bend them through an amplifier, you get the sort of dissonance at full throttle that can move mountains. Born in Ohio in 1909, Smith's method was to discard the violin's lyrical affiliations and turn it into a glorious swing machine, grinding out chords and bearing down hard on the beat, but leaving gaps for the rhythm to sweep through. In the Thirties, he partnered Jonah Jones in a popular small group. In the years before his death in 1967 he regularly toured the circuit. (*Stuff Smith With Dizzy Gillespie and Oscar Peterson* Verve).

TOMMY SMITH

Tommy Smith, born in England in 1967 but brought up in Edinburgh, won a much-publicised scholarship to Berklee College, where he met Gary Burton and worked for a time in his quartet. From his base in Scotland, he has since put together several groups and has greatly extended his composing activities. As a tenor saxophonist, he chopped his style around from an early Coltrane influence, but his recent playing has been better balanced, perhaps a reflection of his writing skills. (Tommy Smith: *Misty Morning And No Time* Linn).

WILLIE 'THE LION' SMITH

A larger-than-life character, Willie 'The Lion' was born in New York in 1897 and became one of the leading members among the so-called 'stride' pianists who flourished in Harlem in the early years of the century. The

The legendary Willie 'The Lion' Smith wrote excellent post-ragtime pieces.

WILLIE SMITH

Regarded as one of the finest alto saxophonists during the Thirties, Willie Smith spent most of his career in big bands, apart from studio work and a spell with Jazz At The Philharmonic. Born in 1910, he joined the Jimmy Lunceford band in 1934, and was a reason why its ensemble work, especially that of the saxophone section he led, has rarely been equalled. After the war, he joined Harry James and remained, apart from a year or two with Duke Ellington, almost up to his death in 1967. His characteristic sound was among the most withering ever produced from an alto. (Willie Smith: *Snooty Fruity* Columbia).

music they played was ragtime, or at least their own derivative of ragtime, while part of the appeal lay in personality – something that Smith had plenty of. He was in fact a pretty good pianist, who also wrote attractively impressionistic tunes, and kept working up to his death in 1973. His nickname came, he said, from his prowess at the front during World War 1. (*Willie The Lion Smith And His Cubs* Timeless).

MARTIAL SOLAL

Still largely unrecognised by the English-speaking jazz world, Martial Solal remains one of the great virtuosi. Born in Algiers in 1927 and arriving in Paris in 1950, he worked with both local musicians and visiting Americans, developing a reputation and improving his already exceptional technique, to the point where his ideas translate effortlessly into notes, governed by an overall formal concept and often imbued with sparkling Gallic wit. Much of his best work has been done in solo, duo or trio formats, However, his compositional and orchestrating skills have led to some remarkable original big-band scores.

(Martial Solal: *Improvise Pour France Musique* JMS).

LEW SOLOFF

After a start with several big bands, Lew Soloff (born New York, 1944) became the trumpet player in the very popular jazz-rock group Blood Sweat And Tears, appearing at festivals and on many of their records. Since then, he has been a key member of several outstanding ensembles, including bands led by Gil Evans and Carla Bley.

He has recently been featured soloist in a revival of the Miles Davis-Gil Evans scores. A splendid technician with a searing tone, he can handle any music, and is consequently much in demand. (Lew Soloff: 'Little Wing' Bellaphon).

EDDIE SOUTH

Born in Missouri in 1904, Eddie South was classically trained on the violin, both in Chicago and in Europe, where he played in the late Twenties.

Muggsy Spanier's sensitive trumpet playing graced many recordings.

Back in the US, he failed to prosper because, it was said, the public did not expect such delicate violin music from a black musician. He returned to Europe until war broke out and recorded some great sides with Django Reinhardt and Stephane Grappelli (South's tone was the more classical). After the war, he worked regularly (including radio and television appearances), though his jazz profile remained low in the period up to his death in 1962. (Eddie South 1923-37 Classics).

MUGGSY SPANIER

A Chicagoan, born 1906, Francis "Muggsy" Spanier was atypical in that he was not part of the Condon set and idolised mainly black musicians, including Louis Armstrong and Tommy Ladnier. He played in the novelty band of clarinettist Ted Lewis for several years and then, after time off for illness, launched his Ragtime Band which, though too early to be part of the New Orleans revival, lasted long enough to record some excellent music. Post-revival, he found regular work in a variety of bands up to his death in 1967. Neither a powerful trumpeter nor a great technician, he played with good time and great feeling. (Muggsy Spanier: *The Ragtime Band Sessions* RCA Bluebird).

JESS STACY

If the average fan remembers Jess Stacy, it's probably for being Benny Goodman's pianist during the King Of Swing days. Born in Missouri in 1904, he was greatly admired for clear-thinking unfussy solos, and for finding the choicest notes to lift jazz ensembles, large and small. He also worked with assorted Bob Crosby bands but, after the war, was reduced to jobs in obscure bars, until a welcome revival in the years before his death in 1994. The recommended album includes that extraordinary unrehearsed extract from Goodman's 1938 Carnegie Hall concert when, it now almost seems, Gene Krupa met Bill Evans. (Jess Stacy: *Ec-Stacy* ASV).

JOHN STEVENS

A catalyst of British jazz, whose energetic drive got so much started, John Stevens was a prime mover on the local freejazz scene. Born in London in 1940, he enjoyed all kinds of jazz but, in the Sixties, became interested in what Ornette Coleman and others were doing. His after-hours club in a tiny West End theatre became the centre of London's avant garde. As a drummer, hard-swinging in a jazz context, Stevens put together all manner of groups, from free-form to fusion. At the time of his death in 1994, he was heavily involved in music education (he wrote a superb manual for use with pupils of mixed ability). (John Stevens: *Re-touch and Quartet* Konnex).

BOB STEWART

Along with Howard Johnson, Bob Stewart has been instrumental in getting the tuba into the front line of jazz. Born in South Dakota in 1945, he switched from trumpet in college and came to New York in the late Sixties, where he found a demand for tuba ensembles. He worked later in the bands of Gil Evans and Carla Bley, and has been part of many groups (including Lester Bowie's Brass Fantasy) and revealing himself as a skilled writer on jazz. He has also led his First Line Band, reflecting some of funk-tuba sounds recently introduced by such groups as the Dirty Dozen. (Christof Lauer: *Bluebells* CMP).

REX STEWART

Every swing trumpeter felt Louis Armstrong's shadow over their shoulders; although Stewart (1907-1967) played cornet, he felt it when he replaced Armstrong with Fletcher Henderson at the age of nineteen. His greatest work was done with Duke Ellington (1934-45), where his incisive muted sound, half-valve effects and powerful open tone were fully accommodated within that orchestra. With Ellington, Stewart co-composed his feature, 'Boy Meets Horn', a simultaneously light-hearted and majestic display of his artistry. With a small band, he made a lengthy European tour (1947-51), before semi-retiring and revealing himself as a skilled writer on jazz. (Rex Stewart And The Ellingtonians Original Jazz Classics).

Playing cornet in Duke Ellington's band, Rex Stewart squeezed notes out by half-depressing the valves.

SLAM STEWART

One of the less-honoured pioneers of jazz, Leroy 'Slam' Stewart started something when he became the first bass player to take a solo that involved simultaneous bowing and humming. Though he usually did it with comic intent, especially when giving a Slim And Slam performance, it took plenty of skill. Apart from those who followed, including Major Holley and the London-based (but Jamaica-born) Coleridge Goode, many bassists have acknowledged his influence on their bowing technique. Born in New Jersey in 1914, Stewart was good enough to

those devoted to solo piano. (Ralph Sutton: *Maybeck Recital* Concord).

STEVE SWALLOW

A leading bass player, who has developed a most distinctive voice on bass guitar, Steve Swallow (born 1940) worked in many contrasting settings in the Sixties, including the Jimmy Giuffre trio and the quartets of Art Farmer and Stan Getz. In Gary Burton's quartet, to fit the rock and country themes, he first began to use the electric bass, on which his gentle, singing sound is far removed from that which is often produced. Apart from reunions with Burton, he has since been most often associated with the various bands led by Carla Bley. Many of his tunes have been recorded by others, and he occasionally leads an album of his own. (Steve Swallow: *Swallow* Watt).

LEW TABACKIN

Born in Philadelphia in 1940, Lew Tabackin has been linked to big bands, from Thad Jones-Mel Lewis to the band led by his wife Toshiko Akiyoshi. Having studied flute at the conservatory, he ranks with anybody on that instrument, though he is probably more associated with the tenor saxophone, which he plays in a style reminiscent in part of the Sonny Rollins who made such records as *Blue Seven* (before his tone grew harder), though he has added plenty of his own. (Lew Tabackin: *What A Little Moonlight Can Do* Concord).

HORACE TAPSCOTT

Hardly an underground figure, Horace Tapscott's commitment to working in his Los Angeles community has restricted his reputation mainly to those who have heard enough about him to buy his records (mostly issued on his own label). Born in Texas in 1934, he played trombone in several West Coast groups before a car accident forced him to

DeJohnette: *The Amazing Adventures of Simon Simon* ECM).

RALPH SUTTON

A founder-member of the World's Greatest Jazz Band along with Billy Butterfield, Bob Wilber, trumpeter Yank Lawson and bassist Bob Haggart, Ralph Sutton has for over 40 years been a leading exponent of ragtime and stride piano. Born in Missouri in 1922, he had worked with New Orleans clarinettist Albert Nicholas and trumpeter Bob Scobey before the WGJB brought his name to a wider public. Much admired for his impeccable playing, he has toured widely and appeared on many excellent small-band records, as well as on

JOHN SURMAN

One of the giants of contemporary European jazz, John Surman has many firsts to his credit. Born in Devon in 1944, he came to prominence with Mike Westbrook's band, in which he played mainly baritone. His control of the instrument's high register was unprecedented anywhere at the time. With the saxophone trio SOS (Surman, Alan Skidmore, Mike Osborne), he was one of the first to use sequencing techniques to set up riffs electronically, while his Westering Home album of 1972 used folk themes in ways that have since become commonplace. Playing baritone, soprano or bass clarinet, he continues to thrive in many settings. (John Surman and Jack

Britain's John Surman, a virtuoso of the baritone saxophone.

play with Art Tatum, and had a more serious but equally productive career before his death in 1987. (Slam Stewart: *Two Big Mice* Black And Blue).

SONNY STITT

Sonny Stitt heard Charlie Parker early on, and became the first alto saxophonist after Bird to seem really at ease playing bebop. Switching to tenor saxophone to avoid obvious comparisons, it became probably his stronger horn. Born in Boston in 1924, he had drug problems in the Forties and drink problems thereafter, but he rarely sounded less than totally committed on stage. Apart from a two-tenor group co-led with Gene Ammons, and a spell in the Sixties with Miles Davis, he generally worked as a single, or in all-star packages where his strong swing and great technique ensured that he was never outclassed. He died in 1982. (Sonny Stitt/ Bud Powell/ J.J. Johnson Prestige).

SUN RA

Born in Alabama, Sun Ra (1914-1993) led a big band for over thirty years that stayed remarkably independent of the 'music business'. His compositions formed the band's library, and were largely experimental – in particular, his *Heliocentric World* albums for ESP affected the vocabulary of free-form bands the world over. From the mid-1980s, the substance of his music was to an extent overtaken by superficial style, as greater popularity encouraged longer tours relying more on the sci-fi trappings that accompanied his appearances. Nevertheless, Ra's stature as an orchestra leader needs to be evaluated alongside such recognised giants as Basie or Ellington. (Sun Ra and the Arkestra: *Outer Spaceways Incorporated* Black Lion).

concentrate on piano. There are obvious parallels with other composer-pianists such as Monk, Herbie Nichols and even Sun Ra, but Tapscott's music is more programmatic. (Horace Tapscott: *The Dark Tree Vols 1 and 2* hatART (2 separate CDs)).

BUDDY TATE

The epitome of the Texas tenor, George 'Buddy' Tate has the big furry sound and affinity for the blues that seem to come with the territory. Born in 1913, he worked in many of the best Southwest bands before joining Basie in 1939, replacing fellow Texan Herschel Evans who had just died. In the Fifties, Tate became renowned for his long stint leading the band at New York's Celebrity Club. By the time the job folded, his kind of jazz was in vogue so that, before illness caused him to stop, he was a very popular tourist on the European scene. (Buddy Tate: *Swinging Like Tate* London).

Buddy Tate epitomised the swing style, taking the big-toned tenor role in the old Basie band and later leading his own group.

ARTHUR TAYLOR

A ubiquitous session drummer of the Fifties, Arthur Taylor was born in New York in 1929 and was part of Bud Powell's trio in 1953. Very much in the Art Blakey mould, he was less domineering and therefore ideal to have on hand for the various hard bop groups that recorded for Blue Note and Prestige. Working in Europe during the Sixties, he started to interview his colleagues, and later published the results as *Notes And Tones*. Back in the US, he eventually revived the group-name Taylor's Wailers for an excellent quintet that was working at the time of his death in 1995. (Arthur Taylor: *Wailin' At The Vanguard* Verve).

BILLY TAYLOR

Reputation without fame could be Billy Taylor's motto. Born in North Carolina in 1921, he was member of an early Dizzy Gillespie group and is classed among bebop pioneers even though he otherwise played mostly with swing stars. Since then, he has chosen the academic life. Active in musical education and the author of books on jazz piano, he tends to get the prestige gigs that don't make headlines. His piano style is a mixture of bebop lines and the even phrasing more suited to less intense forms of music. In recent years, he has composed and performed music for several projects. (Billy Taylor: *Homage* GRP).

CECIL TAYLOR

One could probably call pianist Cecil Taylor a perennial leader of the avant-garde. He was born in New York in 1929, and, from his first record in 1956, he has never deviated from a harmonically atonal, rhythmically percussive world which seems to put the most abstract European music in a context of free rhythms. With both hands flying over the keys, Taylor is utterly amazing to watch. Understandably, he has had few regular partners; apart from bassists and drummers, the most prominent was the late saxophonist Jimmy Lyons. Recently, Taylor has been giving unaccompanied recitals which make more use of light and shade and are, consequently, easier to hear and enjoy. (Cecil Taylor: *For Olim* Soul Note).

JOHN TAYLOR

Born in Manchester in 1942, John Taylor worked with most of the up-coming British musicians of the Sixties, including John Surman, with whom he still plays occasionally. One of many pianists to be influenced by Bill Evans, he has since displayed his own distinct

Jack Teagarden, the top trombonist from Texas.

brand of lyricism in his own groups and a variety of other settings. Perhaps the most familiar over a period has been the trio Azimuth, with Norma Winstone and Kenny Wheeler, and he has also worked with many musicians from the ECM stable, including Jan Garbarek and Miroslav Vitous. (*Azimuth: How It Was Then..Never Again* ECM).

JACK TEAGARDEN

The renowned 'Big T' (1905-1964) came from Texas, and did his best early work in small groups away from his steady jobs with, first, Ben Pollack, then Paul Whiteman's orchestra. With a trombone style that remained largely inimitable, derived from the blues but utilising a complex, refined technique, Jack Teagarden led his own band (1939-46) before joining the Louis Armstrong All-Stars, where his instrumental (and vocal) talents found a congenial haven. Fronting small groups from 1951 until his death, Teagarden was legendary as much for his lifestyle as for his unique abilities. (Jack Teagarden: *That's A Serious Thing* RCA Bluebird).

JACKY TERRASSON

Latest in the line of outstanding French pianists, Jacky Terrasson was actually born in Berlin, in 1966, to a French father and an American mother. He is classically trained, but he became interested in jazz via his mother's records and was soon making his mark. At Berklee College in Boston, he studied for a year, before dropping out to take a gig in Chicago, which lasted nearly a year and broke him in professionally. He has since left France for New York, working for a time with Taylor's Wailers, and then forming a trio, which has made two excellent albums for Blue Note. (Jacky Terrasson: *Reach* Blue Note).

CLARK TERRY

In his suite 'A Drum Is A Woman', Duke Ellington cast the trumpeter Clark Terry, (born in St. Louis in 1920, as the spirit of bebop, but in many ways he belongs in the earlier world of swing. Very fluent on both trumpet and flugelhorn (he has been known to hold one in each hand and play duets), he was a natural to take on Rex Stewart's half-valve effects, notably when Ellington cast him as Puck in his Shakespearean suite. One of the first black musicians to work in TV bands, he has co-led a quintet with the trombonist Bob Brookmeyer, and occasionally puts a big band together. (Clark Terry: Color Changes Candid).

TOOTS THIELEMANS

Very much on his own as a jazzman, Jean 'Toots' Thielemans was born in Brussels, in 1922, and started on accordion, learning the harmonica in his teens and eventually taking up guitar on discovering Django Reinhardt. He played in the US during the Forties and emigrated there a few years later, shortly after touring Europe with Benny Goodman. Since then, he has always had the studios to fall back on, but is deservedly respected throughout the jazz world, especially for his harmonica playing (plus whistle). His tune 'Bluesette' became very popular, not least as a jazz standard. (Toots Thielemans: Do Not Leave Me Stash).

GARY THOMAS

Although involved with everything from playing standards to incorporating hip hop rhythms to leading a group featuring the Hammond organ, Gary Thomas has avoided becoming over-identified with any one approach. Born in Maryland in 1961, he doubles on flute and tenor saxophone and has had spells with Miles Davis and, more successfully, with Jack DeJohnette's Special Edition. His own bands always challenge, without conforming over-much to what is supposed to be challenging. On tenor, his hard, burnished sound often reveals unsuspected warmth. (Gary Thomas: Seventh Quadrant Enja).

BARBARA THOMPSON

Born in Oxford in 1944, Barbara Thompson studied at the Royal College of Music and was a member of the New Jazz Orchestra, a kind of rehearsal band for British jazz musicians in the Sixties. She plays all the saxes and flute, and has led her own groups, notably her long-standing fusion quintet Paraphernalia (featuring her husband, noted drummer Jon Hiseman), worked with musicians throughout Europe and written special works that show a considerable flair for detail, most recently recording, with the Medici String Quartet, her settings of Kurt Weill songs. (Paraphernalia: Everlasting Flame VeraBra).

DANNY THOMPSON

Known as an all-rounder, very popular on the folk circuit and with a background in British R&B, Danny Thompson is a powerful bassist whose aggressive lines recall those of Charles Mingus. Born in Devon in 1939, he played in various groups throughout the Sixties, switching between the modern jazz clubs and gigs with Alexis Korner's Blues Incorporated. More often part of the folk scene since the success of Pentangle, he later formed a group – splendidly titled Whatever – that cocked a snook at categories and came up with a brilliant fusion of jazz and folk. (Danny Thompson: Whatever Hannibal).

KEITH TIPPETT

Born in Bristol in 1947, Keith Tippett made an impact on the London scene with his sextet in the late Sixties. Soon, he branched out into such projects as his fifty-piece band Centipede, that included elements of

LUCKY THOMPSON

A great musician who seemed to find it hard to come to terms with the music business, Eli 'Lucky' Thompson never really found a niche. Born in Detroit in 1924, he soon developed his own style on tenor saxophone, rich-toned in the Hawkins-Byas tradition but put over with a uniquely smooth delivery and showing a level of harmonic awareness that made him feel at home among boppers – probably his best-known recorded solo was on Miles Davis's "Walkin". He spent several years in Paris from the late Fifties, but since then little has been heard of him. (Lucky Thompson: Tricotism Impulse).

HENRY THREADGILL

Henry Threadgill, a Chicagoan (born 1944), can boast a diverse musical history. Playing mostly alto, and composing profusely, he became known through the avant-garde Association For The Advancement Of Creative Musicians, then with Muhal Richard Abrams' Experimental Band and, later, with the co-operative Air. However, his experience also includes playing in a marching band whilst at school and in a rock group during Army service, plus hard-bop and gospel music. His most recent band, Very, Very Circus, manages to integrate something of the anarchy of Ornette Coleman's Prime Time into the retrospective certainties of New Orleans jazz, thus reconciling some of the disparate strands of a rich musical heritage. (Very Very Circus: Spirit Of Nuff...Nuff Black Saint).

A typical shot of Stan Tracey, extracting colour from the piano keys.

free jazz and rock, and much of the work under his own name has tended to use few pre-set structures. As a pianist, he has emerged from an excessively minimalist phase and now gives compulsive solo recitals as well as organising his own groups such as the quartet Mujician. He recently collaborated with musicians from (ex-Soviet) Georgia. (Keith Tippett: *The Dartington Concert Editions* EG).

CAL TJADER

Now best remembered as a pioneer of Latin jazz, Cal Tjader was born in St. Louis in 1925 and began as a drummer, working with the various Dave Brubeck groups while studying in San Francisco. He started playing the vibraphone and joined George Shearing at a time when the pianist was blending the vibes-piano unisons with Latin percussion. Tjader soon formed his own group, which had several hits and featured, at one time or another, Mongo Santamaria, Willie Bobo and Poncho Sanchez. With a renewed interest in Latin-jazz fusions, Tjader remained popular up to his death in 1982. (Cal Tjader: *Monterey Concerts* Prestige).

JEAN TOUSSAINT

Jean Toussaint set a precedent by leaving the American jazz scene and moving to the UK, something that was impossible during the inter-union wrangles of the past, and hardly common since – especially compared to what happens in parts of the European mainland. Born in the Virgin Islands in 1960, he later spent four years with the Jazz Messengers, playing tenor and soprano saxophones and, in time-honoured fashion, ending up as Blakey's musical director. Since taking a teaching job at London's Guildhall,

he has been a significant figure on the scene, not least for the way his own music increasingly reflects what his colleagues are doing. (Jean Toussaint: *What Goes Around World* Circuit).

Woody Herman, Charlie Ventura and Muggsy Spanier during the years 1936 to 1946 but, despite many awards, he remained a frustrated man. He died following a fall in 1948. (Charlie Ventura/Bill Harris Quintet: *Live At The Three Deuces* Jazz Band).

DAVE TOUGH

Although his career was relatively brief and frequently interrupted by illness, Dave Tough nevertheless remained the 'drummer's drummer', respected by both modernists and traditionalists alike. Born near Chicago in 1907, he first became recognised for his work with the Chicago school of the 1920s. Deriving his style from New Orleans drummers, particularly Baby Dodds, he adapted it to big and small bands of whatever genre. He worked with Tommy Dorsey, Benny Goodman,

RALPH TOWNER

Born in Washington in 1940, Ralph Towner played jazz on trumpet while studying composition and classical guitar. He worked with Gary Burton and with Winter Consort, leaving the Consort along with Collin Walcott, Paul McCandless and Glen Moore, who then started Oregon. This became one of the most influential and popular groups of the Seventies, deriving much inspiration from folk material and incorporating classical devices.

Towner's compositions create attractively pastoral moods and, along with the earlier Charlie Byrd and his contemporary Egberto Gismonti, he has moved the guitar away from the usual jazz connotations. (Oregon: *Always, Never and Forever* VeraBra).

STAN TRACEY

Stan Tracey's early career followed the familiar pattern of big bands, while there was jazz to be featured, followed by smaller groups in jazz clubs. Born in London in 1926, he was the house pianist at Ronnie Scott's club for several years, simultaneously running the quartet that recorded his classic *Under Milk Wood* suite. After dabbling with free improvising, he has led groups of all sizes featuring his tunes and arrangements,

whose jagged edges are wholly distinctive, though often idiomatically related to those of his favourites, Ellington and Monk. Likewise his piano solos. His son Clark, an excellent drummer and composer, also runs groups of his own. (Stan Tracey: *Portraits Plus* Blue Note).

ALPHONSO TRENT

Of the territory big bands from the South West that missed out on national fame, pianist Alphonso Trent's was as good as any. Stuff Smith and Sy Oliver passed through the ranks, while among its star soloists, trumpeter Peanuts Holland later built quite a reputation; even better was Snub Mosley, a trombonist in the Higginbotham class who also invented the slide saxophone. Trent, who was born in Arkansas in 1905 (died 1959), worked in a leading Dallas hotel from which he broadcast weekly. The band's masterpiece, 'Clementine'. No records currently available.

LENNIE TRISTANO

Born in Chicago in 1919, and blind from birth, Lennie Tristano claimed he could play anything of Art Tatum's at the piano, and he undoubtedly had a fine technique. By the late-Forties, he was performing his own interpretation of bebop: very long, harmonically advanced lines performed with an even touch. These characteristics he implanted in his pupils, of which the most famous are Lee Konitz and Warne Marsh. Capable of such moving solos as his 'Requiem' for Parker, he could also sound overclinical. His enormous influence on jazz piano comes from being filtered through Bill Evans, who replaced intensity with lyricism. Tristano died in 1978. (Lennie Tristano/*The New Tristano* Rhino). (Lennie Tristano Rhino/Atlantic).

BRUCE TURNER

A legend of postwar British jazz, Bruce Turner (born Yorkshire, 1922) spent the early part of his career playing traditional clarinet with trumpeter Freddie Randall, then joining the more eclectic Humphrey Lyttelton. In the meantime, he had studied with Lee Konitz and Lennie Tristano: as a result, he could play alto saxophone in a style quite close to Konitz's, while sounding more like Hodges on most gigs. He later formed his Jump Band, essentially Hodges-based but taking in other areas. Before his death in 1993, he had rejoined Lyttelton, while occasionally performing in bebop and other contexts. (Humphrey Lyttelton: *Movin' And Groovin'* Black Lion).

JOE TURNER

The uncrowned king of blues shouters, 'Big' Joe Turner (born 1911) was a singing barman in his native Kansas City when he struck up the partnership with pianist Pete Johnson that produced 'Roll 'Em Pete'. Turner made many excellent records in early R&B vein, followed by hit numbers like 'Shake, Rattle and Roll'. In demand almost up to his death in 1985, his irresistibly declamatory style might seem unsubtle, but the timing was great and he never wasted an inflection. Many white rock 'n' rollers did well out of songs he sang originally, but Turner, a genial giant, is unlikely to have lost much sleep over that. (Joe Turner: *Boss Of The Blues* Atlantic).

STEVE TURRE

As players of the trombone once again draw on its potential for exotic effects, few deploy mutes and slide more vividly than Steve Turre. Born in Omaha in 1948, he has worked with the Jazz Messengers and also in Woody Shaw's group. In recent years, he has organised trombone groups somewhat on the lines of Lester Bowie's Brass Fantasy in which, as well as their trombones, the brass double on sea shells (a favourite sound of Turre's) the way members of a saxophone section cover every reed instrument. The album below includes Herbie Hancock, Pharoah Sanders and trumpeter Jon Faddis as guests, and has conches cooing in the background. (Steve Turre: *Rhythm Within* Antilles).

STANLEY TURRENTINE

Born in Pittsburgh in 1934, Stanley Turrentine first worked with a number of rhythm-and-blues bands, including that of Ray Charles. Clearly, this genre influenced his tenor-saxophone style, and from 1965 he moved steadily into popular formats and a wider market, where he was notably successful. Yet he was also capable of extended improvisation in a convincing post-bop manner. His most interesting work derives from when he joined Max Roach, along with trumpeter-brother Tommy, in 1960, and in the recordings after 1961 when he left that group to work as a leader. (Stanley Turrentine: *Up At Minton's* Blue Note).

McCOY TYNER

McCoy Tyner, born in Philadelphia in 1938, played piano in the classic John Coltrane Quartet of the Sixties. Sandwiched between Coltrane and the polyrhythms of drummer Elvin Jones, his clipped yet bouncy right-hand lines, over a plunging left hand, were strong enough to hold their own. After leaving Coltrane, he formed several groups — from trios to big bands — that have toured regularly. As a leader, his most obvious antecedent is Horace Silver, notably in his liking for pieces with a Latin American flavour. His piano style has a few emulators but, untouched by Bill Evans and never adapted to electric keyboards, it is otherwise unique. (McCoy Tyner: *The Turning Point* Birdology).

JAMES 'BLOOD' ULMER

After a period working with organ trios, guitarist James 'Blood' Ulmer (born South Carolina, 1942) came on to the New York jazz scene, where he met Ornette Coleman, studying with him and eventually joining his group. He has since led groups of his own, originally including horns, but more recently working with trios that also feature his singing. Ulmer was among

Pianist McCoy Tyner had a successful career after leaving John Coltrane's quartet.

by wrapping her beautiful tones around it. Her somewhat baroque approach, a tendency to overdo slurs and vibrato, can now be seen as, at worst, a tiny blip on a remarkable career. She died in 1990. (Sarah Vaughan: *Swingin' Easy* Emarcy).

CHARLIE VENTURA

A tenor saxophonist and bandleader, Charlie Ventura made his reputation with Gene Krupa and then, briefly but memorably, led a group whose policy was 'Bop For The People'. Born in Philadelphia in 1916, Ventura came stylistically from Hawkins and tended to overplay in front of large audiences. His own groups, though, included excellent musicians, notably the succession of trombonists that ended with Bennie Green, plus the unique husband-and-wife vocal pairing of pianist Roy Kral and Jackie Cain, whose light-hearted, bop-tinged versions of numbers like 'I'm Forever Blowing Bubbles' still exude more than period charm. Ventura continued working, on and off, up to his death in 1992. (*Gene Norman Presents A Charlie Ventura Concert* MCA).

JOE VENUTI

One of the first jazz violinists, Giuseppe Venuti was born (1903) into an immigrant Italian family, and grew up in Philadelphia. In the mid Twenties, he had a musical partnership with guitarist Eddie Lang, and played with a number of bands, including Paul Whiteman's, where he was a colleague of Bix Beiderbecke and Bing Crosby. He recorded splendid pieces of chamber jazz with Lang, from duets to various combinations of the leading white musicians of the day. Out of the limelight for many years, he eventually joined the touring circuit, on which his combination of lyrical tenderness and ferocious swing was often admired. He died in 1978. (*Joe Venuti and Eddie Lang Volume One* JSP).

heritage. (Andy Sheppard, Steve Lodder, Nana Vasconcelos: *Inclassificable* Label Bleu).

SARAH VAUGHAN

In her combination of range and quality of her voice, plus an ability to improvise, Sarah Vaughan was technically the most gifted jazz singer of all. Born in New Jersey in 1924, she sang in Billy Eckstine's band and recorded with Parker and Gillespie, being linked thereby to bebop. She was, though, essentially a singer of standard songs and one especially able to transform a slow ballad simply

NANA VASCONCELOS

Born in Recife, Brazil in 1944, Nana Vasconcelos played with local bands in the Sixties before joining singer Milton Nascimento. As well as orthodox drums and hand-percussion, he taught himself the berimbau, a one-string instrument increasingly employed for its haunting tone. He has worked with Gato Barbieri, Don Cherry, his Brazilian compatriot Egberto Gismonti and the trio Inclassificable, also performing duets with the Scottish percussionist Evelyn Glennie. As that list implies, he has an open musical mind to go with a great understanding of his own cultural

Brought up on bebop, Sarah Vaughan had the most remarkable voice in jazz.

the first guitarists to transfer the rougher edges of country blues guitar to a jazz world that had become increasingly dominated by the more flamboyant post-Hendrix soloists. (James Ulmer: *Revealing* In & Out).

MICHAL URBANIAK

Born in Warsaw in 1943, Michal Urbaniak is a classically-trained violinist who can also switch to the saxophone if necessary. In the Sixties, he became well known throughout Europe after touring with his own group, featuring his wife, singer Urszula Dudziak. Having won a scholarship to Berklee, he emigrated to the US, where he has participated in several fusion projects (he once led a group entitled Fusion, and now runs Urbanator, with the excellent Al McDowell on bass guitar). His violin these days may resemble a slide rule more than a Stradivarius, but he still made it shimmer like Menuhin while swinging like Grappelli. (Michal Urbaniak: *Songbird* Steeplechase).

WARREN VACHE JR.

Inspired by his bass-playing father, Warren Vache played in Dixieland bands and, as a cornettist, is often cited alongside Ruby Braff as someone who skipped back a generation. Born in New Jersey in 1951, he worked in Eddie Condon's club and has several times teamed up with Scott Hamilton. Compared to Braff, Vache's style is more direct, though with the same virtues of a warm tone and abundant technique. He also fits readily into groups not easy to classify – he played on one of Gerry Mulligan's last albums, and one could imagine him taking the Chet Baker role in some pianoless quartet. (Warren Vache Jr: *Horn Of Plenty* Muse).

MIROSLAV VITOUS

Born in Prague in 1947, bassist Miroslav Vitous played in groups with Jan Hammer (later of the Mahavishnu Orchestra) before studying at Berklee. He remained in the U.S., working with Freddie Hubbard and Herbie Mann before becoming one of the founders of Weather Report, by then playing mostly bass guitar. Leaving the group in 1973, he continued to work on a double-neck version of the electric instrument. Since the mid-Seventies, he has led excellent quartets and reverted to string bass, providing a strong pulse in a variety of settings, rather as Charlie Haden does. (Miroslav Vitous: *First Meeting* ECM).

MAL WALDRON

Listening to a typical Mal Waldron solo, it is hard to imagine him accompanying Billie Holiday, though his ability to do so is well documented. Born in New York in 1926, he worked with Charles Mingus and later recorded with Eric Dolphy, who appeared on his *The Quest*. Since then, he has often used Europe as his base, usually touring as a single. Waldron ignores the kind of melodic improvising associated with bebop and what came after; he treats the piano more percussively, worrying over phrases or chords and making imperceptible changes – almost minimalist, though with a foot-tapping pulse. His tune 'Soul Eyes' has become a standard. (Mal Waldron: *The Quest* Prestige).

BENNIE WALLACE

Bennie Wallace brings together tenor saxophone styles, even more than most. Taking Sonny Rollins as a model while harking back to souful balladeers like Ben Webster causes few shocks today, but Wallace also zigzags between the kinds of spaced out intervals an Eric Dolphy might pick. Born in Tennessee in 1946, he played both jazz and country music – some of this crops up on his albums, and he has recorded successfully with Mose Allison. At his best, an aggressively entertaining performer. (Bennie Wallace: *The Talk Of The Town* Enja).

FATS WALLER

Thomas 'Fats' Waller was one of the most irresistible entertainers of the century: a singer, composer and comedian of effervescent ability. But, during a chaotic life, beset by alcohol and alimony problems, he might write an imperishable song over the telephone, and then sign away the copyright. Born in New York (1904), he became a pupil of James P. Johnson, and one of the greatest of the Harlem stride school, as witnessed by such piano solos as 'Numb Fumblin'' and his popular 'Alligator Crawl', though his great public success came via his sly, genial vocals and general ability to ham it up. He died in 1943. (Fats Waller: *Turn On The Heat* Bluebird (2 CDs)).

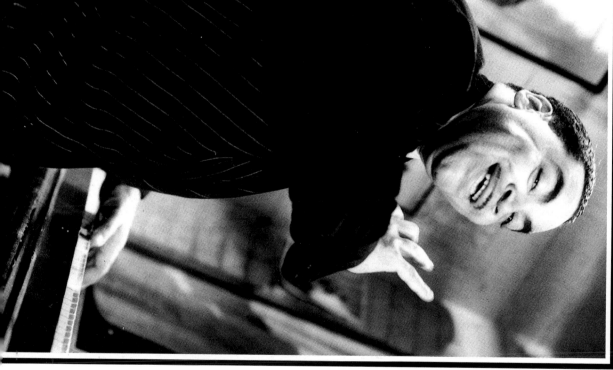

Fats Waller, composer, pianist and all-round entertainer, photographed shortly before his death in 1943.

CEDAR WALTON

Cedar Walton, born in Dallas in 1934, came to prominence as the pianist in one of the great Jazz Messengers groups, backing a front line that included Wayne Shorter and Freddie Hubbard, and writing tunes like 'Mosaic'. He became a busy freelance musician, and later made a not-too-convincing stab at fusion. Since the mid-Seventies, he has taken a quartet on the road, usually with Billy Higgins on drums and a ranking tenor saxophonist out front: George Coleman did it for a while, and more recent incumbents have been Bob Berg, Harold Land and Ralph Moore. (Cedar Walton: *Among Friends* Evidence)

CARLOS WARD

Carlos Ward has not quite broken through to leader status, but he has contributed very positively to groups led by pianists Cecil Taylor and Abdullah Ibrahim in which he is the only horn. Born in Panama in 1940 but raised in Seattle, he worked with the more progressive musicians (as well as the funk group BT Express) before becoming a regular touring member of Ibrahim's various bands. He also stood out in the group Nu alongside Don Cherry. His alto saxophone solos are often passionate, rarely frantic. (Carlos Ward: *Lito Leo*).

WILBUR WARE

A most unusual bassist for his generation, using a percussive method of short notes, massive tone and great rhythmic impact, Ware's work particularly reflected Wellman Braud, the New Orleans bassist who once provided a broad platform for Duke Ellington. Born in Chicago in 1932, Ware came to New York in 1956, and recorded regularly for the Riverside label, though rarely as leader. In 1957, he worked with Thelonious Monk's quartet and also recorded, memorably, with Sonny Rollins and Elvin Jones. Ill-health forced a return to Chicago in 1959. From then he worked on and off until his death in 1979. (Sonny Rollins: *A Night At The Village Vanguard* Blue Note).

DINAH WASHINGTON

Dinah Washington had all the qualities of a soul singer, which she might have become, though for all her gospel background and her way with the blues, even those associated with Bessie Smith, she had a light touch compared to, say, Ray Charles. Hardly the most subtle performer, you can nevertheless understand why jazz musicians enthused over her sense of time and natural swing. Born in Alabama in 1924, and named Ruth Jones, she worked with Lionel Hampton before taking off as a single. This album includes her big hit, 'What A Difference a Day Made', though the best bits are the blues and some cracking small-band sides. (Dinah Washington: *The Original Recordings* Mercury (2 CDs)).

BOBBY WATSON

Born in Kansas in 1953, Bobby Watson played with Blakey's Jazz Messengers for four years and was the musical director when Wynton Marsalis joined. Undervalued at the time, he

has since become a considerable force on the scene, being a founder-member of the 29th Street Saxophone Quartet (arguably the best of the bunch, in jazz terms) and leader of both an occasional big band and an outstanding quintet. A brilliant alto saxophonist, he has written tunes that stay in the mind, such as 'In Case You Missed It' and 'ETA'. (Bobby Watson: *Midwest Shuffle* Columbia).

Marsalis: *Crazy People Music* Columbia).

TREVOR WATTS

Born in Yorkshire in 1939, Trevor Watts was an early member of the free-jazz Spontaneous Music Ensemble along with John Stevens and trombonist Paul Rutherford. At the time, Watts played alto saxophone very much in the style of Ornette Coleman. Over the years, he has been involved with different groups and has changed, both in the way he phrases and in his increasingly singing, highly evocative sound. His current project goes under the name Moire Music, a pleasing variant of minimalism, in which textures, rhythmic and melodic, are given every chance to evolve. (Moire Music *A Wider Embrace* ECM).

JEFF 'TAIN' WATTS

Born in Pittsburgh in 1960, Jeff Watts was the drummer in the Wynton Marsalis quintet. When the Marsalis brothers split up, he continued to play with Wynton, notably on the *Live At Blues Alley* recording, but eventually Watts, bassist Robert Hurst and Kenny Kirkland were reunited under Branford Marsalis. He was at his peak and, behind him, Watts and Hurst made a remarkable team, keeping the beat really tight while the drummer effortlessly piled on the polyrhythms. Not surprisingly Watts (the Tony Williams of his day) is much in demand. (Branford

became the nonpareil big-band drummer despite being short and hunchbacked and having to use special pedals. He began at the Savoy in 1931, and was soon producing excellent music, much of it composed and arranged by Edgar Sampson, including 'Stomping At The Savoy' and 'Blue Lou'. Soon after, Ella Fitzgerald joined and the hits piled up. Sadly, spinal tuberculosis caught up with Webb and he died in 1939. (Chick Webb: *Rhythm Man* Hep).

EBERHARD WEBER

Born in Stuttgart in 1940, Eberhard Weber began as a bassist in a jazz trio, though he also played in jazz-rock groups. His experience of both areas of music caused him to invent his own electric bass, an upright model with extra resonance, from which he could

CHICK WEBB

If ever a bandleader and a venue belonged together, it was William 'Chick' Webb and the Savoy Ballroom. Born in Maryland in 1909, Webb

Drummer Chick Webb (right), was small in stature and hunchbacked, but his band's powerful string captivated dancers at New York's Savoy Ballroom.

extract those great booming tones one now associates with him. He led an outstanding quartet, Colours – with Charlie Mariano on saxophones, John Marshall on drums and Rainer Bruninghaus on piano – and he has also been a regular associate of Jan Garbarek's. His albums often have a pastoral quality, whereas the odd karate chop, tend to be more lively. (Colours: *Silent Feet* ECM).

BEN WEBSTER

As a tenor saxophonist in the Thirties, Ben Webster came up in the shadow of Coleman Hawkins. Born in 1909 in Kansas City, he worked with many of the top bands, including Fletcher Henderson and Cab Calloway, before joining Duke Ellington in 1939 and making such famous records as 'Cottontail'. His tone, always exceptionally full, later developed into one of the glories of the saxophone – rich and creamy, yet ethereal, in the way he could float over the ballads that became his most effective and deeply swinging vehicles. He eventually settled in Europe, where he died in 1973. (Ben Webster: *King Of The Tenors Verve*).

BOBBY WELLINS

Some of the most distinctive sounds in British jazz come from the tenor saxophone of Bobby Wellins, especially a keening wail that some see as the legacy of his Scottish background. Born in Glasgow in 1936, he made his first recordings with drummer Tony Crombie's band, and then joined Stan Tracey's quartet, with whom he was featured on *Under Milk Wood*. During a career that has had ups and downs, Wellins has rarely been well recorded under his own name, but the records that do exist give an indication of the meticulous way he constructs his solos and, especially on standard tunes, his dry musical humour. (Stan Tracey: *Under Milk Wood Blue Note*).

DICKY WELLS

Trombonist Dicky Wells, one of the great stylists, is associated with a particular band and a particular series of records. Born in Tennessee in 1907, he joined Count Basie in 1938, having worked with Fletcher Henderson and Benny Carter and travelled with Teddy Hill to Paris, where he made some classic recordings with Django Reinhardt and others. His style, one of the most humorously expressive ever produced on that expressive instrument, was replete with slurs, smears and off-pitched notes, all done with the tightest control. Never quite the same after the war, he managed to stay on the circuit up to his death in 1985. (Dicky Wells: *Swingin' In Paris Le Jazz*).

MIKE WESTBROOK

Born in Buckinghamshire in 1936 and brought up in Devon, Mike Westbrook led a big band during the Sixties that reflected the times, from his anti-war *Marching Song*, to the album *Release* that used swing-era material, to the jazz-rock of *Metropolis*. He later expanded the concept of setting words to music and, in collaboration with his wife Kate, produced *The Cortege* and *London Bridge Is Broken Down*, stunning orchestral masterworks full of great songs and great tunes. Westbrook currently runs a big band, and has written two operas, plus several works for smaller groups, including settings of songs by the Beatles. (Mike Westbrook: *The Cortege Enja*).

RANDY WESTON

One of the first pianists to reflect the influence of Monk and Ellington, Randy Weston has always been among the more self-contained musicians. Born in New York in 1926, he began in the Sixties to work mostly outside the US, living for a time in Africa and using it as a base for gigs, often as a single, in Europe and Japan. Weston writes appealing tunes (some, including 'High Fly' and 'Little Niles' have become standards), often with an African or West Indian lilt, that benefit from good arrangements, while at the piano he draws out their harmonic richness. (Randy Weston: *Saga Verve*).

KENNY WHEELER

A rare mix of trumpeter and composer/arranger, Kenny Wheeler overlays all his work with a kind of beautiful melancholia, perhaps redolent of his native Canada's open spaces. Born in Toronto in 1930, he has been based in the UK since 1952. After several years of working as a studio musician, finding time to fill his many outside engagements, he now works full-time in jazz. His tone and style on trumpet were inspired by the playing of Booker Little and, like Little, he excels particularly at metres other than 4/4. Among his notable affiliations have been Dave Holland's groups and the trio Azimuth. (Kenny Wheeler: *Music For Large And Small Ensemble* ECM (2 CDs)).

Ex-Bechet pupil, Bob Wilber, plays a different shape of soprano saxophone.

BOB WILBER

Master of the curved soprano and the most illustrious pupil of the legendary Sidney Bechet, Bob Wilber later studied with Lennie Tristano, which gives some idea of his breadth of vision. Born in New York in 1928, his strongest links are with the jazz of the

Twenties and Thirties, but he was among the first to promote the educational value of repertory bands, an idea that has since found its time, and won an award for his Ellington re-creations in the film *The Cotton Club*. His playing on clarinet and soprano is marked by an infectious lyricism. (Bob Wilber: *Summit Reunion* Chiaroscuro).

COOTIE WILLIAMS

Born in Alabama in 1911, and a professional musician at 14, Charles 'Cootie' Williams worked in touring bands until he got to New York, where he joined Duke Ellington in 1929. Probably the greatest of all 'growl' players, as well as providing an exhilarating Armstrong-influenced open horn, he stayed with Ellington until 1940.

Forming his own big band, he introduced compositions by Thelonious Monk and also employed Bud Powell as pianist. With the decline of big bands, his career drifted until, in 1962, he rejoined Ellington, reprising his 'Concerto For Cootie' and featuring in much new music. He died in 1985. (Duke Ellington: *The Duke's Men – Small Groups Vol.I* Columbia).

JESSICA WILLIAMS

Another musician coming late to fame, Jessica Williams (born Baltimore, 1948) settled on the West Coast in the Sixties and made several records on obscure labels. For a time she was the house pianist at San Francisco's Keystone Korner, playing behind the likes of Stan Getz and Bobby

Joining Andy Kirk's band as pianist, Mary Lou Williams became its chief arranger.

Hutcherson. Her reputation began to spread in the Nineties, largely through an exceptional talent for playing without accompaniment. She has the technique for complex runs but never seems to be rushing them, while her respect for Monk ensures, among other things, that solos hang together and have plenty of humour. (Jessica Williams: *The Next Step* Hep).

JOE WILLIAMS

As the blues singer with Count Basie in the Fifties, Joe Williams made the big-selling 'Every Day' that helped widen the band's appeal. On such blues material, his big voice put one in mind of Joe Turner: if he didn't have Big Joe's inimitable timing, he was much more of an all-round singer and

has since done well with ballads. Born Joseph Goreed in Georgia in 1918, he has mixed jazz gigs, including Basie reunions, with a presence in other areas of show business. (*Count Basie Swings, Joe Williams Sings* Verve).

MARY LOU WILLIAMS

Her writing and playing for Andy Kirk's Clouds of Joy established Mary Lou Williams as making the most notable contribution of its kind by a woman during the swing era. Born in Atlanta in 1910, she joined Kirk, in 1931, untrained as an arranger, but by the time she left her reputation was such that she wrote for Goodman and Ellington. Unfortunately, her orchestral work 'Zodiac Suite' is now only available by her trio. Her luminous piano style was formed in the Thirties, but her harmonic depth, and friendship with the leading bebop pianists, let her cross that particular boundary with ease. She died in 1981. (*The Chronological Mary Lou Williams, 1927-40* Classics).

ROY WILLIAMS

When part of Britain's traditional jazz movement detached itself, edging closer to swing and even beyond, the band led by Alex Welsh was in the vanguard. Roy Williams, born in Lancashire in 1937, played trombone in the band during those years when the Welsh band regularly shared the stage with visiting American swing stars. He later worked with Humphrey Lyttelton and co-led some intriguing small bands, also finding himself in demand as a freelance. His ringing yet velvety sound and effortless phrasing come over as something of a cross between Jack Teagarden and Jimmy Knepper. (Brian Lemon/Roy Williams: *A Beautiful Friendship* Zephyr).

TONY WILLIAMS

Tony Williams rather missed out on the jazz-rock boom, despite forming a group (Lifetime) in 1969 that included both John McLaughlin and Jack Bruce. Before that, he had sparked the Miles Davis rhythm section, spanning Davis's modal and abstract periods and becoming probably the most admired and imitated drummer of the Sixties, for his whiplash beat and mastery of polyrhythms. Born in Chicago in 1945, he was only 17 when he joined Davis, staying with him for seven years. Most recently, he has led an acoustic quintet which underlines how effectively he now writes for such a group. (Tony Williams: *Native Heart* Blue Note).

Tony Williams, the most influential drummer of the Sixties and later a jazz-rock pioneer.

STEVE WILLIAMSON

Like many young British jazz musicians during the Eighties, when media interest reached an unusual high, Steve Williamson had to develop as a musician under the public gaze. As a saxophonist, born in London in 1964, he came to prominence in the wake of Courtney Pine and, though less obviously Coltrane-influenced, he played with the same energy. After trying various things, he is currently taking the M-Base route of angular tunes and streetwise rhythms, recording with American trumpeter Graham Haynes and, at home, often accompanying rap artists. (Graham Haynes: *Transition* Verve).

CASSANDRA WILSON

The most distinctive of the younger jazz singers, Cassandra Wilson is versatile enough to have appeared with Steve Coleman and associates, then expertly handle straight jazz material and, as of now, come up with a new accompaniment built largely around the unamplified guitar. Born in Mississippi in 1955, she pitches her voice deeper than one usually finds with jazz singers, reminding one a little of a cooler, less abrasive Nina Simone. Her most recent albums, *Blue Light 'Til Dawn* and *New Moon Daughter*, include classics by blues legend Robert Johnson among an unusual collection of songs. (Cassandra Wilson: *New Moon Daughter* Blue Note).

TEDDY WILSON

Born in Texas in 1912, Teddy Wilson was a leading piano stylist of the Thirties, his relaxed stride patterns and melodic right-hand phrases looking ahead to bebop. Wilson came to fame as the pianist in the Benny Goodman Trio of 1935, but his abiding legacy is a series of group sessions featuring most of the great musicians of that era. After leaving Goodman in 1939, he led a big band that failed to take off. Wilson was still playing with style in the Fifties, though in his final decade he seemed to lack something (there were rumours that he suffered from muscular problems). He died in 1986. (Teddy Wilson: *Fine And Dandy* Hep).

Where jazz meets world music, some of the most captivating sounds come from Aziza Mustafa Zadeh.

NORMA WINSTONE

Born in London in 1941, Norma Winstone sang in many of the bands that came up in the Sixties, in the process developing a new approach to fit essentially new music. Her voice was often used instrumentally by such composers as Kenny Wheeler. At the same time, when singing words, she did not, as most did, try hard to sound American. As her confidence grew and she began to write more of her own lyrics, she become one of the best, and most original, of contemporary singers. Lately, she has become more identified with standards (which she has always sung) following her album with pianist Jimmy Rowles. (Norma Winstone: *Somewhere Called Home* ECM).

PHIL WOODS

Among the Charlie Parker followers of the Fifties, Phil Woods (together with Cannonball Adderley) filtered the barrage of notes through a more even-paced attack that owed more to Benny Carter. Born in Massachusetts in 1931, he was much in demand for New York sessions before moving to Europe, where he was one of the first to see the commercial advantages of a multinational group. Back in the US, he has led excellent groups (acoustic, to the point of discouraging microphones) which have variously included Tom Harrell and Hal Galper, with his brother-in-law Bill Goodwin a fixture on drums. (Phil Woods: *Real Life* Chesky).

YOSUKE YAMASHITA

Yosuke Yamashita, born in Tokyo in 1942, learnt to play the piano by ear and has always preferred to keep his music spontaneous. He discovered bebop through Hampton Hawes, then free jazz through Cecil Taylor. His Taylor-like group caused a sensation at a European festival in 1974 and was described by ecstatic scribes as the kamikaze trio (they also brought up karate, kung-fu and samurai, Yamashita now recalls). He has various projects back home, including a big band, and each year revives his American trio, to play music that is structured, but allows much room for freedom. (Yosuke Yamashita: *Kurdish Dance* Verve).

JIMMY YANCEY

The early master of blues and boogie piano, Jimmy Yancey actually began in vaudeville and danced before King George V in London during the First World War. Born in Chicago in 1894, he returned there after the war, earned his living as a groundsman for the White Sox and played piano in the evenings. His technique was rudimentary and he could play few tunes, but his timing was innate, he varied his bass patterns skilfully and he could invest the simplest solos with tremendous feeling. Those who came

Saxophonist John Zorn became a leader of New York's avant garde.

after added excitement, but none surpassed him where it mattered. He lived until 1951, long enough to be acclaimed during the revival. (*Barrelhouse Boogie* RCA Bluebird).

LARRY YOUNG

Born in New Jersey, in 1940, Larry Young (later known as Khalid Yasin Abdul Aziz) studied piano and worked with rhythm-and-blues bands before arriving in New York as an exponent of the Hammond organ. Signed to Blue Note Records in 1964, he recorded in a variety of settings before, late in 1965, he unveiled a spectacular Coltrane-influenced shift of style with his album *Unity*, breaking the hegemony imposed on the organ in jazz by Jimmy Smith's pioneering work. Subsequently diversifying into jazz-rock, Young recorded with Miles Davis and John McLaughlin, and was part of Tony Williams's group Lifetime. He died in 1978. (*The Art Of Larry Young* Blue Note).

TRUMMY YOUNG

As happened to many stars of the Thirties, James 'Trummy' Young's career was split in two. Born in Georgia in 1912, his trombone technique and ability to reach the high notes impressed Earl Hines and then Jimmy Lunceford. His speciality number with Lunceford, 'Margie', became a show-piece, and he was also part of the various vocal groups the band featured. After the war, it was Dixieland, though he later enjoyed playing trombone in rock. Subsequently diversifying into jazz-rock, Louis Armstrong's group for a while. Most of the time up to his death in 1984 he was living and occasionally playing in Hawaii. (Louis Armstrong: *Satch Plays Fats* Columbia).

AZIZA MUSTAFA ZADEH

The late father of Aziza Mustafa Zadeh, Vagif, invented a kind of fusion between jazz and the folk music of Azerbaijan, and she has continued in the same vein. Born in 1969, her appearances at various European events led to her being signed by a major record company. She brings to her kind of jazz a headlong attack, especially in her explosive solo performances, that, in intensity if not style, recalls the early bebop pianists. This is especially marked during her very fast scat singing where one gets the wildest interplay between voice and piano – often over metres strange by Western standards but more common in Baku. (*Aziza Mustafa Zadeh* Columbia).

JOE ZAWINUL

Born in Vienna, Austria, in 1932, Joe Zawinul studied at the local conservatory, but later became interested in jazz. In 1959, he won a scholarship to Berklee College in Boston, and was soon touring with Maynard Ferguson's band. He subsequently joined Cannonball Adderley, where he wrote the hit 'Mercy, Mercy, Mercy'. Miles Davis recorded his 'In A Silent Way' on a legendary recording, and, shortly afterwards, Zawinul formed Weather Report, with Wayne Shorter. By avoiding the easy options, this remained the most blue-blooded of electric groups, with Zawinul, increasingly, the dominant driving force. He has since formed his own groups, all controlled from his seat at the keyboard. (Weather Report: *Heavy Weather* Columbia).

JOHN ZORN

The current idol of the iconoclasts, alto saxophonist John Zorn sets out to be hard to classify. Born in New York in 1953, he has been involved with most aspects of improvising, working with guitarists Fred Frith and Bill Frisell. At the same time, he does compose and use themes by others, while the contexts vary from relatively orthodox jazz trios to Japanese noise bands to a kind of free-improvising by numbers, extending the idea of musicians being given roles rather than notes. The album cited includes George Lewis (not the clarinettist) and Bill Frisell. (John Zorn: *News For Lulu* hatART).

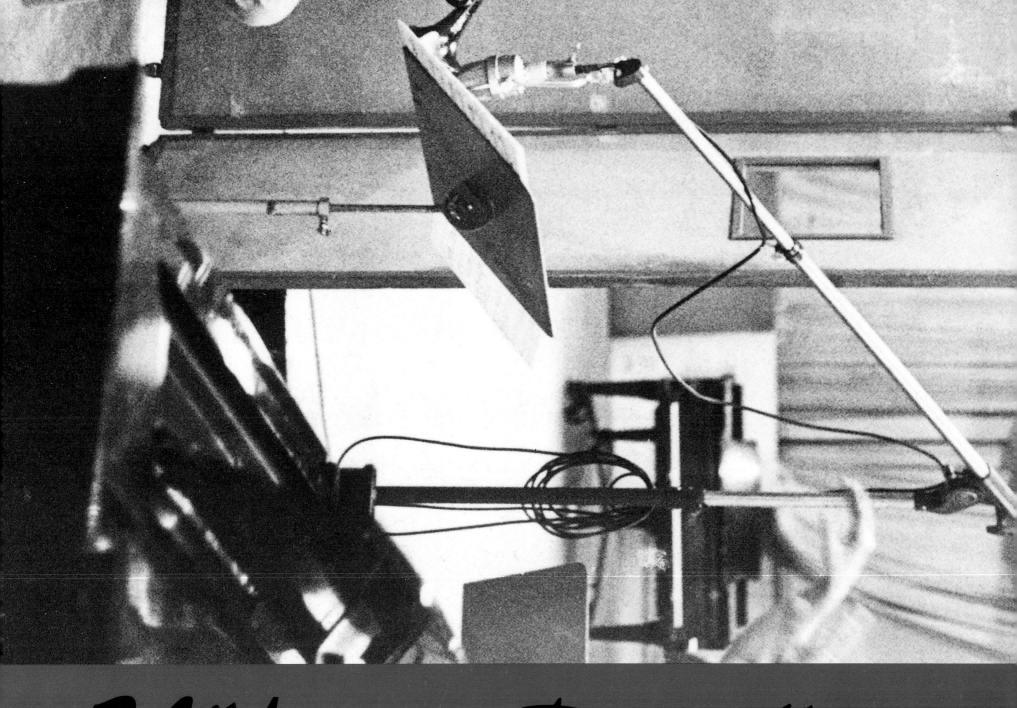

Milestone Recordings

Jazz and the Record Industry

Mike Westbrook, the British composer, recalls the night he agreed a deal with the top executive of a very big record company. Arriving at the firm's headquarters next morning to sign the contract, he found the executive fired and his office dismantled. Events like these contribute to the suspicion felt throughout jazz for the industry that grew up alongside it

and without which, because of the nature of jazz, it could barely exist.

How would European classical music fare if every version of a Mozart symphony could be compared aurally with its first-ever performance? Because its masterpieces often exist independently of any written score, recordings became the main yardstick by which to evaluate jazz. Where clas-

sical composers remained largely aloof from the narrow demands of the three-minute shellac disc, the works of Jelly Roll Morton and, for much of his career, Duke Ellington were conditioned by them.

By the time jazz arrived, the industry had just about established itself among the technological phenomena of the age. Battles between cylinder and disc, and between rival opera singers, that had enlivened the early years, were over when the Original Dixieland Jazz Band hit the streets with 'Livery Stable Blues' and 'Dixie Jass Band One-step'. They recorded that million-seller for Victor

Records on the February 26, 1917 – not their first studio session, as on January 31 they had been recorded by the rival Columbia, who, no doubt to their eternal shame, dithered about releasing the results.

The next landmark came in February 1920 when blues singer Mamie Smith recorded for Okeh. This first recording by a black artist came

The Original Dixieland Jazz Band made the first jazz record and then triumphed in London. Larry Shields is on clarinet, Nick La Rocca on trumpet and Tony Spargo on drums.

about largely through the songs' composer Perry Bradford, who fought hard on behalf of Mamie Smith when Okeh were inclined to favour Sophie Tucker. Smith's hugely successful follow-up record of 'Crazy Blues', where the backing group included such New York musicians as trumpeter Johnny Dunn and Willie 'The Lion' Smith on piano, opened doors: not long afterwards, in 1922, a group of New Orleansians in Los Angeles under the direction of trombonist Kid Ory made the first jazz record by black musicians. Around this time, the term 'race records' was invented by Okeh to describe records aimed primarily at black buyers, and it remained in use for about 20 years.

Jazz has been quick to benefit from technical breakthroughs. Microphones came too late for Oliver's Creole Jazz Band (who had to play into a large horn, with a stylus at the other end), but in time for the Red Hot Peppers and the Hot Fives. Several years later, the Prestige company in New York celebrated the longer playing time by letting Miles Davis and group loose for a whole side of a 10-inch vinyl disc.

With few exceptions, the commercial record industry has served jazz well, when judged in terms of coverage, if not of how musicians themselves have been treated. Most are adequately documented. A few gaps were filled by tapings, usually unofficial, of live events, such as Charlie Christian with Monk in 1940 and the eventual issue of a club performance by Paul Bley's quintet with Ornette Coleman. Releases of radio broadcasts by Charlie Parker added to what we knew of his work in the studios, almost all for independent record labels.

JAZZ SPECIALISTS

Until the Forties, jazz tended to rely on the big companies, who might be persuaded by such influential patrons as John Hammond to do justice to new talent. Hammond also introduced British composer Spike Hughes to some of the top musicians in New York, with whom he then recorded – the first substantial transatlantic collaboration. A few years on, records supervised in New York by French critic Hugues Panassié helped to launch the New Orleans revival.

The first important independent of modern times was Commodore, founded in 1938 by enthusiast Milt Gabler and run from his New York record store. Gabler set the tone for the best of his innumerable successors: all-round emphasis on quality, a sense of direction for the label and an identity that created a trend rather than followed one. The same applied to various labels started later by Norman Granz, to record artists appearing on his Jazz At The Philharmonic shows.

Blue Note, founded in 1939, recorded Thelonious Monk in depth and then came into its own in the Fifties with Art Blakey, Horace Silver and Jimmy Smith. Contemporary and Pacific Jazz documented the West Coast scene. Atlantic recorded Charles Mingus and then Ornette Coleman, by which time Prestige had lost the in-demand Miles Davis to Columbia. None of these labels now exist as independents, but most of the names are still used by the firms that took them over, even for newly recorded works.

Among the companies today, many based in Europe and Japan specialize in recording American artists. Others exist purely to record local talent, much easier to promote now that jazz has become genuinely international, though records sold in the US still account for at least 65% of the jazz market. Perhaps the independent firm closest to the old Blue Note in terms of impact and quality is the German ECM, even if you can't get much further from the Jazz Messengers than Jan Garbarek.

MARKETING JAZZ RECORDS

During the last decade, there has been a jazz revival among the biggest firms, themselves often the result of mergers and takeovers. Sudden U-turns over policy have become less extreme and, for the first time, people in executive positions are given specific responsibility for the music, one of them being Richard Cook, Head of Jazz for Polygram/Verve U.K. He says that the lack of anyone doing his job in the past meant that jazz was woefully undersold. "Many parts of the record market have reached saturation point, while jazz is a growth area in that very little effort has previously been put into, for example, having sales representatives who actively push jazz to retailers."

He disputes the official industry figures for the U.K., which give jazz about 1% of the market, claiming that they fall down on the thorny question of what counts as jazz. The large retail record stores estimate their sales at between 5% and 8%, a substantial slice that corresponds with his own experience at Verve, where business has just been a 30% increase in turnover over the previous year, achieved without any increase in the number of jazz records actually released.

INVESTING IN JAZZ

For companies with any sense, the durability of jazz should be sufficient attraction. Initial sales may be insignificant compared to those which top the pop charts. Yet the potential for building a back catalogue in the following years, when the fairly modest cost of the session will have long since been absorbed, can be seen on the racks of any record store.

The period of mechanical copyright (i.e. before the company loses exclusive rights to the recording, so that anybody with a decent pressing to tape from can release the same material) is long enough – 75 years in the US and 50 years in the U.K. – to justify several reissues.

The converse has resulted in another thriving industry, notably in the UK with its shorter copyright period, of firms that compile their own reissues from out-of-copyright material. Some of the reissues cited throughout this book are U.K. compilations that will not be available in the same form in the U.S. This only applies to a few recordings over 50 years old, as anything below that is copyright in both countries. International communications are now such that a record officially withdrawn from sale in one country can be imported from some central warehouse somewhere if a copy exists.

TOWARDS A JAZZ RECORD LIBRARY

The 600 or so albums listed earlier under the names of musicians give a cross-section of the jazz century. What follows is a kind of supplement. Included are some albums that did not make the lists, for various reasons. There are also CD compilations of several individual albums, some of which were recommended in the entry under the artist's name.

Mosaic Records compile their own multi-CD issues, usually in collaboration with the company that made the original recordings. Because these are limited editions, apart from one mammoth set of Charlie Parker in-person performances, stock of many excellent items has long since gone. The address for mail orders is: MOSAIC RECORDS, 35 Melrose Place, Stamford, Connecticut 06902 USA Tel: (203) 327-7111.

ABBREVIATIONS:

trumpet = t; cornet = c; trombone = tb; tuba = tu; clarinet = cl; soprano saxophone = ss; alto saxophone = as; tenor saxophone= ts; baritone saxophone = bs; flute = f; piano = p; keyboards = key; violin = vn; guitar = g; vibraphone = vib; bass = b; drums = d; percussion = perc.

LOUIS ARMSTRONG
The Complete Recordings of Louis Armstrong and The Blues Singers 1924-30,
Affinity (5 CDs)

Personnel includes: Perry Bradford, Butterbeans and Susie, Lillie Delk Christian, Blanche Calloway, Seger Ellis, Coot Grant, Bertha 'Chippie' Hill, Alberta Hunter, Margaret Johnson, Billy Jones, Maggie Jones, Virginia Liston, Baby Mack. Ma Rainey, Jimmie Rodgers, Clara Smith, Bessie Smith, Trixie Smith, Victoria Spivey, Eva Taylor, Hociel Thomas, Clarence Todd, Sippie Wallace, Nolan Welsh, Wesley Wilson (v); Tommy Dorsey, Charlie Green, Charlie Irvis, Kid Ory, (tb); Sidney Bechet (cl, ss); Don Redman (as); Buster Bailey; Jimmy Dorsey, Jimmie Noone (cl); Coleman Hawkins (ts); Lil Armstrong, Fletcher Henderson, Earl Hines, James P Johnson, Richard M. Jones, Hersal Thomas, Clarence Williams (p); Joe Venuti (vn); Eddie Lang (g); Johnny St. Cyr, Mancy Cara (banjo); Kaiser Marshall, Zutty Singleton (d).

The early part of the Twenties was the heyday of the classic blues singers. Following the success of Mamie Smith and 'Crazy Blues', the door opened for Bessie Smith, Ma Rainey and many others to make records that sold very well. From the time he came to New York to join Fletcher Henderson in 1924, Louis Armstrong was naturally in demand as accompanist on these sessions. It has been said, with some truth, that he was too imperious to dovetail closely with the singers: Joe Smith is a trumpeter who excelled at that. However, Armstrong's solo spots are as pertinent as you would expect, and have the benefit of making tracks by the lesser singers worth hearing. Included are his early jousts with Sidney Bechet, the closest thing pre-bebop to Parker meeting Gillespie.

CHET BAKER
Chet Baker:
The Pacific Jazz Years
Pacific Jazz (4 CDs)

Personnel includes: Don Fagerquist (t); Bob Brookmeyer, Frank Rosolino (tb); Herb Geller, Art Pepper, Bud Shank (as); Stan Getz, Bill Holman, Jack Montrose, Bill Perkins, Phil Urso (ts); Russ Freeman, Pete Jolly, Bobby Timmons (p); Monty Budwig, Red Mitchell, Carson Smith, Leroy Vinnegar (b); Larry Bunker, Chico Hamilton, Mel Lewis, Shelly Manne, Bob Neel (d); Annie Ross (v).

Chet Baker's meteoric rise to fame followed his role in Gerry Mulligan's quartet, as heard on some tracks here – notably on the live version of 'My Funny Valentine', the number most associated with him at the time. The rest splits between his regular quartet, tailored to his unfussy lyricism and usually with Russ Freeman at the piano, and sessions where leading musicians based on the West Coast in the early Fifties join in. The latest tracks, from 1957, document his reunion with Mulligan.

CHARLIE BARNET
Charlie Barnet: Drop Me
Off At Harlem
MCA/Decca

Personnel includes: Roy Eldridge, Peanuts Holland, Al Killian, Paul Webster (t); Eddie Bert, Lawrence Brown, Tommy Pederson (tb); Buddy

In his younger days, Louis Armstrong often recorded with the popular blues singers.

De Franco, Les Robinson (as); Dave Matthews (ts); Danny Bank (bs); Al Haig, Dodo Marmarosa (p); Barney Kessel, Turk Van Lake (g); Howard Rumsey (b); Cliff Leeman (d); Kay Starr, Frances Wayne (v).

Among the later swing band-leaders, Charlie Barnet enjoyed a reputation among jazz buffs higher than most. He hired good musicians, greatly admired Duke Ellington and played the saxophones in a style obviously inspired by Johnny Hodges. One of his hits, the smoothly stream-lined 'Skyliner' turns up here and still evokes the swing era better than almost anything. Apart from the obviously big names in the personnel, such as Eldridge and Brown, note the excellent but, in career terms, some-

what erratic Dodo Marmarosa at the piano.

COUNT BASIE
Count Basie:
The Original American Decca Recordings
MCA/Decca (3 CDs)

....

Personnel includes: Buck Clayton, Shad Collins, Harry Edison, Ed Lewis, Bobby Moore, Carl Smith (t); Eddie Durham, George Hunt, Dan Minor, Benny Morton, Dicky Wells (tb); Caughey Roberts, Earl Warren (as); Chu Berry, Herschel Evans, Lester Young (ts); Jack Washington (bs); Freddie Green (g); Walter Page (b); Jo Jones (d); Helen Humes, Jimmy Rushing (v).

Basie's early band on these recordings, made between 1937 and 1939, contained, arguably, the soloists one would be keenest to hear

in such a context. They also evoked the sense of contrast one gets from the Ellington band, most notably among the saxophones where Lester Young, the ultimate individual, crossed swords with his friend Herschel Evans, who had the breathy Hawkins-type tone. Tunes and arrangements were simple, their theme song 'One O'Clock Jump', typifying the blues feeling and the naturally riffing style that simply flows from the music. The ultra-relaxed 'Jive At Five', with Young's superb opening statement, is another marvel.

SIDNEY BECHET
Sidney Bechet:
The Bluebird Sessions, 1932-43
Bluebird (5 CDs)

....

Personnel includes: Henry 'Red' Allen, Sidney de Paris, Tommy Ladnier,

Henry Levine, Charlie Shavers (t); Rex Stewart (c); Vic Dickenson, J.C. Higginbotham, Claude Jones, Sandy Williams (tb); Albert Nicholas (cl); Mezz Mezzrow (cl, ts); Happy Caldwell, Lem Johnson (ts); Hank Duncan, Earl Hines, Cliff Jackson, Willie 'The Lion' Smith, Sonny White, Jelly Roll Morton (p); Teddy Bunn, Everett Barksdale (g); Wellman Braud, John Lindsay (b); Big Sid Catlett, Kenny Clarke, Warren 'Baby' Dodds, J C Heard, Manzie Johnson, Zutty Singleton (d); Herb Jeffries, William Maxey (v).

These include all the Feetwarmers sides with Tommy Ladnier, the Mezzrow sessions organized by Hugues Panassié that in part helped to launch the revival in New Orleans-styled music and were issued under Tommy Ladnier's name, and the classic 'Blues In Thirds' with Earl Hines. Also a unique 'Sheik Of Araby',

Art Blakey, pictured at New York's Café Bohemia in 1956 during a gig by the original Jazz Messengers. His drum kit appears spartan by current standards.

entirely solo but with instruments overdubbed. More inclined to use the clarinet in those days and less obviously autocratic, Bechet is generally in peak form. As with many such compilations, versions rejected at the time are included. Musicians themselves tend to disapprove of this, but they can be very illuminating for listeners, especially long after the event when the scholarly aspect becomes part of the pleasure.

ART BLAKEY

The History Of Art Blakey And The Jazz Messengers
Blue Note (3 CDs)

Personnel includes: Clifford Brown, Kenny Dorham, Bill Hardman, Freddie Hubbard, Wynton Marsalis, Lee Morgan, Valery Ponomarev, Woody Shaw (t); Howard Bowe, Robin Eubanks, Curtis Fuller (tb); Lou Donaldson, Jackie McLean, Sahib Shihab, Bobby Watson (as); Benny Golson, Carter Jefferson, Hank Mobley, Billy Pierce, Wayne Shorter, Dave Schnitter (ts); Branford Marsalis, Ernie Thompson (bs); Walter Bishop, Walter Davis, Sam Dockery, Horace

Silver, Bobby Timmons, Cedar Walton, James Williams (p); Kevin Eubanks (g); Laverne Barker, Micky Bass, Spanky De Brest, Charles Famborough, Dennis Irwin, Jymie Merritt, Curley Russell, Doug Watkins, Reggie Workman (b); John Ramsey, Tony Waters (perc).

With few exceptions, the early-Sixties Riversides and some of his Eighties work, all the best of Art Blakey's Jazz Messengers is found on Blue Note. This compilation includes the pre-Messenger Birdland session of 1954 with Clifford Brown, and ends with selections from the time after Bobby Watson and Wynton Marsalis joined. All great stuff, powered by the commanding figure at the drums.

Highlights would definitely include the Wayne Shorter band, as much as anything else because of the tunes he and others brought in.

CARLA BLEY

Carla Bley: Escalator Over The Hill
JCOA (2 CDs)

Personnel includes: Don Cherry, Michael Mantler, Enrico Rava, Michael Snow (t); Sam Burtis, Jack Jeffers, Jimmy Knepper, Roswell Rudd (tb); Bob Carlisle, Sharon Freeman (Frh); Howard Johnson (tu); Perry Robinson (cl); Jimmy Lyons (as); Gato Barbieri (ts); Chris Woods (bs); Don Preston (key); Karl Berger (vib); Sam Brown,

John McLaughlin (g); Leroy Jenkins, Calo Scott (vn); Jack Bruce (b, v); Charlie Haden, Ron McLure (b); Paul Motian (d); Paul Jones, Sheila Jordan, Jeanne Lee, Linda Rondstadt, Viva (v).

There were few parallels for *Escalator Over The Hill* when it came out in the early-Seventies – somehow, the work Carla Bley used to describe her opera, chronotransduction, indicated that this was no ordinary event. The lyrics by Paul Haines still defy analysis, but the settings, the songs put over by everyone from popular singers (Rondstadt, Jones) to the composer herself, and the splendid work by, in particular, Cherry and

Barbieri, have lost nothing. The long overture in itself makes it worthwhile.

BOOGIE WOOGIE
Various Artists:
Boogie Woogie Stomp
ASV

Personnel includes: Albert Ammons, Count Basie, Cleo Brown, Blind Leroy Garnett, Earl Hines, Meade Lux Lewis, Pete Johnson, Tommy Linehan, Jay McShann, Avery Parrish, Howard Smith, Pinetop Smith, Jess Stacy, Jimmy Yancey, Bob Zurke (p). Ammons, Lewis and Yancey are in the book's main section. This

includes other seminal tracks and personalities, notably Smith and his 'Pinetop's Boogie Woogie'. Wisely avoiding wall-to-wall eight beats to the bar, the compilers have broken up the piano solos and duets by examples of big bands cashing in on the short-lived craze. Every jazz fan should also have this original version of "Roll 'Em Pete" where Joe Turner, backed by Pete Johnson's piano, sings the phrases that launched a thousand blues shouters. Best from the bands is that languid masterpiece, 'After Hours', featuring Avery Parrish with Erskine Hawkins.

ANTHONY BRAXTON
Anthony Braxton:
Willisau (Quartet) 1991
hatART (4 CDs)

Personnel includes: Marilyn Crispell (p); Mark Dresser (b); Gerry Hemingway (d).

Braxton's quartet has grown more involved and intricate, the use of written scores more pronounced,

A writer of memorable tunes and a brilliant arranger, Carla Bley produced a one-off with 'Escalator', begun in 1967 and recorded over four years.

Multi-instrumentalist Anthony Braxton, at the cutting edge of contemporary improvized music.

even as a way of inspiring different ways of performing the same piece. Two of the albums come from a concert, where Braxton's habit of swapping between five or six instruments – from alto saxophone up to flute and down to contra-bass clarinet – in itself adds to the spectacle. This was his regular working group, with Crispell in notably fine form.

CLIFFORD BROWN

Clifford Brown: Brownie
EmArcy (10 CDs)

Personnel includes: Maynard Ferguson, Clark Terry (t); Herb Geller, Joe Maini (as); Walter Benton, Harold Land, Paul Quinichette, Sonny Rollins (ts); Herbie Mann (f); Kenny Drew, Jimmy Jones, Junior Mance, Richie Powell (p); Joe Benjamin, Keter Betts, Curtis Counce, George Morrow (b); Roy Haynes, Max Roach (d); Helen Merrill, Sarah Vaughan, Dinah Washington (v).

The jewel in the crown is obviously the Roach-Brown quintet, on such tracks as 'Delilah' and 'Dahoud' with Harold Land on tenor, and all those recorded when he was replaced by Sonny Rollins. In his short life, Clifford Brown managed to record in a variety of contexts, so between 1954 and 1956 you have his rather straight-laced work with strings juxtaposed with his usual bubbly high spirits during the carefree jamming on the Dinah Washington session, where he is joined by Terry and Ferguson.

DAVE BRUBECK

*Dave Brubeck:
Time Signatures –
A Career Retrospective*
Columbia (4 CDs)

Personnel includes: Dick Collins (t); Bob Collins (tb); Perry Robinson, Bill

Smith (cl); Paul Desmond, Bobby Militello (as); Jerry Bergonzi, Dave Van Kreidt (ts); Gerry Mulligan (bs); Darius Brubeck, Billy Kyle (p); Cal Tjader (vib); Norman Bates, Joe Benjamin, Chris Brubeck, Ron Crotty, Charles Mingus, Wyatt Reuther, Jack Six, Eugene Wright (b); Dan Brubeck, Lloyd Davis, Alan Dawson, Joe Dodge, Randy Jones, Joe Morello (d); Howard Brubeck (perc); Louis Armstrong, Lambert, Hendricks and Ross, Carmen McRae, Jimmy Rushing (v); New York Philharmonic Orchestra cond. Leonard Bernstein.

This is a real cross-section, including material from the mid-Forties, long before Brubeck became a Columbia recording artist. Both his octet and his trio are featured, before the first appearance of of the quartet with Paul Desmond on a radio broadcast from 1951. Obviously, the tracks that, for many people, introduced jazz to time-signatures other than 4/4 are here, not least 'Take Five' itself, though Desmond tends to be more invigorating on the earlier quartet tracks. Pretty tunes, such as 'La Paloma Azul', bring out Brubeck's more delicate touches.

CHARLIE CHRISTIAN

Charlie Christian:
Live Sessions At
Minton's Playhouse
Jazz Anthology

Personnel includes: Dizzy Gillespie, Joe Guy, Hot Lips Page (t); Rudy Williams (as); Don Byas (ts); Thelonious Monk, Kenny Kersey (p); Nick Fenton (b); Kenny Clarke, Taps Miller (d).

These sessions from 1941 give a priceless insight into the transition from swing to bebop. Historically, Gillespie tries to get his new style together and sometimes succeeds. The album's glory, though, is Charlie Christian. Not a bebopper, at least not yet, he stretches out with relaxed abandon over the punchy Monk-Clarke rhythm team. The track titled 'Swing Top Bop', where Christian grooves to a more supple beat in between piling on the riffs, superbly contrasts the old with the new.

ORNETTE COLEMAN

Ornette Coleman: Beauty Is
A Rare Thing
Atlantic (6 CDs)

Personnel includes: Don Cherry, Freddie Hubbard (t); Robert DiDominica (f); Eric Dolphy (as, f, bass clarinet); Bill Evans (p); Eddie Costa (vib); Jim Hall (g); George Duvivier, Charlie Haden, Scott LaFaro (bs); Ed Blackwell, Sticks Evans, Billy Higgins (d).

Dave Brubeck at the piano, before the famous partnership with Paul Desmond, pictured in 1950 at the Haig in Los Angeles.

Recorded between 1959 and 1961, these contain known tracks from epoch-making sessions plus a few not released before. The quartets, and the double-quartet 'Free Jazz' (both versions) are legendary, while, as a so-called Third Stream operation, bringing in a string section and looking to entwine jazz and classical, the 'Jazz Abstractions' project can be considered ahead of its time. From the violent abstractions of part of 'Free Jazz', to the folksy 'Ramblin'' to the aching romanticism of dirges like 'Lonely Woman', the future was here.

LEE COLLINS

Lee Collins, and others:
Sizzling The Blues
Frog

Personnel includes: Lee Collins, Sharkey Bonano (t); Louis Dumaine (c); Earl Humphrey (tb); Sidney Arodin, Willis Joseph (cl); Hal Jordy, Theodore Purnell (as); David Jones (ts); Johnny Miller (p); Eddie Jackson (tu); Al Morgan (b); Leo Adde, Monk Hazel, Joe Strode (d); Ann Cook, Genevieve Davis (v).

This album, recorded between 1927 and 1929, collects some of the important bands that stayed in New Orleans. Of the trumpeters, Lee Collins has the more developed solo style. The band he led jointly with David Jones (the Astoria Hot Eight, named after the dance hall where they performed) benefits from the comparative rarity for the time of a string bass that gives the tunes that typically bouncy New Orleans beat. The appearance on this session band of Sidney Arodin, who does elsewhere an excellent job on 'High Society',

A recent action photograph of Ornette Coleman, whose Prime Time performances have expanded to include a light show and a rapper.

with Monk Hazel, made it the first racially mixed session in what was then a segregated city.

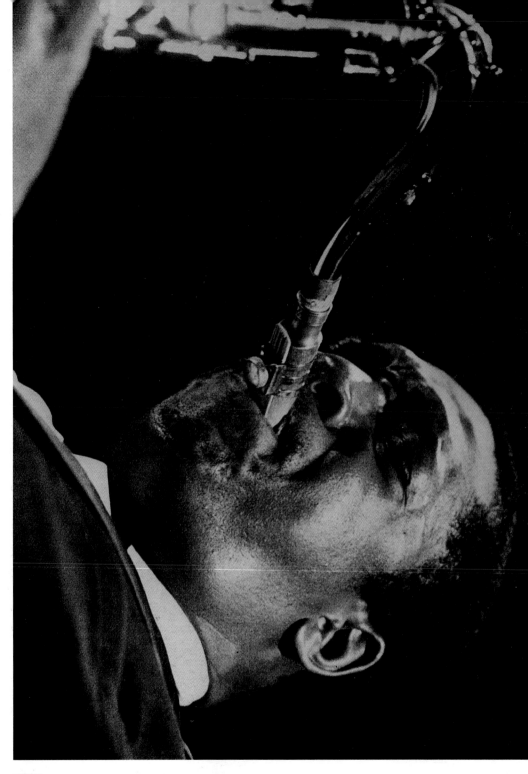

John Coltrane, pictured here in Amsterdam in 1962, regularly appeared with his quartet throughout Europe during the Sixties.

JOHN COLTRANE

John Coltrane: The Heavyweight Champion
Atlantic (7 CDs)

Personnel includes: Don Cherry, Freddie Hubbard (t); Eric Dolphy (as, fl); Tommy Flanagan, Hank Jones, Wynton Kelly, McCoy Tyner, Cedar Walton, (p); Milt Jackson (vib); Paul Chambers, Art Davis, Steve Davis, Reggie Workman (b); Jimmy Cobb, Lex Humphries, Elvin Jones, Connie Kay, Arthur Taylor (d).

The *Giant Steps* album, the hit version of 'My Favourite Things', 'Ole', with a larger group including Dolphy, and the tracks with Milt Jackson are here, with all the other Atlantics, recorded between 1959 and 1961 when Coltrane signed with Impulse. The 1959 sessions, which include 'Naima', 'Mr. PC', 'Like Sonny', 'Some Other Blues' and 'Giant Steps', themselves set an exalted level for Coltrane that he could only reach again by doing something else. One of the CDs is a kind of bonus, full of versions of these tunes not issued at the time.

AL COOPER

Al Cooper: The Savoy Sultans 1938-41
Classics

Personnel includes: Pat Jenkins, Sam Massenberg (t); Rudy Williams (as); Irving Brown, George Kelly, Ed McNeil, Sam Simmons (ts); Cyril Haynes, Oliver Richardson (p); Paul Chapman (g); Grachan Moncur (b); Alex Mitchell (d); Helen Proctor, Evelyn White (v).

A band that contained few musicians who made a reputation elsewhere, Williams being the best known, the Savoy Sultans had a fearsome reputation on their home territory, and many famous names who played opposite them at the Savoy had a hard battle to win over the dancers. With Al Cooper as the clarinet-leader, they built excitement out of simplicity, as did the Basie band in a different way. The driving beat laid down by the rhythm section explains part of the reason.

MILES DAVIS

Miles Davis: The CBS Years 1955-85
Columbia (4 CDs)

Personnel includes: Dave Liebman (ss); Julian 'Cannonball' Adderley, Gary Bartz (as); John Coltrane, George Coleman, Hank Mobley, Wayne Shorter (ts); Chick Corea, Bill Evans, Victor Feldman, Red Garland, Herbie Hancock, Keith Jarrett, Wynton Kelly, Joe Zawinul (p, key); John McLaughlin, John Scofield, Mike Stern (g); Ron Carter, Paul Chambers,

Dave Holland (b); Kenny Clarke, Jimmy Cobb, Billy Cobham, Jack DeJohnette, Al Foster, Elvin Jones, Philly Joe Jones, Lennie White, Tony Williams (d); Airto Moreira, Collin Walcott (perc).

One hesitates to recommend a sampler in the case of Miles Davis. However, he did record so much for so long during his spell at Columbia, that a four-volume digest is maybe justified as something that acts as more than a simple introduction. Material comes from several albums: while 'Flamenco Sketches' represents *Kind Of Blue*, the version of 'So What' is the Gil Evans arrangement from Carnegie Hall. Expected high-lights, from 'Summertime' to 'My Funny Valentine' to 'Miles Runs The Voodoo Down' are all here.

Miles Davis And Gil Evans, The Complete Columbia Studio Sessions
Columbia (6 CDs)

Personnel includes: John Carisi, Johnny Coles, Bernie Glow, Taft Jordan, Ernie Royal (t); Jimmy Cleveland, Rod Levitt, Frank Rehak, Joe Bennett (tb); Willie Ruff, Julius Watkins, Gunther Schuller (Frh); Bill Barber (tu); Lee Konitz (as); Romeo Penque, Jerome Richardson (f); Julian 'Cannonball' Adderley, Lee Konitz (as); Danny Bank (bs); Wynton Kelly (p); Janet Putman (harp); Paul Chambers (b); Jimmy Cobb, Elvin Jones, Philly Joe Jones, Arthur Taylor (d).

Possibly the most ambitious exhumation project of its kind to date, this combines the four long-playing albums with Gil Evans arrangements issued originally – including *Quiet*

In his last years, Miles Davis, playing here at London's Royal Festival Hall in 1988, attracted big audiences from well beyond the field of jazz.

Twenty years after his death, Duke Ellington's music is increasingly being performed by big bands that give their interpretations of his original scores.

Nights, that Davis was never happy to see released. There are few questions about the rest: *Miles Ahead*, *Porgy And Bess* and *Sketches Of Spain*. All of them provide marvellous examples of concertos for trumpet and orchestra and, significantly, each differs from the other. What sets this apart from previous reissues is that, aside from different versions of the tunes as released, there are extracts from rehearsals and alternative endings.

JIMMY DORSEY
Jimmy Dorsey: Contrasts
MCA/Decca

Personnel includes: Toots Camarata, Ray Linn, Phil Napoleon, Shorty Sherock (t); Bobby Byrne, Joe Yukl, Andy Russo (tb); Herbie Haymer, Dave Matthews, Sam Rubinwich, Babe Russin (reeds); Johnny Guarnieri, Joe Lippman, Freddy Slack (p); Allen Reuss (g); Bill Miller (b); Ray McKinley, Buddy Schutz (d); Bob Eberly, Helen O'Connell, June Richmond (v).

Overshadowed among jazz fans by his brother Tommy, Jimmy Dorsey's claim to fame in this context is the technical admiration of his peers. As an alto saxophonist, he had some influence on Lester Young and Charlie Parker, while others as different as Johnny Hodges and Ornette Coleman have praised his abundant technique. There are plenty of examples here, notably on the band's theme song, which otherwise showcases one of the better swing bands between 1936 and 1943. The later sides include a splendid 'King Porter Stomp'.

DUKE ELLINGTON
Duke Ellington: The Duke's Men, Vol. 1
Columbia (2 CDs)

Personnel includes: Freddie Jenkins, Rex Stewart, Cootie Williams (t); Lawrence Brown, Juan Tizol (tb); Joe 'Tricky Sam' Nanton, Juan Tizol (tb); Barney Bigard (cl); Otto Hardwick, Johnny Hodges (as); Harry Carney (bs); Tommy Fulford (p); Bernard Addison, Freddie Guy (g); Hayes Alvis, Wellman Braud, Billy Taylor (b); Sonny Greer (d).

Ellington's small-band sides of the Thirties are among the best of the era, high praise at a time when the miniature swing band, from the Holiday-Wilson classics to the Hampton jam sessions, was at its height. In fact, Ellington was not the nominal leader, the honour often going to Barney Bigard, Rex Stewart or Cootie Williams, though he was clearly the brains behind the venture. Among the best-known tracks are 'Stompy Jones' and 'Caravan', in its original version, under Bigard, and 'Echoes Of Harlem', by Cootie Williams.

Duke Ellington: The Blanton-Webster Band
(3 CDs)

Personnel includes: Wallace Jones, Ray Nance, Cootie Williams (t); Rex Stewart (c); Lawrence Brown, Joe 'Tricky Sam' Nanton (tb); Barney

Bigard (cl); Otto Hardwick, Johnny Hodges (as); Chauncey Haughton, Ben Webster (ts); Harry Carney (bs); Billy Strayhorn (p); Freddie Guy (g); Jimmy Blanton, Junior Raglan (b); Sonny Greer (d); Ivie Anderson (v).

By common consent the greatest of Ellington's bands, the one where compositional flair, individual strength and ensemble drive came together in a way that perhaps was never surpassed. He had been coming close, but the catalyst appears to have been the arrival of bassist Jimmy Blanton, just that little more propulsive as a rhythm than anyone else. Between 1940 and 1942, a regular stream of masterpieces was produced. The futuristic blues textures of 'Koko', the explosive swing of 'Harlem Air Shaft' and the ultimate trumpet feature, 'Concerto For Cootie' are just the icing on the cake.

Duke Ellington:
Fargo, 1940
Vintage Jazz Classics (2 CDs)

Personnel includes: Wallace Jones, Ray Nance, Cootie Williams (t); Rex Stewart (c); Lawrence Brown, Joe 'Tricky Sam' Nanton (tb); Otto Hardwick, Johnny Hodges (as); Ben Webster (ts); Harry Carney (bs); Freddie Guy (g); Jimmy Blanton (b); Sonny Greer (d); Ivie Anderson, Herb Jeffries (v).

Another of those nights when amateur recording engineers got a historical scoop. In November 1940, the Ellington band stopped off to play for dancers in the town of Fargo in North Dakota. Most of what survives was taken down by a couple of fans in the audience. It's a typically mixed live set, but some of the famous numbers are here in different versions, as are Webster, Blanton and Ray Nance, who apparently had just joined. The sound quality is, of course, not ideal, but perfectly acceptable in the circumstance, this being a great band that, in this form, was not together for very long.

EUREKA BRASS

Eureka Brass Band:
New Orleans Funeral
And Parade
American Music

Personnel includes: Percy Humphrey, Willie Pajeaud, Eddie Richardson (t); Sunny Henry, Albert Warner (tb); George Lewis (cl); Reuben Roddy (as); Emanuel Paul (ts); Joseph 'Red' Clark (sousaphone); Robert Lewis, Arthur Ogle (d).

Marching brass bands are part of the New Orleans myth. For obvious reasons, there were few recordings of outdoor events in the Twenties, so one cherishes this session from 1951 by arguably the best band of the period, led by trumpeter Percy Humphrey with George Lewis brought in as guest. The ragged but delightfully loose swing typifies New Orleans music in all its manifestations, while the wailing funeral sounds represented by 'West Lawn Dirge', ultra-traditional though they be, look forward to Ornette Coleman and Albert Ayler.

ELLA FITZGERALD

Ella Fitzgerald:
The Complete Song Books
Verve (16 CDs)

Personnel includes: Benny Carter (as); Ben Webster (ts); Oscar Peterson, Paul Smith (p); Stuff Smith (vn); Herb Ellis, Barney Kessel (g); Ray Brown, Joe Mondragon (b); Alvin Stoller (d). Plus orchestras of Buddy Bregman, Duke Ellington, Billy May, Nelson Riddle, and Paul Weston.

These songbooks, dedicated to the major American popular composers, now seems a staggering achievement for which producer Norman Granz deserves all our thanks – the more so, as not all fans of the time approved of Ella Fitzgerald being taken out of the strict jazz milieu. Beginning in 1956, when the Cole Porter songs were recorded, and ending with Johnny Mercer in 1964, the format was generally a big band (including Duke Ellington's for his own songs). What hindsight also makes clear is that, however you measure it, Ella Fitzgerald was then at her peak.

The original Benny Goodman quartet with, left to right, Lionel Hampton, Teddy Wilson, Goodman and Gene Krupa.

STAN GETZ

Stan Getz:
The Bossa Nova Years
Verve (4 CDs)

Personnel includes: Doc Severinson, Bernie Glow, Clark Terry, Nick Travis (t); Ray Alonge (Frh); Tony Studd, Bob Brookmeyer, Willie Dennis (tb); Romeo Penque (f); Hank Jones, Steve Kuhn (p); Gary Burton (vib); Laurindo Almeida, Luis Bonfa, Kenny Burrell, Charlie Byrd, Joao Gilberto, Jim Hall (g); Keter Betts, George Duvivier, Don Payne, Gene Cherico (b); Dave Bailey, Milton Banana, Jose Carlos, Edison Machado (d, perc); Astrud Gilberto, Joao Gilberto, Maria Toledo (v).

The bossa nova proved the biggest career boon to Stan Getz – he once credited 'Desafinado' as having paid his children's way through college. Although he did not actually introduce the undulating Brazilian rhythms to the wider public, his records in this style made between 1962 and 1964 ultimately did most to popularise it, together with the fortuitous vocal appearance that launched the career of Astrud Gilberto. It was a project bound to succeed, as few musicians in any sphere can rival Getz in extracting so much poetry out of pretty tunes.

BENNY GOODMAN
Benny Goodman: The Birth Of Swing
RCA Bluebird (3 CDs)

Personnel includes: Bunny Berigan, Sterling Bose, Pee Wee Irvin, Manny Klein (t); Red Ballard, Jack Lacey, Murray McEachern (tb); Toots Mondello, Hymie Schertzer (as); Vido Musso, Arthur Rollini (ts); Frank Froeba, Jess Stacy (p); Allan Reuss, George Van Eps (g); Harry Goodman (b); Gene Krupa (d).

This set presents the band before Harry James joined, but he had a more than capable predecessor in Bunny Berigan, whose solo on 'King Porter Stomp' sets his stamp on the music. Goodman had hired the best swing arrangers, notably Fletcher Henderson, who had perfected the art rather late in the day when he was struggling to keep his own band together. The effortless swing of 'Blue Skies' and of the various numbers arranged by Jimmy Mundy and Edgar Sampson helped Goodman launch the swing era, though his poised clarinet solos did more than a little to nudge it along.

LIONEL HAMPTON
Lionel Hampton: Flying Home
MCA/Decca

Personnel includes: Cat Anderson, Wendell Culley, Karl George, Al Killian, Joe Morris, Jimmy Nottingham, Lamar Wright, Snooky Young (t); Fred Beckett, Al Hayes, Vernon Porter, Jimmy Wormick (tb); Earl Bostic, Herbie Fields, Ben Kynard, Bobby Plater, Marshall Royal (as); Arnett Cobb, Johnny Griffin, Dexter Gordon, Illinois Jacquet, Al Sears, Charlie Fowlkes, Jack McVea (ts); Milt Buckner, Dardanelle Breckenridge, John Mehegan (p); Irving Ashby, Billy Mackel (g); Ray Perry (vn); Vernon Alley (b); George Jones (d); Dinah Washington (v).

The album title stands for one of the legendary rabble-rousers of jazz, an ordinary riff tune that lives on through the fervent but, by rock'n'roll and later standards, really quite tasteful solo by Illinois Jacquet. Many times copied, it became part of the arrangement and helped both Hampton and Jacquet in their subsequent careers. There are two versions here, Jacquet's and Arnett Cobb's, plus a representative sample of early (1942-45) orchestral Hampton: pounding happily at the vibraphone and showing off his two-fingered piano style on 'Hamp's Boogie Woogie'.

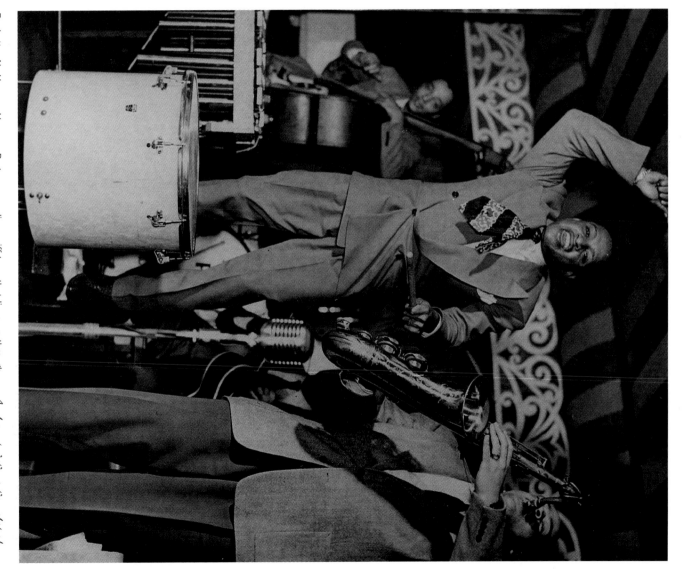

A characteristic action shot of Lionel Hampton, about to bring a number to a shattering climax.

COLEMAN HAWKINS
Coleman Hawkins: The Complete Recordings, 1929-41
(6 CDs)

Personnel includes: Henry 'Red' Allen, Muggsy Spanier, Bobby Stark (t); J.C.

whole, one has to concur with the view expressed by some of the band's members that the records didn't capture the way they sounded on the gig. The age of swing, the addition of a string bass and the fact of Fletcher and his brother Horace finally being forced to write new musical arrangements brought new musical life to the band, as is clear from the tracks after 1931. How ironic that this tale is most often told in the form of Benny Goodman reaping the benefit.

Butch Warren, Buster Williams, (b); Roy Brooks, Joe Chambers, Billy Drummond, Al Foster, Roy Haynes, Al Harewood, Al Heath, Roger Humphries, Elvin Jones, Clarence Johnson, Pete La Roca, Mel Lewis, Mickey Roker, Tony Williams (d).

JOE HENDERSON

Joe Henderson:
The Blue Note Years
Blue Note (4 CDs)

Personnel includes: Donald Byrd, Johnny Coles, Kenny Dorham, Freddie Hubbard, Lee Morgan, Woody Shaw (t); Garnett Brown, Curtis Fuller, Jimmy Knepper, Benny Powell, Julian Priester (tb); Hubert Laws (f); Eric Dolphy, Jerry Dodgion, James Spaulding (as); Eddie Daniels, Jerome Richardson (ts), Pepper Adams, (bs) Barry Harris, Tommy Flanagan, Herbie Hancock, Roland Hanna, Steve Kuhn, Renee Rosnes, Horace Silver, Cedar Walton (p); Bobby Hutcherson (vib); Grant Green (g); Ron Carter, Ira Coleman, Bob Cranshaw, Richard Davis, Eddie Khan, Herbie Lewis,

Elevated rather late in his career to what, in jazz terms, is almost super-star status, Joe Henderson has always had the respect of his colleagues. Essentially a post-Rollins tenor saxophonist, he could perform from the start with something of the delicacy of Stan Getz; his latter-day album of Jobim tunes has its roots in his early collaborations with Kenny Dorham, often dominated by Latin-style tunes. The strongest parts of this compilation, spanning 1963 to 1990, tend to be concentrated in the Sixties, though note the excerpts from the outstanding *State Of The Tenor* album from 1985.

BILLIE HOLIDAY

Billie Holiday:
The Voice Of Jazz
Affinity (6 CDs)

Personnel includes: Bunny Berigan, Buck Clayton, Roy Eldridge, Bobby Hackett, Jonah Jones, Frankie Newton (t); Benny Morton, Jack Teagarden, Dicky Wells, Trummy

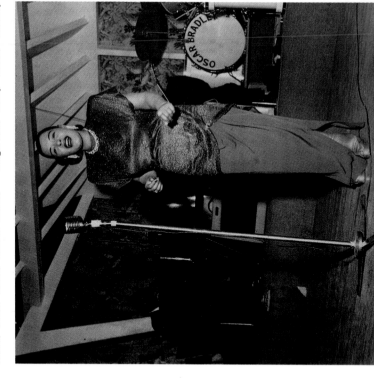

Tenor saxophonist Joe Henderson has become one of the most popular jazz musicians since his album of Billy Strayhorn songs.

Higginbotham, Claude Jones, Glenn Miller, Dicky Wells (tb); Benny Goodman, Pee Wee Russell (cl); Hilton Jefferson, Jimmy Dorsey (as); Horace Adrian Rollini (bass-sax.); Horace Henderson, Buck Washington (p); Bernard Addison (g); Pops Foster, John Kirby, Al Morgan (b); Walter Johnson, Gene Krupa (d). Plus the Jack Hylton Orchestra and The Ramblers.

There are grounds even today for claiming that Coleman Hawkins was at his peak around the time he sailed for Europe in 1934, with such numbers as 'Hello Lola' and 'I've Got To Sing A Torch Song' under his belt. His five years in Europe, documented on three of these discs, put him into many contexts, though he shines especially when pitted against fellow-expatriate Benny Carter. Then it was home again, and almost immediately the triumph of 'Body And Soul'.

FLETCHER HENDERSON

Fletcher Henderson:
A Study In Frustration
Columbia (3 CDs)

Personnel includes: Henry 'Red' Allen, Louis Armstrong, Roy Eldridge, Rex Stewart (t); Charlie Green, Jimmy Harrison, J.C. Higginbotham, Benny Morton (tb); Buster Bailey (cl); Benny Carter, Hilton Jefferson, Russell Procope, Don Redman (as); Chu Berry, Coleman Hawkins, Ben Webster (ts); Fletcher Henderson, Horace Henderson, Fats Waller (p); Israel Crosby, John Kirby (b); Walter Johnson, Sid Catlett (d).

In a strange way, Fletcher Henderson's finest band came after his period of fame. As the man who put big band jazz on the map, he hired the best soloists, and they are enough to make his early records fascinating beyond the fact of their prime historical significance. On the

The quality of her voice may have coarsened over the years, but Billie Holiday never lost the ability to transfix an audience.

Young, (tb); Buster Bailey, Benny Goodman, Irving Fazola, Edmund Hall, Cecil Scott, Artie Shaw (cl); Benny Carter, Johnny Hodges, Hilton Jefferson, Tab Smith (as); Babe Russin, Joe Thomas, Ben Webster, Lester Young (ts); Joe Bushkin, Sonny White, Teddy Wilson (p); Bernard Addison, Dave Barbour, Al Casey, John Collins, Freddie Green, Lawrence Lucie, Allan Reuss (g); Artie Bernstein, Milt Hinton, John Kirby, Walter Page (b); Cozy Cole, J.C. Heard, Jo Jones, Gene Krupa, Yank Porter (d).

In a set that includes Billie Holiday's first records made in 1933 and extends to her first Commodore session of 1940, the one that produced 'Strange Fruit' (which her own company of the time was unwilling to risk), this could be the ultimate compilation of jazz singing. If the material was hardly the best from an era rich in popular songs, her ability to make something called 'A Sailboat In The Moonlight' tug the heartstrings still seems incredible. The backing groups, with Lester Young shadowing her all the way, are alone worth more than a listen.

SPIKE HUGHES

Spike Hughes: High Yellow
Largo

Personnel includes: Henry 'Red' Allen, Shad Collins, Leonard Davis Norman Payne, Leslie Thompson (t); Lew Davis, Wilbur de Paris, George Washington, Dicky Wells (tb); Billy Amstell, Benny Carter, Wayman Carver, Harry Hayes, Howard Johnson (as); Chu Berry, Buddy Featherstonhaugh, Coleman Hawkins (ts); Eddie Carroll, Red Rodriguez, Luis Russell, (p); Lawrence Lucie (g); Ernest Hill (b); Sid Catlett, Kaiser Marshall (d).

British jazz in its formative years owed much to Spike Hughes. His New York recordings of 1933, with the likes of Benny Carter and Red Allen playing his arrangements, are justly famous, apart from anything else, as being among the first and best to show the influence of Duke Ellington. Nine of these tracks turn up here. A well-known leader of the time, he had, by 1930, begun to model his dance band on the great black orchestras. The moody 'Harlem Symphony' and the stomping 'Six Bells Stampede' are two outstanding examples of Hughes putting his personal stamp on the emerging big band scene.

KEITH JARRETT

Keith Jarrett: Sun Bear Concerts
ECM (6 CDs)

Keith Jarrett (p)

A phenomenon of the past two decades was the success of the solo piano recital as conceived by Keith Jarrett. These bore little relation to what one thinks of normally as jazz piano. Totally improvised, they often drew on classical European principles, as Jarrett hit on a phrase or motif and spun it out for several minutes before proceeding to the next bit, with few pauses in between. Only an exceptional virtuoso could have pulled it off. These concerts, given on five days in Japan between November 5 and 18, 1976, were among the earliest.

Among his other achievements, Keith Jarrett put the piano recital on the map.

STAN KENTON

Stan Kenton: Retrospective
Capitol (4 CDs)

Personnel includes: Chico Alvarez, Buddy Childers, Conte Candoli, Maynard Ferguson, Sam Noto, Shorty Rogers, Jack Sheldon, Marvin Stamm, Stu Williamson (t); Milt Bernhart, Eddie Bert, Carl Fontana, Frank Rosolino, Kai Winding (tb); Gene Roland (ss); Gabe Baltazar, Lee Konitz, Charlie Mariano, Boots Mussulli, Lennie Niehaus, Art Pepper, Dave Schildkraut, Bud Shank (as); Bob Cooper, Sam Donahue, Richie Kamuca, Don Menza, Bill Perkins, Zoot Sims (ts); Bob Gioga (bs); Laurindo Almeida, Ralph Blaze, Sal Salvador (g); Don Bagley, Eddie Safranski (b); June Christy, Nat King Cole, Chris Connor, Ann Richards, Jean Turner (v).

Given his image as a restless seeker, Stan Kenton's career shows appropriate changes of mood. This compilation extends from 1943, virtually the start, to 1968, by which time the innovations had run out. There are enough spirited jazz performances, including such Shorty Rogers specialities as 'Jolly Rogers', and excellent solos from the various stars to please those who may not relish Bob Graettinger's futuristic 'City

RAHSAAN ROLAND KIRK

Rahsaan Roland Kirk: Rahsaan – The Complete Mercury Recordings
Mercury (11 CDs)

Personnel includes: Virgil Jones (t); Tom McIntosh (tb); Tubby Hayes, James Moody (ts); Walter Bishop, Jaki Byard, Andrew Hill, Wynton Kelly, Harold Mabern, Tete Montoliu, Horace Parlan, Richard Wyands (p); Art Davis, Richard Davis, Sam Jones, Niels-Henning Orsted Pederson (b); Roy Haynes, J.C. Moses, Walter Perkins, Charlie Persip (d); Sonny Boy Williamson (harmonica).

Of all jazz musicians, Roland Kirk had to be seen, and one hopes there is enough film around to enliven the documentary that is the very least his memory deserves. As a performer

The amazing line-up of Rahsaan Roland Kirk, fully equipped with (left to right) manzello, stritch, tenor saxophone, siren and flute.

Of Glass', now increasingly regarded as a pioneering work and represented here by a single movement, or who find the plummy sound of the brass mellophoniums not to their taste.

who made the most of his ability to play three saxophones at once, he was utterly unique, though there may be echoes of the one-man-band street entertainers of the past. These CDs collect all his albums for the Mercury label between 1961 and 1965, including *We Free Kings* and the much-admired *Rip, Rig And Panic*, with a judicious choice of unissued tracks and rejected versions.

MCKINNEY'S COTTON PICKERS

McKinney's Cotton Pickers: The Band Don Redman Built
RCA Bluebird

Personnel includes: Leonard Davis, Sidney de Paris, John Nesbitt, Joe Smith (t); Rex Stewart (c); Ed Cuffee, Claude Jones (tb) ; Benny Carter, Don Redman (as); Coleman Hawkins, Ted McCord, Prince Robinson, George Thomas (ts); Todd Rhodes, Fats Waller (p); Dave Wilborn (g); Ralph Escudero, Billy Taylor (tu); Cuba Austin, Kaiser Marshall (d).

After leaving Fletcher Henderson and before setting up on his own, Don Redman became musical director of McKinney's Cotton Pickers, a band with some good musicians and a talented arranger in trumpeter John Nesbitt. Redman turned it almost into what one now calls an arranger's band, cutting across the sections and aiming for a light yet full sound that, in some ways, looks ahead to the Miles Davis nonet. Such big names as Benny Carter and Fats Waller were added as guests for the sessions, made between 1928 and 1930.

MINGUS BIG BAND

Mingus Big Band: Gunslinging Birds
Dreyfus

Personnel includes: Randy Brecker, Philip Harper, Ryan Kisor (t); Jamal Haynes, Ku-lumba Frank Lacy, Earl McIntyre (tb); David Lee Jones, Steve Slagle (as); Craig Handy, Chris Potter, John Stubblefield (ts); Gary Smulyan (bs); Kenny Drew Jr. (p); Andy McKee (b); Adam Cruz (d).

Remembered for his belting blues or churning gospel rhythms, Charles Mingus was essentially a linear composer who enjoyed spinning a tune to ultimate lengths. His compositions often cry out for orchestration, and The Big Band, formed in 1991 following the revival of *Epitaph*, surround these melodies and riffs with swirling textures and add exceptionally strong soloists in a way that does Mingus proud. Much of their earlier album consisted of arrangements which Mingus either wrote or approved. This one has been largely put together by members, four of the tunes being arranged by saxophonist Steve Slagle, and you can't spot the difference.

KIPPIE MOEKETZI

Kippie Moeketzi and others: Jazz In Africa, Vols. 1 and 2
Kaz (2 separate CDs)

Personnel includes: Hugh Masakela (t); Jonas Gwangwa (tb); Kippie Moeketsi, Dennis Phillips, Robbie Jansen (as); Basil Coetzee, Duke Makasi, Barney Rachabane (ts); Abdullah Ibrahim, Christopher Joseph, Pat Matshikiza, Tete Mbambisa, John Mehegan (p); Lionel Beukes, Sipho Gumede, Alec Khaoli, Claude Shange (b); Nazier Kapdi, Gene Latimore, Sipho Mabuse, Gilbert Matthews (d); Ray Shange (pennywhistle).

For obvious reasons, South Africa would be high on any list of countries where jazz or an equivalent should emerge. These albums, from between 1959 and 1962, include a couple of names in Abdullah Ibrahim and Hugh Masakela that have since become familiar throughout the world, though at the time Kippie Moeketsi was equally well-known in his homeland. Volume 1 is largely straight jazz : the tracks with American pianist Mehegan first appeared under his name and include several standards. The kwela rhythms and overlapping melodies are far more pronounced on the second volume.

THELONIOUS MONK

Thelonious Monk: Complete Blue Note Recordings
Blue Note (4 CDs)

Personnel includes: Kenny Dorham, Idrees Sulieman, George Taitt (t); Lou Donaldson, Sahib Shihab, Danny Quebec West (as); John Coltrane, Sonny Rollins, Lucky Thompson (ts); Milt Jackson (vib); Nelson Boyd, Paul Chambers, Al McKibbon, Ahmed Abdul Malik, Bob Paige, Gene Ramey, John Simmons (b); Art Blakey, Roy Haynes, Max Roach, Shadow Wilson (d); Kenny Hagood (v).

Thelonious Monk's Blue Note period got a posthumous extension, when a hitherto unknown recording was discovered, from the Five Spot, by the quartet with Coltrane. The rest dates from 1947 to 1952 and includes the first, and often the best, versions of such remarkable pieces as 'Criss Cross', 'Straight No Chaser' and the famous 'Round Midnight'. His partnership with Milt Jackson on 'Mysterioso', 'Epistrophy' and 'Evidence' exploited the jangling sound of piano-plus-vibes in a way no one has bettered. A real oddity, long before *Time Out*, is the 6/4 rhythm underpinning the old pop song 'Carolina Moon'.

Thelonious Monk, wrists flat over the keys while the impetus comes from forearm and fingers.

JELLY ROLL MORTON

Jelly Roll Morton:
Complete Victor Recordings

RCA Bluebird (5 CDs)

....

Personnel includes: Henry 'Red' Allen, Ed Anderson, Sidney de Paris, Bubber Miley, Ward Pinkett (t); Wilbur de Paris, Charlie Irvis, J.C. Higginbotham, Claude Jones, Kid Ory, Fred Robinson (tb); George Baquet, Barney Bigard, Johnny Dodds, Darnell Howard, Albert Nicholas, Omer Simeon (cl); Paul Barnes (ss); Stump Evans, Russell Procope, Walter Thomas (as); Happy Caldwell, Joe Garland, Joe Thomas (ts); Rod Rodriguez (p); Clarence Black, J. Wright Smith (vn); Lee Blair, Johnny St. Cyr (banjo); Bernard Addison, Lawrence Lucie (g); Wellman Braud, Pops Foster, John Lindsay, Billy Taylor (b); Bill Benford, Pete Briggs (tu); Paul Barbarin, Tommy Benford, Cozy Cole, Andrew Hilaire, Manzie Johnson, Zutty Singleton (d); Lew LeMar (v).

These contain everything Morton recorded as a leader for the Victor company between 1926 and 1939, although there is a gap of nine years from 1930 that accurately measures the decline in his fortunes. All the music is worth hearing, though the really great orchestral compositions

are those recorded by the Red Hot Peppers before Morton moved to New York. Others have fine solos from the likes of Allen and Bechet, while the piano solos and the delightful trios with Dodds and Bigard also stand out. Note that a couple of the supposedly different versions (those of 'Original Jelly Roll Blues' and 'Freakish') are in fact repeated.

BENNY MOTEN

Benny Moten: Kansas
City Orchestra 1930-32

Classics

....

Personnel includes: Joe Keyes, Ed Lewis, Hot Lips Page, Booker Washington (t); Eddie Durham, Thamon Hayes, Dan Minor (tb); Eddie Barefield, Harlan Leonard (as); Woody Walder, Ben Webster (ts); Jack Washington (bs); Count Basie (p); Buster Moten (accordion); Leroy Berry (g); Vernon Page (tu); Walter Page (b); Willie McWashington (d); Jimmy Rushing (v).

Since the transfer from vinyl to CD, the main links missing in the historical chain are, at the time of

writing, the territory bands of the South West. Moten's, the best known and the most prolifically recorded, provides the obvious exception, and this is the great period before its almost seamless transformation into the Count Basie band. Local fans preferred rugged, blues-rooted music and were unimpressed by the sophisticated stuff purveyed by the Ellington or Henderson when these bands visited the area. Once the bass of Walter Page replaces the tuba of his namesake, that familiar drive emerges on 'Moten Swing' and 'Toby' (ironically, the dancers of Kansas City at first deplored the change).

Throughout the world, the jazz big band continues to evolve, without jettisoning completely the swing and the brass-reed riffs that set it apart in the first place. Members of the New York Composers Orchestra include some key players from the progressive end: Ray Anderson, Bobby Previte and Wayne Horvitz are just three who lead prominent groups under their own names but occasionally pool their resources. Anthony Braxton, Lenny Pickett and Elliott Sharp contribute pieces from outside; the others are by Robin Holcomb, Horvitz and Previte.

NEW YORK COMPOSERS ORCHESTRA

New York Composers
Orchestra: First Program
In Standard Time

New World

....

Personnel includes: Eddie Allen, Steven Bernstein, Jack Walrath (t); Ray Anderson, Art Baron (tb); Vincent Chancey (Frh); Robert DeBellis, Cleave Guyton Jr (as); Marty Ehrlich, Doug Wieselman (ts); Sam Furnace (bs); Robin Holcomb (p); Wayne Horvitz (key); Lindsey Horner (b); Bobby Previte (d).

CHARLIE PARKER

The Complete Charlie
Parker On Verve

Verve (10 CDs)

....

Personnel includes: Buck Clayton, Kenny Dorham, Harry Edison, Roy Eldridge, Dizzy Gillespie, Benny Harris, Howard McGhee, Red Rodney, Charlie Shavers (t); Benny Carter, Johnny Hodges, Willie Smith (as); Coleman Hawkins, Flip Phillips, Ben Webster, Lester Young (ts); Walter Bishop Jr., Al Haig, Hank Jones, Kenny Kersey, John Lewis, Thelonious Monk, Oscar Peterson, Mel Powell, Arnold Ross (p); Irving Ashby, Billy Bauer, Barney Kessel (g); Ray Brown, Billy Hadnott, Percy Heath, Teddy Kotick, Charles Mingus, Tommy

Charlie Parker, identified, with
other Metronome poll winners
recording in 1948.

A happy Jelly Roll Morton
seated at the piano in 1940,
shortly after his career revived.

With Dizzy Gillespie in the trumpet section, the band also recorded the first version of 'Night In Tunisia' under the title 'Interlude'.

DJANGO REINHARDT
Django Reinhardt: Swing In Paris 1936-40
Affinity (5 CDs)

Personnel includes: Phillipe Brun, Bill Coleman, Red Stewart (t); Benny Carter, Andre Ekyan (as); Frank 'Big Boy' Goudie, Alix Combelle, Coleman Hawkins, Bertie King, Hubert Rostaing (ts); Stephane Grappelli, Eddie South, Michel Warlop (vn); Pierre Ferret, Joseph Reinhardt (g); Wilson Myers, Louis Vola (b); Pierre Fouad (d); Freddy Taylor (v).

These cover the period when Django Reinhardt was at his peak. Alongside Grappelli during the early recordings by the celebrated Quintet of the Hot Club, effervescent, unpredictable phrases erupted from his guitar and received major international recognition alongside Hawkins, Carter, Dicky Wells and other passing Americans. He also gets a chance to play with other violinists, both South and the Frenchman Warlop offering a contrast to Grappelli. Note, incidentally, how well the other Frenchmen acquit themselves when pitched against top Americans.

BUD POWELL
Bud Powell: The Complete Blue Note and Roost Recordings
Blue Note (4 CDs)

Personnel includes: Fats Navarro (t); Curtis Fuller (tb); Sonny Rollins (ts); Paul Chambers, George Duvivier, Sam Jones, Pierre Michelot, Tommy Potter, Curly Russell (b); Kenny Clarke, Roy Haynes, Philly Joe Jones, Max Roach, Arthur Taylor (d).

For much of the later part of his career, Powell's personal difficulties affected his piano playing, so that the virtuoso heard on the opening session from 1947, where his extraordinary touch imparts an almost staccato effect to each note even at speed, hardly appears after the early Fifties. However, the point about all his American Blue Note sessions (those from 1963 were recorded in Paris) is that they each produced fascinating new compositions, showing that his musical mind was as acute as ever.

BOYD RAEBURN
Boyd Raeburn: Boyd Meets Stravinsky
Savoy

Personnel includes: Tommy Allison, Dizzy Gillespie, Ray Linn (t); Johnny Mandel, Ollie Wilson, Trummy Young (tb); Johnny Bothwell (as); Ralph Lee, Frank Socolow (ts); Ike Carpenter, Dodo Marmarosa (p); Harry Babasin, Oscar Pettiford (b); Shelly Manne, Jackie Mills (d); David Allyn, Ginny Powell (v).

Boyd Raeburn had it in him musically to become a rival to Stan Kenton in the progressive stakes of the time. These tracks were recorded between 1945 and 1947. Those furthest out were arranged by George Handy, a pianist who later played for Zoot Sims but wrote such pieces as 'Dalvatore Sally' and arranged 'Over The Rainbow' as a futuristic collage.

SONNY ROLLINS
Sonny Rollins: The Complete Prestige Recordings
Prestige (7 CDs)

Personnel includes: Clifford Brown, Miles Davis, Kenny Dorham, Art Farmer (t); Bennie Green, J.J. Johnson (tb); Julius Watkins (Frh); Jackie McLean (as); John Coltrane, Charlie Parker (ts); Walter Bishop Jr., Ray Bryant, Kenny Drew, Tommy Flanagan, Red Garland, Elmo Hope, Wade Legge, John Lewis, Thelonious

In public and on record, Oscar Peterson usually performs in a trio context.

Potter, Curly Russell (b); Max Roach, Arthur Taylor, Lee Young (d); Machito, Chano Pozo, Carlos Vidal (percussion); Ella Fitzgerald, Dave Lambert Singers (v).

Whereas Parker's recordings for Savoy and Dial revolved around his small groups, his later work for Verve was more varied. Label boss Norman Granz, who had previously used Parker on some of his Jazz At The Philharmonic tours (as on the 1946 'Lady Be Good'), recorded him with big bands and strings as well as quartets and quintets. Though some of the more experimental pieces don't quite succeed, and it is impossible to miss the decline shown in his playing towards the end, most of this is typically exhilarating stuff from one of the real improvising geniuses.

ART PEPPER
Art Pepper: The Complete Galaxy Recordings
Galaxy (16 CDs)

Personnel includes: George Cables, Stanley Cowell, Tommy Flanagan, Hank Jones (p); Howard Roberts (g); Ron Carter, Tony Dumas, Charlie Haden, Red Mitchell, David Williams (b); Carl Burnett, Al Foster, Roy Haynes, Billy Higgins (d); Kenneth Nash (perc); string section.

All the music comes from 10 sessions between 1978 and 1982, and nearly half the tracks never emerged on LP. They are fully representative of Art Pepper's later period, the searing emotional content and the more corrosive sound he produced from the alto hitting harder than his more lyrical solos from the Fifties, while also being more unpredictable. Never afraid of a challenge, he is the only horn soloist present, taking some solos without accompaniment or in duets with pianist Cables.

OSCAR PETERSON
Oscar Peterson: Exclusively For My Friends
Verve/MPS (4 CDs)

Personnel includes: Ray Brown, Sam Jones (b); Bobby Durham, Louis Hayes, Ed Thigpen (d).

These tracks were recorded between 1963 and 1968 in Germany, at the home of the MPS boss, a Peterson admirer who managed to produce an atmosphere more relaxed than one often finds in the studio. They constitute an ideal balance, because the various trio sessions, themselves representative, were followed by some solo piano. Peterson is one of the few who can claim to follow in Tatum's footsteps with total conviction, but it is a skill he has all too rarely exercised in concert or on record.

Sonny Rollins poses for the camera outside Ronnie Scott's Club, London, while making his debut there in January 1963.

Monk, Richie Powell, Horace Silver (p); Paul Chambers, Leonard Gaskin, Percy Heath, George Morrow, Tommy Potter, Doug Watkins (b); Art Blakey, Kenny Clarke, Roy Haynes, Philly Joe Jones, Willie Jones, Max Roach, Arthur Taylor (d); Earl Coleman (v).

Most of the early recordings by Sonny Rollins were made for Prestige. They begin in 1949 and gradually work up to the sessions with Monk, Silver or Elmo Hope on piano, when his mature style is all but there. It duly appears after his return in 1955, beginning with the *Worktime* album and then on to *Saxophone Colossus*, with its much-analysed 'Blue Seven' solo. For another example of thematic development on the blues, but done at speed and with bags of humour, try 'Ee-Ah'. The inclusion of 'Sonny Boy' begins a series of rhapsodies on unlikely pop songs continued when Rollins moved to other labels.

ART TATUM

Art Tatum: The Complete Pablo Solo Masterpieces

Pablo (7 CDs)

Art Tatum (p).

Recorded between 1953 and 1956, over four long sessions, these solo piano performances were Tatum's magnificent swan song. With so much time at his disposal, he recorded several songs, including 'You're Blasé' and 'I've Got A Crush On You' that do not turn up elsewhere, as well as such familiar items as 'Tea For Two' and 'Elegie'. Most of the tunes are well enough known and delightful to follow. The trick is to get behind the obvious bravura and the endless stream of arpeggios and then appreciate the intellectual complexity behind it all.

Virtuoso pianist Art Tatum gets ready to send his fingers flying over the keys.

In the early Fifties, a need was seen to record musicians from the pre-bop era, who had often been overlooked in the squabbling between factions. The Vanguard label took the lead in this, and these sessions were among the results. His own style a cross between Basie and bop, pianist Sir Charles Thompson leads the rhythm section with aplomb, and there are excellent solos from Newman, Morton and the rather under-valued Emmett Berry. An inevitable highlight is the Hawkins solo on 'It's The Talk Of The Town'.

SIR CHARLES THOMPSON

Sir Charles Thompson: His Personal Vanguard Recordings

Vanguard (2 CDs)

Personnel includes: Emmett Berry, Joe Newman (t); Benny Morton, Benny Powell (tb); Pete Brown, Earl Warren (as); Coleman Hawkins (ts); Skeeter Best, Freddie Green, Steve Jordan (g); Aaron Bell, Gene Ramey (b); Osie Johnson (d).

Before the Birth Of The Cool came Claude Thornhill's society band. Leading from the piano, Thornhill used French horns, plus tuba as a melody instrument, when they were rare in the jazz world. He hired Gil Evans and Gerry Mulligan as arrangers, included upcoming stars like Lee Konitz and ended by mixing such bebop tunes as 'Anthropology' with 'La Paloma', both expertly arranged on these radio transcriptions by Gil Evans. Mulligan later adapted his arrangement of 'Godchild' for Miles Davis.

CLAUDE THORNHILL

Claude Thornhill: The Song Is You

Hep

Personnel includes: Johnny Carisi, Louis Mucci, Gene Roland, Ed Zandy (t); Allan Langstaff, Johnny Torick (tb); Sandy Siegelstein, Walter Weschler (frh); Bill Barber (tb); Danny Polo, Lee Konitz (as); Mickey Folus, Brew Moore (ts); Gerry Mulligan (bs); Joe Derise (g); Joe Shulman (b); Bill Exiner (d).

Jazz Media

Live Jazz

Major jazz festivals in the U.S., starting with Newport, often include historical surveys and make room for jazz of all kinds on the fringes.

Festivals are the current success story of jazz. While rock has no rival at getting fans to fill giant stadiums or similar events, the jazz festival has several acres of the countryside, jazz is ideal for the urban setting. Music can readily be divided among several halls, clubs, bars, and can even take to the streets. Jazz festivals are of the right type, the right size, and draw people who fit the right image, to attract sponsorship from local and/or central government funds and from local businesses, so that offering support of whatever kind is seen increasingly as making a positive impact on the community's well-being.

Festivals tend to encompass the whole of jazz so, unsurprisingly, the most likely starting date was the late Thirties. Benny Goodman at Carnegie Hall and the two Spirituals To Swing concerts presented jazz in the round. Perhaps the closest to a modern festival took place in 1938 at New York's Randall's Island. It ran for less than a day, but among those squeezed in were Duke Ellington, Gene Krupa, Eddie Condon, Slim Gaillard and future film star Betty Hutton, then the vocalist with the Vincent Lopez Orchestra.

Europe's involvement grew after the war. A week in Nice in 1948, under the auspices of the somewhat blinkered French critic Hugues Panassie, included no bebop; next year, however, both Sidney Bechet and Charlie Parker appeared at the Paris Festival. The modern age began in 1954, one summer's weekend in Newport, Rhode Island. The importance of a festival to a town, in putting it on the map, was acknowledged by the mayor in his opening address.

Surviving a brief period when crowd trouble affected both Newport and similar events, the jazz festival has become established world-wide. Among literally hundreds, a few feature almost entirely local musicians while others might specialize – from very traditional to very progressive to the interface with other musics. Bassist Jyrki Kangas, now artistic director at Pori in Finland, was among those enthusiasts who launched the festival in 1966. Topping the bill in early years were George Russell and the Art Ensemble of Chicago. As it mushroomed, so were Chaka Khan and Ringo Starr invited. But even if headline acts of this kind are used here and elsewhere to attract crowds well beyond the committed fans, the wise programmer makes available a generous representation of jazz, in assorted venues, for at least part of the time.

In the U.S., leading festivals include those in New York (the eventual successor to the original Newport), Monterey, New Orleans, and Detroit, which has links with a major European festival at Montreux. Because European events in summer are driven by tourism, ten major festivals from different countries have formed a Jazz Festivals Association to coordinate bookings of American stars. Their festivals all take place around the same time in June-July, so Association members can combine in negotiating fees. This also enables others to book musicians on days when they are not appearing for the 'big ten' (who stretch, geographically, from Glasgow to Istanbul and from Molde to Vitoria), without having to pay the full travel costs.

Although the touring American band is very important in Europe and elsewhere – and why not, as this could be the only chance fans get to see them? – those from other countries often hold their own, not just musically but also as commercial attractions. The ease of modern transport allows musicians of all nationalities to team up regularly, while the practice of getting a distinguished (not necessarily American) musician to lead a group of locals has been very successful.

Festivals carry the highest profile, but most jazz gigs are still in clubs, with concerts becoming more frequent, helped by the amount of smaller halls available. Older-established clubs, such as the Village Vanguard and the Blue Note in New York and Ronnie Scott's in London, book well-known groups for weeks at a time. Some newer clubs change the bill almost nightly. These tend to be more informal, while their flexible policy suits those musicians who do not wish to be tied to a venue, or who are available for just one or two nights of a long tour.

There are venues for all tastes, from New York's progressive Knitting

A regular performer at festivals throughout the world, Duke Ellington had his biggest success when the band appeared at Newport in 1956.

Factory to the Lord Napier pub in South London that caters for tradition. Jazz as functional music has been on the decline, though trends, including the rapprochement with hip hop, have led to a revival of clubs where people dance to it. Most people now go just to listen, just as most musicians perform in public because they want to be heard. As we have seen, when all else has failed, the enterprising often take the initiative and book the place themselves.

In New York, Sam Rivers organized performances in his loft. The first home for free jazz in Sixties London was a private theatre, situated in a tiny attic in the West End, where John Stevens put on nightly sessions after the show closed.

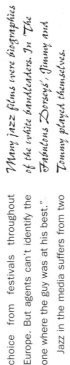

The Media

While festivals take strongly to jazz, the media play harder to get. A sudden flurry of interest will put musicians on the front of magazines and lead to profiles in unlikely parts of newspapers, possibly even to interviews on prime-time chat shows. Sandwiched between classics and pop, and without the industry muscle of either, jazz otherwise has to struggle for space. What ought to count in its favour are the demographic considerations that so attract festival promoters and advertisers. Research classifies a majority of fans as of the appropriate social brackets and financial standing, and of the right age – 25-54. Their tastes are relatively stable so, once hooked, they don't immediately succumb to the next craze.

That, plus the music's sheer longevity and staying power, has just about preserved jazz coverage in the newspapers. Hollywood has produced the occasional biography. Radio has remained supportive: jazz features on over a dozen stations in New York, England's Jazz FM has recovered its nerve after a shaky period and the radio big bands in Germany and Scandinavia are legendary. The obvious potential for jazz as a niche product has encouraged the U.S. media/entertainment group Black Entertainment TV to open a dedicated jazz and blues channel on cable television, showing for the moment mainly archive material.

Europe's NBC Super Channel includes current groups on its half-hour programme *Talkin' Jazz*, on satellite and cable. That apart, very little current television involves new, considered programming. John Jeremy, who directed excellent jazz documentaries when these were commissioned more regularly, runs the worldwide Campaign For Jazz On Television. He says that almost the only filming today is of festivals, so the same people keep turning up. "If I needed live footage of some musicians, there is an embarrassment of choice from festivals throughout Europe. But agents can't identify the one where the guy was at his best."

Jazz in the media suffers from two handicaps. Yesterday's jazz fans are found more often among promoters and recording executives than among

Many jazz films were biographies of the white bandleaders. In The Fabulous Dorseys', Jimmy and Tommy played themselves.

those commissioning press articles or television shows, who are likely to see jazz as unnecessarily complicating the three verities: rock, classical and the rest, mostly defined as amorphous world music.

Since the sex 'n' drugs era, jazz has barely surfaced in the mass-circulation press. Now, the quality papers are obsessed by how to replace readers when they die. This has led to what the U.K. Press Gazette described as, "The shift from intelligence and intellect, the relative neglect of the arts – except by some twist of the concept to embrace low-grade film and rock – because it will frighten young people. . . the absence of a sense of history beyond about 1980."

A sensitive film treatment of jazz, its musicians and fans: Round Midnight, starring Dexter Gordon.

The Magazines

Articles on jazz and record reviews appear in a variety of magazines covering every type of music. Below are listed a few, drawn from around the world, that specialize in jazz. Anyone wishing to learn more and to keep up with the latest releases will find the mass of detail, however indigestible at first, a stepping-stone to future expertise.

For an art form originating exclusively within the U.S., it took the indigenous population a long time to develop anything like an academic interest. Europeans began the documenting process, with books published in Germany as early as 1922, followed by Portugal in 1924, before the first American title in 1926. In the Thirties, Hilton Schleman and Charles Delaunay invented the art, or science, of jazz discography.

The same with magazines. Orchestra World was first published in the U.S. in 1925, followed by Down Beat, but in the U.K. alone over a dozen titles were published before the war. Melody Maker started in January 1926 and Rhythm in September 1927. The French Jazz Hot claimed to be the world's first dedicated Jazz magazine. They may be right, as their predecessors mainly reported on dance-swing bands; with some 'hot jazz' thrown in.

CADENCE – USA

Cadence Building, Redwood, NJ 13679-9612, USA.

Founded 1976 – Monthly – Text in English.

Predominantly reviews of jazz, blues and creative improvized music, both new releases and reissues. Also book reviews, readers' letters, in-depth interviews and musicians' responses to a standard questionnaire. Large record sales section.

CODA – CANADA

Coda Magazine, Box 1002, Station 'O', Toronto, M4A 2N4, Canada.

Founded 1958 – Bi-monthly – Text in English.

Declared aim is to cover 'all aspects of the art of jazz and improvized music' which it achieves through articles, interviews and festival, book and record reviews. Takes a non-partisan approach with strong coverage across the musical spectrum, including European as well as North American issues.

DOWN BEAT – USA

Maher Publications, 102 N. Haven Road, Elmhurst, IL 60126-3379, USA.

Founded 1934 – Monthly – Text in English.

Covers jazz and blues with the occasional foray into popular music. Features mainly contemporary sounds and trends, in articles and interviews. Strong CD review section, live event reviews, musical transcriptions, readers' letters and blindfold test.

JAZZ HOT – FRANCE

Jazz Hot Publications, 66 Rue Villiers-de-l'isle-Adam, BP405, 75969, Paris, France.

Founded 1935 – Monthly (11 issues per year) – Text in French.

American musicians hold sway, but also includes European artists. Coverage of jazz, blues and improvized music by way of interviews and articles, plus concert, book and record reviews. Some items of discographical interest.

JAZZ JOURNAL INTERNATIONAL – UK

1-5 Clerkenwell Road, London, EC1M 5PA.

Founded 1948 – Monthly – Text in English.

Bias towards jazz that is both American and acoustic, but covers the full range. Reviews most albums released in the UK.

Interviews, book reviews, opinion pieces, jazz on film/TV/video, discographical information, two pages of readers' letters.

JAZZ PODIUM – GERMANY

Verlags GmbH, Vogelsangstrasse 32, 70197 Stuttgart, Germany.

Founded 1952 – Monthly – Text in German.

Concentrates on the domestic scene, but includes articles on American and other European musicians. Several pages of brief items under the title of Jazz News, plus concert, festival and record reviews. Provides a detailed guide to coming events under the headings Jazz Clubs and Concerts, Radio, On The Road and Festivals.

MUSICA JAZZ – ITALY

Rusconi Editore, Via Vitruvio 43, 20124 Milan, Italy.

Founded 1945 – Monthly – Text in Italian.

Primarily covers the American jazz scene and musicians through articles and the occasional discographical piece. Contains several pages of readers' letters, news items and record reviews, plus surveys of contents of other jazz periodicals.

ORKESTER JOURNALEN – SWEDEN

Box 4206, 10265 Stockholm, Sweden.

Founded 1933 – Monthly (11 issues per year) – Text in Swedish.

American musicians feature prominently, though there is some coverage of homegrown talent and other Europeans. Articles, interviews and items of discographical interest. Record and book reviews.

SWING JOURNAL – JAPAN

Swing Journal Co. Ltd. 3-6-24 Shibakoen, Minato-Ku, Tokyo, Japan.

Founded 1947 – Monthly – Text in Japanese (Some headlines in English).

Probably the largest jazz periodical in the world, weighing in at several pounds. Tends to concentrate on US artists with album and CD reviews, concert reports and coverage of book and video releases. Has long section entitled 'Hot News Around The World'. Hi-Fi equipment reviews and much advertising.

On the Internet

The explosion on the Internet has already made an impact on jazz. There have been a number of sites in the USA for some time, and sites have since been set up in Europe and the UK. You can get information about gigs, clubs, festivals, records, radio stations, magazines, workshops, archives and tuition, along with details about individual musicians, and much else.

One way to access jazz is to use Web browsing software (such as Galaxy on http://galaxy.einet.net) and then enter a search word (e.g. 'jazz').

With this method, you may have to trawl through many useless sites that are thrown up by the search. Established jazz and music sites will have done some of this trawling, so try:

USA: http://www.music. indiana.edu/music_resources/jazz

EUROPE: http://www.xs4all.nl/ ~centrale/jazz

UK: http://ds.dial.pipex.com/ town/square/ad663/

UK: http://www.cerbernet.co.uk/fly

As for sound on the Internet, some companies have dipped their toes in the water, but the hardware involved, particularly over the speed of domestic modems and the storage capacity of most personal computers, is not up to sending music 'live' down the line. The company probably furthest advanced in this is Cerberus (http://cdj.co.uk/) who offer a CD jukebox: you purchase music per track, and it is then transmitted down the line on to your computer, enabling you to listen to it.

Learning to Play

Jazz as a subject for tuition is commonplace today, with colleges all over the world offering degrees or diplomas. In the early days, many people took the view that jazz could not be taught. Musicians might have studied an instrument at school, but they learnt how to play jazz on the job, moving from band to band as their ability and/or commitment improved.

There might be a causal link between the rise of jazz education and the decline of regular band employment in the Sixties, when well-known musicians began to move into the education field. Colleges such as Berklee in Boston and bands such as the North Texas University jazz orchestra began to receive mentions. Publicity surrounding Gary Burton, an ex-pupil whose association with Berklee continues today in an official capacity, also helped draw attention to the idea of formal training.

Since then, the educational acceptance of what in the U.K. is called 'creative music making' has led to a sizeable majority of musicians being involved, either as teachers or as pupils, or both. One reason for going to music colleges is to meet like-minded musicians. Some students drop out as soon as they get a gig; others discover enough to learn and stay the course.

Of the two main supra-national bodies, the International Association of Jazz Educators (IAJE) acts as a resource centre for teachers, awards, fellowships and scholarships, and

Britain's National Youth Jazz Orchestra (NYJO) has spawned many offshoots. All material is written by past and present members.

organizes clinics. It claims an individual membership of around 7,000 in 35 countries. The International Association of Schools of Jazz (IASJ) has, as the name implies, institutional members spread over several countries, and one of its aims is to improve the quality of jazz teaching by keeping members informed about what the others are doing.

An in-depth survey of jazz education in America was carried out in 1993 by the composer Graham Collier, who is currently Artistic Director of the Jazz Department at London's Royal Academy of Music, an IASJ member. His account, published in the IASJ magazine, raised many issues, including those of content and motivation. Why should young jazz musicians today be taught how to play bebop? Are orchestral competitions, as Collier quotes someone saying, an extension of the school's athletics programme? Do most pupils participate simply to gain credits?

These and similar questions get to the heart of the old-versus-new argument, so prevalent since Wynton Marsalis came along (thanks to Marsalis and Jazz At Lincoln Center, contemporary versions of jazz classics are made available to American public radio as educational instruction, are available on mail-order from:

Many musicians offer individual tuition. As a tribute to his teaching, jazz musicians with recognizable styles, including pillars of unorthodoxy, as well as many who do other things (in and out of music) but retain a love of jazz.

For those wishing to practice alone there are tutors that simulate the jazz environment. Among the most popular is the Jamey Aebersold Play-a-Long instructional series, where you learn to construct a jazz solo over a pre-recorded rhythm section. These, and many other aids to self-instruction, are available on mail-order from:

JAMEY AEBERSOLD, PO Box 1244C, New Albany, IN 47151-1244 USA. Tel: 1-800-456-1388

JAZZWISE, 2(b) Gleneagle Mews, London, SW16 6AE, England. Tel: 0181-769-7725

things from studying privately with Joe Henderson. Bill Saxton says Henderson beefed up his classical technique, while Teodross Avery says he taught him to play by ear. The most pertinent comment on motivation comes perhaps from guitarist Bill Frisell, who studied at Berklee and is nobody's idea of a conformist. Whenever he was advised not to use a particular note in voicing a chord, he made a point checking out to see if, in fact, he liked the sound.

Israeli and British students record 'Adam's Marble', by Graham Collier (second from right, back row). Guest clarinettist Harold Rubin is in the front row, extreme left.

Glossary

Terms commonly used in books, magazines and articles about jazz.

Acid Jazz

Invented to describe jazz, often on record, which clubs for dancers started to feature in the Eighties. The music was largely taken from funk/soul recordings made in and around the period 1955 to 1965.

Arrangement

Those who organize or write down a piece of music to be performed by a band are called arrangers, especially if they did not compose the tune in question - an example is the Miles Davis recording of *Porgy And Bess*, where the tunes are composed by George Gershwin but arranged by Gil Evans. An arrangement put together collectively and subsequently reproduced is called a 'head arrangement' ('head', for short).

Ballad

Describes a piece, usually in the form of a popular song, that is taken at a slow tempo. Sometimes used for any song in this form that is taken at anything other than breakneck speed.

designed to make the maximum impact upon the part that follows. Arrangements often allow for breaks — 'Night In Tunisia' has a passage designed for two-bar or four-bar breaks, memorably exploited by Charlie Parker. A tune with breaks built into its structure is 'Bugle Call Rag', in this case memorably exploited by Louis Armstrong. See also 'Stop-time'.

Chase

When two or more musicians swap phrases throughout one or several choruses, each leap-frogging over the other, this is called a chase. Depending on the number of bars each plays before the next takes over, they can be said to swap 'fours', 'eights' or any number from one to sixteen.

Chicago

See 'Dixieland'.

Chorus

A chorus describes the totality of the part of a tune that is used as a structural base for improvization. In many cases, that would be the tune itself. Exceptions include such multi-thematic compositions as 'King Porter Stomp' and 'Weary Blues', where the improvization is based on just one of the themes. Once the chorus (usually 12, 16 or 32 bars long) is completed, the soloist goes back to the beginning until the solo finishes. In such cases, a musician is said to take a solo of x choruses, x being the number of times the structure recurs.

Bebop

Often abbreviated to 'Bop' (the variant 'Rebop' survives only in the words of some songs). Ideally, should describe only the music Parker, Gillespie and those in their circle played during the Forties. Usage has been carelessly extended to cover almost any post-Parker performance on which the participants improvize on the harmonies of a tune.

Blues

Phrases such as 'blue tonality' identify music in which the minor, or flattened, notes (the 'blue notes'), are used extensively compared to the major notes of the scale. Such music frequently evokes a kind of melancholy, 'blue' feeling. Also describes a musical form of anything between 10 and 16 bars in length, but usually of 12 bars, by far the most common and readily identifiable blues form.

Boogie-Woogie

First used on record by Pine Top Smith on his 'Pine Top's Boogie Woogie', the phrase caught on in the late Thirties. The so-called boogie bass is simply a means whereby a solo blues pianist keeps a regular rhythm in his left hand, usually a rolling eight-beats-to-the-bar. During its popular period, this rhythm was even taken up by big bands.

Breaks

Gaps between one chorus and the next, or between different segments of a tune, can be used for breaks. The beat provided by the rhythm section is suspended temporarily while the soloist invents a phrase

Cool

The term 'hot' was coined to define jazz as played by the likes of Louis Armstrong and Coleman Hawkins and especially to differentiate it from ordinary dance music performed by ordinary dance bands. Its opposite, 'cool jazz',

came along later to describe music where the emotional content was more subtle and less up-front than hot jazz. From being a term of approbation, 'cool' then became for a time a synonym for 'effete' or 'emotionless', though today both hot and cool temperatures are regarded as valid.

Dixieland

Dixieland can cover any kind of jazz played by the traditional front line of trumpet, clarinet and trombone or any variant thereof (including larger bands), especially if the base rhythm is 2/4 rather than 4/4. Sometimes used instead of 'Chicago' to describe bands playing music associated with either Chicago bands of the Twenties or with those linked to Eddie Condon in later years. Musicians from New Orleans sometimes call what they play 'Dixieland' - very rarely 'New Orleans'.

Energy Music

Invented in the Sixties for jazz that was freely improvized and extremely loud.

Free

A simple definition of free improvization would be music where solos do not revolve around a succession of choruses or scales. Sometimes it is not completely free of any pre-determined structure: there might be a motif, derived from a tune played before the improvization begins, or some guidelines may be built into the performance (e.g. a particular rhythm, or a fixed order of soloists). At other times, there are no tunes and no guidelines. The term 'free jazz' usually implies some kind of rhythmic support and some kind of governing system, however loosely conceived and applied.

Funk

An old word reactivated in the Fifties as a marketing term for blues-oriented jazz that employed plenty of flattened 'blue' notes and/or emphasized a back beat or some other pronounced rhythmic effect that differed from a straight 4/4. Also used to describe some of the secularized gospel music inspired by Ray Charles. Interchangeable in this respect with 'soul'. Examples on record would include 'Moanin' by the Jazz Messengers and 'This Here' by Cannonball Adderley, both written by pianist Bobby Timmons.

Fusion

Can refer to any kind of merger between jazz and some other identifiable form of music, but reserved generally for the use of electric guitars and keyboards and rock-derived rhythms in a jazz context, which is also called 'jazz-rock'.

Hard Bop

The more varied music that bebop became in the Fifties instead of, as before, being dominated by both the types of tunes and the phraseology associated with Charlie Parker.

Harmolodic

A term invented by Ornette Coleman to describe music in which there is supposed to be no clear distinction between the melody and the rhythm instruments: both now have melodic and rhythmic responsibilities.

Harmonics

See 'Multiphonics'.

Hot

See 'Cool'.

Improvization

In its widest sense, improvization describes music

that is not completely predetermined, i.e. neither written on manuscript paper nor re-created note-for-note. The most common form of jazz improvization is still based on the chorus (see above), and derives more often from the underlying harmonic structure of the tune than from the tune directly. Some solos, especially when slotted into a big band arrangement, may be partly improvized. Louis Armstrong tended to develop solos he approved of and thereafter stick closely to them. From a recording session in 1950 involving Bud Powell and Sonny Stitt, there are two superb versions of the tune 'Fine And Dandy'; each has completely different solos but the seemingly ad-lib piano introductions by Powell are almost identical.

MAINSTREAM

The term was applied in the Fifties to jazz that had its roots in the swing era, before bebop came along. Thirty years on, the mainstream has broadened to include jazz whose roots in an earlier time are obvious to all. This, of course, includes jazz related to bebop.

MODAL

In the Fifties, a move away from reliance on improvizing over the ever-shifting chords of the average popular song or jazz standard led to the use of modes, and to modal jazz. The idea was to free the soloist from having to run from one chord to the next: now, there was just a scale from which any note could in theory be chosen. An example is 'So What', by Miles Davis, built around just two scales. Then there is 'Flamenco Sketches', also by Davis, with five. Sometimes, there are no structural limits and the scale written by a jazz musician, as doesn't change, as in the improvized 'vamp' part of John Coltrane's version of 'My Favourite Things'.

MODERN JAZZ

Used in the Forties and Fifties, to describe bebop and anything that derived from it. Still applied to that music today.

MULTIPHONICS

The term 'multiphonics' covers all systems whereby a musician simultaneously plays more than one note on a wind or brass instrument. So-called harmonics are produced either by fingering or by special blowing techniques. These can be supplemented by extra notes produced by humming and blowing simultaneously. The technique of circular breathing, whereby the musician continues blowing without taking a breath, can result in overlapping notes that have a similar effect.

MUTES

Devices used in conjunction with any brass instrument, but associated mainly with the trumpet and trombone, to distort the sound. They come generally in three types: those that are fitted into the bell, sometimes extending into the bore itself; those that are fixed on to the outside of the bell; those that are manipulated by the hand in front of the bell. The same mute can have more than one function, and two mutes (i.e. one fixed, the other hand-operated) can be used at the same time. Before manufactured mutes became common in jazz, musicians would use bathroom plungers, hats or just their hands.

ORIGINAL

Specifically used for tunes composed by the leader or by other members of the band. Can extend to almost any tune written by a jazz musician, as opposed to those by a songwriter from outside the world of jazz. See also 'Standard'.

REVIVALIST

The most common usage relates to the New Orleans revival of the Forties, when bands with trumpet-clarinet-trombone line-ups in the New Orleans style were called revivalist, irrespective of nationality. The term has since been extended to cover any musician considered to play jazz that comes from any earlier era.

RIFF

A simple, repeated phrase that can be part of a tune or an arrangement, usually in a big-band context, or it can be made up on the spot. If incorporated into the tune, it can coexist with another riff, played by another section of the band, and the two are said to answer each other in a call-and-response fashion. An example is Count Basie's 'Jumpin' At The Woodside'. Sometimes there is just one riff, such as Count Basie's 'Swingin' The Blues'. The riff may also be a device to spur on a soloist, generally towards the end of the solo.

SCAT

Singing without words, often with syllables substituted. First done on record by Louis Armstrong. Exponents include Ella Fitzgerald, Betty Carter and Bobby McFerrin.

SECTION

The jazz orchestra usually divides into four sections: trumpet, trombone, reed and rhythm.

SOLO

An improvized statement made by a jazz musician. Despite the name, most solos take place with some accompaniment, from a single instrument to a big band. If just the one musician is involved, it could be referred to as an unaccompanied solo.

SOUL

Modern jazz with gospel or blues connotations. See 'Funk'.

STANDARD

A tune that is regularly improvized upon by jazz musicians. Sometimes implies a tune written by non-jazz composer, as opposed to 'original'. However, both 'Lady Be Good' by George Gershwin and 'Confirmation' by Charlie Parker deserve to be called standards.

STOP-TIME

Instead of playing all the beats in a bar behind a soloist, the rhythm section plays (usually) just the first beat, thus creating a feeling of suspension. An outstanding example is Louis Armstrong's 'Potato Head Blues'. Another piece with stop-time passages built into the arrangement is 'Lester Leaps In' as played by Lester Young.

SWING

Jazz of the Thirties, by both big bands and smaller groups, is often called Swing. Music that is said 'to swing' is easier sensed than defined. Ingredients include a regular tempo (4/4, 3/4 etc.), a relaxed beat whatever the tempo and the ability of all concerned to time everything correctly. Straightforward examples of swing include such tunes as Ellington's 'C Jam Blues' and anything that features the four members of a Count Basie rhythm section.

SYNCOPATION

Distorting a basic beat. The most obvious example of syncopation is the cakewalk rhythm that is incorporated into ragtime. Syncopated notes are common in jazz, but as part of a solo or an overall structure and not, as with some ragtime, as a main ingredient.

TRADITIONAL

Traditional jazz is a term sometimes applied to anything that might otherwise be called New Orleans, Chicago or Dixieland. The abbreviation 'Trad' has been used in the UK. Recently, the term 'tradition' implies any jazz whose history stretches back several years.

VOCALESE

Putting words to jazz solos, and/or to jazz originals that were not written for that purpose. Exponents of vocalese include King Pleasure, Annie Ross, Eddie Jefferson and Jon Hendricks. The most determined examples were the words written by Hendricks to recordings by Count Basie (including themes, solos and riffs) and performed by himself, Annie Ross and Dave Lambert.

WEST COAST

This style of jazz was played by musicians around Los Angeles in the early Fifties. It had a tendency to be cool in concept and, on a head-for-head count, it was arranged more tightly than one would expect from a New York group. Today, the term West Coast can be used to describe any music that is seen to reflect that particular style.

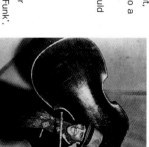

Picture credits

The publishers would like to thank the following sources for their kind permission to reproduce the pictures in this book:

Corbis
Bettmann/UPI

Frank Driggs Collection

Mary Evans Picture Library

Hulton Getty

London Features International
David Boehm
Martin Esseveld
Herb Snitzer

Peter Newark's Pictures

Pictorial Press
David Corio
Polygram

Redferns
Rico D'Rozario
Brigitte Engl
William Gottlieb
Tim Hall
Mick Hutson
Max Jones Files
Thomas Krebs
Elliott Landy
Marc Marnie
Leon Morris
Michael Ochs Archives
Andrew Putler
David Redfern
Bob Willoughby

Peter Symes.

Thanks are also due to Nancy White at Redferns.

Every effort has been made to acknowledge correctly and contact the source and/or copyright holder of each picture, and Carlton Books Limited apologises for any unintentional errors or omissions which will be corrected in future editions of this book.

Author's acknowledgements

To Jack Cooke for some of the biographies, Graham Langley (British Institute of Jazz Studies) for details of magazines and Steve French (Jazz Services) for sorting out the Internet. Some pieces first appeared in The Guardian in different form and are used with permission.

For interviews and/or particular help, thanks to Sharon Kelly (Sony/Columbia), Debbie Ballard and Amadu (Coalition), Angus Trowbridge (TCB), John Jeremy, Richard Cook (Polygram), Derek Gorman (Glasgow Jazz Festival), Jeanie Bergin (Jazz FM), and Charles Alexander (Jazzwise).

Thanks also to John Fordham, Martin Gayford, Stan Britt, John Jack, (Cadillac), Alastair Robertson (Hep), Celia Wood (Jazz Services), Chris Wellard, Mike Dodds (AFP), Kerstan Mackness (New Note), Jodi Howard (Arabesque), Pat Tynan (Koch), John Crosby (Ace), Grainne Devine (RCA/BMG), Becky Stevenson (Polygram), Trevor Mainwaring (Harmonia Mundi), Nod Knowles, Marion Piras (Inclinaisons), Andrea Gibbs (Atlantic), Graham Collier, Rosie Jarvis (SW Jazz), Colin McLeod (Assembly Direct), Harriett (Topic), and Celeste (B&W).

Special thanks to everyone at Carlton for putting up with the author's vagaries: Lorraine Dickey, Charlotte Bush, Zoë Maggs and especially Duncan Noble for spotting the mistakes.